AF705585

The 2-Minute Transformation

The 2-Minute Transformation

How Small Habits Build Big Lives

Lina Vermeer

Mindful Pages

Published in 2025

ISBN: 9789362921727 (PB)
ISBN: 9789362928764 (eBook)

Published by

Mindful Pages
Imprint of Alpha Editions LLC
312 W. 2nd St #1834
Casper, WY 82601, USA

All rights reserved.
No part of this publication may be reproduced, distributed, or transmitted in any form or by any means — including photocopying, recording, or other electronic or mechanical methods — without the prior written permission of the publisher, except in the case of brief quotations used in reviews or permitted by applicable copyright law.
This book was developed using advanced writing tools to support the drafting and ideation process. All content has been thoughtfully curated, refined, and reviewed to ensure quality and relevance.

Content

Introduction
The Power of Tiny Steps

Change is so often cast as a sweeping act—a reinvention, a dramatic turning of the page that demands grit, resolve, and perhaps a touch of heroic zeal. We're drawn, almost instinctively, to the allure of a clean slate: fresh starts, bold routines, and life-altering masterplans. And yet, when that initial burst of enthusiasm wanes—as it inevitably does—so too does the grand vision. What if, contrary to popular belief, the key to lasting transformation lies not in dramatic overhauls, but in something far more unassuming? The 2-Minute Transformation leans into precisely this notion: that real change is quiet, incremental, and disarmingly simple.

At its core lies a deceptively powerful idea—micro habits. Not flashy, not difficult, not even particularly time-consuming. Just small, deliberate actions, easy to repeat and designed to align with our deeper intentions. Traditional goal-setting, with its emphasis on outcomes and its reliance on fleeting motivation, often collapses under its own ambition. Micro habits take a gentler approach: they bypass the psychological resistance we associate with big commitments and instead invite us to just begin. They're the kind of habits that make you laugh at their simplicity—flossing one tooth, writing a single sentence, sitting in silence for two short minutes. It feels almost absurd not to try.

This isn't about downsizing your dreams or settling for less. It's about meeting human nature where it lives—in the realm of the doable. Behavioural psychology backs this up. We are far more likely to act when the task before us doesn't provoke anxiety, avoidance, or dread. The brain is not designed for constant heavy lifting; it seeks shortcuts, efficiency, comfort. Grand goals often demand cognitive effort we can't always summon. But micro habits? They slip quietly into our routines, creating a kind of behavioural Trojan horse. Suddenly, small isn't insignificant—it's strategic.

That distinction changes everything. Much of the personal development advice floating around is well-meaning but flawed—dream big, plan thoroughly, aim high. And then reality hits: life is busy, motivation is fickle, and expectations can quickly become burdens. Micro habits invert the model. They ask not what you might do someday, but what you can do now—this moment, with the resources and energy available. Their genius lies in how low the bar is set. So low, in fact, that failure almost doesn't apply. When the task is brief and undemanding, consistency follows naturally. You don't feel the sting of missed days; you simply begin again.

And then there's the Two-Minute Rule—elegant in its minimalism. The idea? Any habit worth developing should start in a form so compact, so manageable, that it takes no more than two minutes. Want to get back into reading? Read a single paragraph. Want to exercise? Lace your trainers and step outside. It's not about staying at that level forever, but about easing into action. The greatest obstacle to change is often just starting. This rule clears that hurdle. Once the routine becomes a reflex, expanding it happens almost of its own accord.

Beyond the neuroscience and habit theory, there's something quietly profound about the ripple effects these micro shifts produce. Habits, after all, rarely exist in isolation. A small change in one domain can nudge others along with it. That glass of water first thing in the morning? It may not seem like much, but it can lift your energy, which sharpens your focus, which affects how you show up for others. A brief moment of gratitude might gently alter your emotional tone, deepening your connections and enhancing your resilience. These changes don't march in a straight line—they compound, diverge, spiral outward.

It's not unlike compound interest. The magic isn't in the first deposit—it's in the patient accumulation over time. Micro habits, like sound investments, grow their impact gradually. For weeks, perhaps even months, they remain beneath the surface, quietly shaping your days. But then, seemingly all at once, the results start to show. The line between trivial and transformational blurs.

Perhaps the most underestimated benefit of this approach lies in what it does to how we see ourselves. Each time we carry out a micro habit, however small, we affirm something: I am the kind of person who does this. It's subtle, but powerful. One sentence scribbled before bed, and you begin to think of yourself as a writer. A two-minute jog, and you inch toward seeing yourself as someone who moves. Identity, it turns out, is forged not through grand gestures but repeated action. We do not rise to the heights of our ambitions; we settle into the systems we build. Micro habits offer a system—reliable, resilient, and tailored for real life.

This book doesn't claim to hold all the answers. It isn't a sermon or a rigid plan. Think of it more as a framework—a companion of sorts. There are no ultimatums, no "one true way" to succeed. Instead, you'll find practical strategies drawn from behavioural science, grounded in real-world experience, and versatile enough to meet you where you are. You'll be encouraged to begin, however imperfectly, and to build from there. It is an invitation, not a command.

The structure of the book is deliberate. It begins with the science—why habits matter, and how the micro variety works. From there, it moves into application: how to start, what to watch out for, and how to adjust when life throws its inevitable curveballs. Along the way, you'll see how these ideas touch every area of human experience—our health, our work, our relationships, our sense of purpose. The emphasis is always on practicality, but without losing sight of the deeper emotional and psychological stakes.

In its final stretch, the book turns to stories—real ones. Not sensational accounts of overnight reinvention, but quieter tales of steady, persistent effort. These are people who didn't wait for perfect conditions or superhuman resolve. They just started. Their transformations are a testament not to magic but to method. The lesson is clear: change is possible, not when we master motivation, but when we make it irrelevant. When the bar is low, we stop tripping over it.

The 2-Minute Transformation is not a call to revolution, but to rhythm. It's not about overachieving; it's about not stopping. This is change at human scale—sensible, forgiving, and lasting. Let the pages guide you, challenge you, and remind you: you don't need to do everything, just something. And if that something takes two minutes? Even better. Because that's where change begins—not with a bang, but with a breath.

Chapter 1
Understanding Habits – The Building Blocks of Change

At first glance, habits tend to go unnoticed—those quiet, automatic behaviours that weave themselves into the fabric of our everyday existence. We brush our teeth without thinking, scroll through our phones before we've even fully woken up, sip our coffee, lock the front door. Routine, yes—but hardly trivial. Beneath their outward simplicity, habits hold a deeper, more consequential influence: they don't merely punctuate our days; they shape them. They mould who we are, how we choose, and ultimately, the lives we come to live. In truth, habits form the unseen scaffolding of our lives. And if we're to talk seriously about change—not fleeting novelty, but real, lasting change—we must begin here.

A habit, stripped to its essence, is a behaviour repeated often enough to become automatic. It no longer demands focused attention; instead, it moves in rhythm with our days, looping from trigger to action to satisfaction almost on cue. From the standpoint of behavioural science, this is the brain's way of conserving energy. Instead of deliberating afresh each time, it scripts routines for efficiency. This mental economy is both clever and perilous: while it frees us to think and act creatively elsewhere, it also means that we can find ourselves repeating behaviours—helpful or harmful—without realising they're steering the ship.

This is why the idea of the "habit loop" is so critical. Introduced and expanded upon by figures like Charles Duhigg and supported by decades of empirical research, the habit loop consists of three moving parts: cue, routine, and reward. The cue—some environmental signal or internal sensation—triggers the behaviour. The routine is the behaviour itself. And the reward is what your brain registers as a payoff, something reinforcing enough to make the behaviour worth repeating. Do it often enough, and it becomes encoded, neurologically speaking, into your wiring. Consider this simple example: your alarm goes off (cue), you brew coffee (routine), and you feel awake and soothed (reward). Rinse and repeat—and you're no longer choosing that routine, you're embodying it.

What makes this loop so potent, and at times so slippery, is how it circumvents conscious thought. Before you even register the cue, your brain is already predicting the reward and priming you to act. The basal ganglia—an ancient structure buried deep in the brain—plays a pivotal role in this process. It's responsible for recognising patterns and executing motor functions, and as a habit becomes more deeply engrained, it shoulders more of the burden. So much so that the more deliberate parts of your brain begin to quiet down during the habit. This is why you can arrive at your destination after a long drive and realise you remember almost nothing of the journey.

From this neurological underpinning, two truths emerge—each carrying weight. First: habits are far more embedded than we'd like to admit. They're physiological as much as psychological, and no amount of gritted-teeth determination will consistently overcome their pull. Second: habits are not fixed. They can be dismantled and rebuilt—but only if we work *with* the habit loop, rather than against it. That means identifying what triggers the behaviour, redesigning the response, and ensuring the new behaviour still offers a meaningful reward. It's not easy, but it's possible.

Here's where micro habits enter the frame, offering a kind of behavioural judo. Rather than relying on grand gestures or overhauls, micro habits begin with actions so small they barely register as effort. That's intentional. The aim is to reduce the friction, to make the start so ridiculously easy that there's no excuse not to begin. The brain balks at the prospect of difficult change—but it rarely objects to a two-minute action. Fill a water bottle. Open your notebook. Roll out a yoga mat. These are wins so modest they can almost slip in unnoticed—but therein lies their genius.

And these tiny actions do something else, something deeply valuable: they reduce the burden of choice. Every day, we're faced with thousands of decisions, and each one subtly drains our capacity to think, act, and persevere. This is the phenomenon known as decision fatigue. It's why we reach for snacks at 4 p.m., or scroll mindlessly late at night—we're just too tired to choose better. Micro habits help because they *remove* the need to decide. They create a default. When you know your morning starts with a two-minute journal entry or a short walk, you're not negotiating with yourself. You're executing. And that's what the most effective people understand—not because they're paragons of self-control, but because they're pragmatic. They remove friction where they can.

Still, motivation continues to get all the headlines. The myth that change begins with motivation is deeply embedded in modern culture—the stirring quote, the dramatic movie montage, the promise of personal reinvention sparked by sheer desire. But motivation, as anyone who's tried to rely on it knows, is deeply unreliable. It's moody, fickle, weather-prone. If your strategy hinges on "feeling inspired," you're building your future on sand.

What works instead? Structure. Systems. Environments tailored to your goals. Say you want to eat better: the most practical move isn't to read another nutrition blog; it's to replace what's in your kitchen. Want to start stretching daily? Put the mat in plain sight where you'll see it each morning. By shaping your surroundings, you remove the need for daily resolve. The habit becomes part of the landscape, not a moral dilemma.

This is what distinguishes habit-building from goal-chasing. Goals are aspirational—they point to what we *hope* to achieve. Systems are operational—they shape what we *actually* do. A good habit system operates regardless of mood, helping us default to better behaviour even on low-energy days. Each repetition reinforces neural pathways. Over time, effort gives way to instinct. That's where sustainability lives.

Take writing, for instance. A goal might be to complete 1,000 words a day. But life intervenes: deadlines, tiredness, a child's cold. The ambitious plan falters. But a micro habit—say, one sentence a day—requires no grand conditions. You sit. You write. Some days, that sentence becomes a paragraph, even a page. Other days, it's just the sentence—and that's fine. Because what matters is not volume, but continuity. The identity of "I'm a writer" remains intact.

This logic applies widely: fitness, learning, budgeting, meditation, relationships. The most transformative habits often don't announce themselves. They're not impressive at first glance. But they last. And because they last, they accumulate.

This chapter serves as a foundation—not just for the book, but for the larger project of changing your life. If you can view habits as the underlying operating system of who you are and how you live, then learning to craft and refine them becomes the most worthwhile investment you can make. You don't need an epiphany. You don't need to transform overnight. You just need to understand behaviour—what initiates it, how it embeds itself, and how it can be subtly redirected. Begin small—so small the mind doesn't resist. Let the change root itself gently, quietly.

Understanding habits isn't merely useful; it's essential. It is the starting point for all real change. And from this foundation, we will move forward—to building, refining, and scaling habits that can, over time, transform not only how you act, but who you believe yourself to be. Because in the end, it's not the grand gestures that remake a life. It's the small, repeated choices—the ones you barely notice—that quietly determine everything.

What Are Habits?

To understand the mechanics of change, one must begin with a clear understanding of habits—not as a vague notion or a buzzword in the self-help lexicon, but as a concrete behavioural pattern grounded in neuroscience and psychology. A habit, at its simplest, is a behaviour that has become automatic through repetition. It is a learned routine or action that we perform with minimal conscious thought, often triggered by specific contexts or cues. From brushing our teeth each morning to checking our phones every time we hear a notification, habits streamline our daily existence by reducing the cognitive load required to navigate life.

The human brain, marvellously efficient yet inherently lazy, seeks to conserve energy wherever possible. This inclination for economy underpins our habitual behaviours. Rather than expending mental effort on recurring decisions—what to eat for breakfast, whether to exercise, how to respond to a stressful email—the brain creates shortcuts. These shortcuts allow us to operate on autopilot, freeing up mental resources for novel problems and complex reasoning. In this way, habits are not merely useful—they are indispensable. They are the silent architects of our routines, choices, and ultimately, our identities.

Take, for instance, the act of tying one's shoelaces. As a child, this task requires focus and deliberate sequencing. Over time, with enough repetition, the behaviour becomes instinctive. The same principle applies to more complex behaviours: the route we take to work, the way we respond to emotional triggers, or even how we initiate conversations. Each repeated action, when cued consistently and reinforced through reward, becomes embedded in neural pathways. These pathways, like well-trodden trails in a forest, make future repetitions faster and easier. The more frequently a behaviour is enacted, the more automatic it becomes.

The significance of habits, then, extends far beyond convenience. Habits shape who we are because they determine what we do consistently. While motivation might inspire action once or twice, it is habit that sustains it over the long term. The distinction between who we are and who we hope to become is often the difference between our daily routines and our aspirations. An individual who writes for five minutes each day is, functionally, a writer—regardless of whether they've published a book. A person who stretches every morning is cultivating a lifestyle of health, whether or not they have run a marathon. Identity, over time, is constructed through repeated behaviour. We are, quite literally, what we repeatedly do.

Consider the story of Darren, a mid-level manager who found himself perpetually fatigued and stressed. Determined to make a change, he began experimenting with waking up 30 minutes earlier to read, reflect, and plan his day. Initially difficult, the habit gradually became second nature. Over time, Darren noticed a marked improvement in his mood, decision-making, and productivity. What seemed like a small shift—a quiet start to the morning—had profound ripple effects. This is the power of habit: small actions, repeated consistently, can reshape not only our behaviours but the quality of our lived experience.

From a scientific standpoint, habits are not just behavioural phenomena; they are neurobiological constructs. When a habit is formed, it is encoded within the basal ganglia, a cluster of nuclei in the brain associated with emotion, procedural learning, and routine behaviours. This region is deeply involved in the formation of habits because it allows certain actions to become automatic, sparing the more energy-intensive parts of the brain—like the prefrontal cortex—from constant decision-making. This is why habits feel so effortless once ingrained: the brain has delegated the task to its more primitive, efficient machinery.

But the same mechanism that allows us to develop productive habits also permits the entrenchment of destructive ones. Habits do not differentiate between what serves us and what undermines us—they are neutral by design. Whether it's biting nails under stress or snacking late at night, the habit loop functions the same way: a cue triggers a behaviour, which yields a reward, reinforcing the loop. It is this neutrality that makes habits so powerful, and why cultivating awareness around them is essential for personal growth.

The daily impact of our habits cannot be overstated. Studies suggest that nearly 40 to 50 percent of our actions on any given day are habitual. These behaviours are not the result of active choices but of established routines operating in the background. This means that nearly half of our lives is governed by systems we've put in place—consciously or unconsciously. It also means that any attempt to change our lives without addressing our habits is likely to be superficial at best. Real, enduring transformation requires altering the default settings of our behaviour.

To appreciate the cumulative power of habits, imagine two people who begin with identical routines but make a minor shift in behaviour. One decides to read for five minutes before bed each night, while the other scrolls through social media. The effect on day one is negligible. But compound that choice over a year, and the difference becomes stark. One has completed multiple books, expanded their thinking, and improved their sleep; the other has fed distraction and perhaps even compromised their mental wellbeing. This divergence, sparked by what seemed like an inconsequential decision, illustrates how habits are the compound interest of self-improvement.

The key to this compounding effect lies in consistency, not intensity. Popular culture often glorifies dramatic acts of change—intense workouts, digital detoxes, or overnight business success. But the research tells a different story. Sustainable change is usually quiet, often unglamorous, and deeply rooted in habitual action. It is not the one-off achievement that changes a life but the daily practice that seems almost too simple to matter.

This truth underpins the methodology of micro habits, which we will explore throughout this book. Micro habits are small by design. Their effectiveness lies in their low barrier to entry. A habit that takes two minutes to complete is far more likely to be done than one that demands twenty. More importantly, these small acts are not trivial—they are foundational. They teach the brain consistency. They create a sense of reliability. And over time, they act as gateways to more substantial behaviours.

For example, someone wishing to cultivate a writing habit might begin by opening their laptop and writing one sentence. This minimal task seems inconsequential, but its real value lies in creating a mental association: when I sit at this desk, I write. Over time, the habit expands—not by force, but by the natural desire to continue once the action has begun. The initial two minutes serve as a behavioural trigger, nudging the mind and body into motion. This is how habits scale organically, without relying on unstable bursts of inspiration.

Understanding what habits are—and how they function—grants us agency. It allows us to step back and examine our lives not through the lens of willpower or personal failings, but through patterns. It invites us to become behavioural architects rather than accidental consumers of routine. When we recognise that our habits are malleable, we realise that change is not a matter of personality but of practice.

This perspective also liberates us from the binary thinking of success and failure. Missed a day? The habit hasn't failed—it's merely paused. Fell into an old pattern? That's data, not defeat. The work of transformation is not about perfection but about reorientation. Every habit can be adjusted, reinforced, or replaced with intention and patience. And that work begins with awareness.

To examine your habits is to study yourself with curiosity, not criticism. It is to notice what you do when you're tired, distracted, anxious, or hopeful. It is to ask not just what you do but why—and what purpose it serves. Are your habits aligned with your values? Do they move you towards or away from the person you hope to become? These questions are not rhetorical; they are the foundation of deliberate living.

In defining habits, then, we are not simply labelling behaviour—we are uncovering the structure of human life. Habits are how goals become reality. They are how intentions survive the chaos of daily life. They are the bridge between who we are and who we can be. To understand them is to unlock the most powerful lever for change available to us. And as you'll discover throughout this book, the smallest habits—those that take just two minutes to perform—often hold the greatest potential for transformation.

The Habit Loop

Every habit we form, whether beneficial or detrimental, follows a structure—one so predictable and universal that it operates beneath our conscious awareness. This structure, known as *the habit loop*, is the backbone of behavioural psychology's understanding of how actions become automatic. First introduced into popular discourse by researchers and later crystallised by authors like Charles Duhigg, the habit loop provides a clear framework for analysing and altering the behaviours that shape our lives. Comprised of three fundamental components—cue, routine, and reward—this loop offers both a diagnosis and a roadmap for meaningful behavioural change.

At its core, the habit loop begins with a *cue*: a trigger that tells the brain to initiate a particular behaviour. This cue can be internal, such as a feeling of boredom or anxiety, or external, like the time of day, a specific location, or even a particular sound. The cue is the spark that ignites the habitual sequence, and it often slips beneath conscious recognition. Yet once identified, the cue becomes a powerful point of intervention, a lever through which the entire behavioural sequence can be influenced.

Following the cue is the *routine*—the behaviour itself. This is the action we take in response to the trigger. It may be as simple as checking a smartphone when a notification pings, or as complex as preparing a detailed report when prompted by a calendar alert. The routine is what we commonly think of as the habit, the visible part of the sequence. It is the behaviour we repeat, often without considering why we do it or what led us to start.

Finally, the loop concludes with the *reward*: the outcome that reinforces the behaviour and makes the brain more likely to repeat it in the future. Rewards are not always obvious. Sometimes they are tangible—a sugar rush after eating chocolate. Sometimes they are psychological—a sense of relief after venting frustration. The reward serves a crucial role: it teaches the brain that the behaviour was worthwhile. Over time, the brain begins to anticipate the reward as soon as it encounters the cue, which is why the loop strengthens with repetition.

To illustrate this in real terms, consider the habit of checking your phone upon waking. The cue might be the act of opening your eyes in the morning. The routine follows—reaching for the phone, scrolling through emails or social media. The reward could be a sense of connection, stimulation, or simply satisfying curiosity. Because the brain receives this positive reinforcement, it strengthens the association between waking up and phone use, making it more likely you'll repeat the behaviour tomorrow—and the day after that.

What makes the habit loop particularly compelling is its ability to operate with remarkable efficiency. Once established, the brain shifts the responsibility for executing the routine from areas associated with decision-making and attention (such as the prefrontal cortex) to deeper, more automatic regions like the basal ganglia. The basal ganglia are responsible for procedural learning, emotion, and routine behaviours. This neurological delegation allows the brain to conserve cognitive resources, but it also means that habits—good or bad—become deeply ingrained and harder to dislodge through sheer willpower alone.

This has important implications for both personal development and behavioural change. It reveals that habits are not arbitrary but highly conditioned loops that follow consistent neurological rules. More importantly, it shows that by understanding and altering one component of the loop, we can reshape the entire pattern. For example, if you identify the cue that triggers an unwanted behaviour, you can work to substitute the routine with a more constructive alternative—provided the new routine satisfies the same reward.

This is precisely the technique that behavioural scientists and habit coaches use when helping individuals change entrenched behaviours. Take, for instance, the common habit of snacking in the afternoon. Many people find themselves reaching for sugary treats at around the same time each day. The cue might be a slump in energy or a break in the workday. The routine is the act of snacking. The reward could be a temporary boost in energy or a moment of mental escape. If the goal is to reduce sugar intake, the key is not to eliminate the habit outright but to re-engineer it. One might replace the snack with a brisk walk or a handful of nuts—behaviours that satisfy the underlying need without the unwanted consequences.

The same principle can be applied to positive habit formation. Suppose you wish to build a habit of daily reading. The process begins by selecting a reliable cue—perhaps finishing breakfast or commuting home. The routine would then be to read for a set period, even if it's just two minutes. The reward could be the pleasure of the story, a sense of progress, or the satisfaction of honouring a personal goal. With enough repetition, this behaviour loop becomes self-sustaining. The cue automatically leads to the routine, and the reward reinforces the entire sequence.

It's important to note that cues are highly personal. What triggers one person's behaviour may have no effect on another. Some cues are sensory—the smell of coffee, the sound of a certain song. Others are emotional—stress, loneliness, anticipation. And some are social—the presence of a particular person or a shared environment. The effectiveness of the habit loop depends on recognising these patterns in one's own life. Awareness is the first step. Once we become aware of what prompts our habits, we gain the power to alter them deliberately.

Understanding the habit loop also sheds light on why bad habits are so difficult to break. Because the cue and the reward often remain constant, the brain clings to the loop even when the routine becomes harmful. Smokers, for example, may light up not simply out of nicotine dependence, but because the act serves as a break from work (cue), with a reward of relaxation or social interaction. If one tries to quit smoking without replacing the underlying reward, the habit loop remains unsatisfied—and relapse becomes highly likely. Successful habit change, then, requires satisfying the craving behind the habit, even if the behaviour itself changes.

One of the most profound insights about the habit loop is that it provides a structure for deliberate design. Rather than relying on motivation—which is notoriously inconsistent—we can engineer our environments and routines to support desired behaviours. This involves embedding cues into our surroundings, simplifying routines to reduce resistance, and identifying rewards that align with our values and objectives. When a habit loop is consciously crafted, it transforms from an unconscious pattern into a tool of personal agency.

Consider the case of Nadia, a university student struggling with procrastination. She noticed that every time she sat at her desk to study, she would end up scrolling through social media instead. Upon analysis, she realised the cue was the sight of her phone, the routine was distraction, and the reward was temporary relief from academic pressure. By removing the phone from her workspace and replacing it with a printed schedule and a visual tracker of completed study sessions, she restructured the habit loop. The cue remained (sitting at the desk), but the routine changed (focused study), and the reward became the sense of accomplishment. Over time, the new habit took root—because the loop had been rewired.

This example underscores a critical takeaway: habit loops are not fate. They are flexible. They can be reshaped through intention, experimentation, and self-awareness. They are not obstacles to success—they are the instruments by which success is achieved. When we learn to work with them, rather than against them, we unlock a more reliable and sustainable path to behavioural change.

Moreover, understanding the habit loop invites a shift in how we judge ourselves. Many people carry guilt over failed resolutions, lapses in discipline, or recurring negative behaviours. But these "failures" are often not reflections of character—they are the natural outcome of misaligned or misunderstood habit loops. By taking a more scientific and compassionate approach to our behaviours, we move from self-blame to self-understanding. We become observers and designers of our routines, rather than victims of them.

As we continue to explore the architecture of habit formation throughout this book, the habit loop will remain a foundational model. It is not a passing theory, but a practical framework with real-world applications. Whether you want to exercise more, reduce stress, improve focus, or simply feel more in control of your day, the habit loop is the mechanism through which change occurs. It provides the language, the structure, and the strategy.

By learning to identify cues, craft effective routines, and reinforce them with meaningful rewards, you take control of the behavioural scripts that guide your life. You shift from living reactively to acting intentionally. You become not just a participant in your habits, but their author. And in that shift lies the beginning of true transformation—measured not in radical overhauls, but in small, deliberate loops repeated over time.

The Science of Habit Formation

At the crossroads of psychology and neuroscience lies one of the most transformative understandings of human behaviour: how habits are formed. Far from being accidental routines we fall into, habits are the product of precise neurological processes that govern how we learn, adapt, and navigate the complexity of daily life. They are not just behavioural patterns but deeply ingrained mental shortcuts that free up our cognitive capacity for other tasks. To understand habit formation is to understand how the brain builds efficiency, how behaviour becomes automatic, and how change can be systematically engineered from within.

The development of habits is neither mystical nor entirely mysterious. It is rooted in the brain's drive for efficiency. Every conscious action we perform requires mental energy. Decision-making, impulse control, and focused attention are cognitively expensive processes. In order to conserve resources, the brain seeks to automate frequent behaviours through repetition. Once a behaviour is repeated often enough in the same context, it becomes encoded as a habit—a shortcut that allows the brain to delegate the task to a lower-cost system. This transfer from conscious effort to automaticity is what makes habits both so helpful and so difficult to change.

The primary brain structure responsible for this shift is the basal ganglia, a cluster of nuclei located deep within the cerebral hemispheres. This region plays a crucial role in movement, learning, and routine behaviours. When a new task is being learned—riding a bicycle, for example—the prefrontal cortex is highly active. This part of the brain is responsible for executive functions: planning, decision-making, problem-solving. But as the task becomes more familiar through repetition, activity in the prefrontal cortex diminishes. Simultaneously, the basal ganglia take over, streamlining the action into a smooth, automatic sequence.

This neurological handover is what enables us to perform complex tasks without consciously thinking about every step. Think about the first time you drove a car. Every movement required focus: adjusting the mirrors, checking blind spots, pressing the pedals with precision. But after sufficient repetition, those actions become instinctive. You can now drive while holding a conversation, listening to a podcast, or even planning your day ahead. The underlying behaviour has not changed—what's changed is the brain's allocation of effort.

This process—encoding behaviour into the basal ganglia—is not reserved for physical activities alone. It applies to emotional responses, decision-making habits, and even self-talk. If, for example, you routinely respond to stress by reaching for your phone or avoiding difficult tasks, those responses become neural patterns just as robust as brushing your teeth. What began as a conscious coping mechanism becomes an automatic response, triggered without reflection. Understanding this allows us to appreciate that many of our struggles with behaviour are not moral failings or personality flaws—they are deeply conditioned responses embedded in neural pathways.

The process of forming a habit can be mapped through a feedback loop known as the cue-routine-reward cycle, which we examined in the previous section. But the neurological substrate that underpins this loop deserves closer attention. When a cue is encountered—say, the smell of coffee in the morning—the brain lights up in anticipation. Dopamine, a neurotransmitter associated with pleasure and motivation, is released not at the moment of reward, but in anticipation of it. This anticipation primes the brain to perform the behaviour, strengthening the neural connection each time the routine is successfully executed and rewarded. It is this release of dopamine that makes habits so sticky. The brain not only remembers the behaviour—it *wants* to repeat it.

Crucially, repetition is the mechanism through which these neural pathways are reinforced. The axiom "neurons that fire together, wire together" summarises the process of synaptic strengthening: when two neurons are activated repeatedly in close succession, the connection between them becomes stronger. This is known as long-term potentiation, and it is the biological basis of learning and memory. In the context of habit formation, each time a habit loop is completed, the brain becomes slightly more efficient at executing it. The synaptic connections involved become faster, more reliable, and eventually, automatic.

This neurological foundation also explains why consistency is more effective than intensity when establishing new habits. A behaviour performed briefly but frequently is more likely to become hardwired than one performed sporadically with great effort. Consider someone trying to build a writing habit. Writing one paragraph every day, at the same time and place, does more to create a habit than writing ten pages once a fortnight. It is not the volume of the behaviour that matters most, but its frequency and contextual stability.

The implications of this understanding are profound. They suggest that habit formation is not about willpower but about architecture—about constructing an environment and routine that cue the desired behaviour, make it easy to perform, and reward it in a meaningful way. For example, if your goal is to develop a reading habit, placing a book on your pillow each morning serves as a cue that's hard to ignore. The act of reading even one page becomes the routine, and the sense of relaxation or accomplishment that follows becomes the reward. Repeat this process over several weeks, and the brain will begin to anticipate and crave the experience, embedding it into your daily rhythm.

But the science of habit formation also presents a more nuanced truth: not all habits form at the same rate, and not all individuals build habits in the same way. Studies suggest that on average, it takes around 66 days to form a new habit—but this number varies widely depending on the complexity of the behaviour, the individual's environment, and their psychological predispositions. Simple habits like drinking a glass of water after waking may become automatic in a few weeks. More complex habits, such as exercising for thirty minutes or learning a new language, may require months of repetition before becoming routine.

Moreover, emotional context plays a vital role in habit consolidation. Habits that are emotionally reinforced—those linked to positive emotions, social validation, or relief from discomfort—tend to stick more readily. This is why many habits are formed during emotionally charged periods of life: moving to a new city, starting a new job, becoming a parent. These transitions create opportunities to rewire routines because the usual cues and contexts are disrupted. When old patterns are broken, new ones are easier to form—if we seize the opportunity with awareness.

This insight is particularly valuable for those looking to break old habits and form new ones simultaneously. It is not enough to simply stop a behaviour. The brain resists vacuums. If a cue still exists and the reward is still desired, the brain will seek out a replacement routine. Therefore, the key to breaking a habit is not eradication but substitution. For instance, if stress at work triggers the habit of eating junk food, the underlying cue (stress) and reward (relief) remain. By substituting the routine with a healthier alternative—such as taking a short walk or practising breathing exercises—the habit loop can be preserved and redirected in a healthier direction.

The malleability of the brain, often referred to as *neuroplasticity*, is what makes all of this possible. Far from being fixed after childhood, the adult brain retains a remarkable capacity to adapt and rewire itself in response to new behaviours. This plasticity means that it is never too late to change habits. With deliberate effort, structured repetition, and a supportive environment, even the most deeply entrenched behaviours can be reshaped. What's more, each successful habit change strengthens the brain's capacity to adapt, creating a virtuous cycle of personal growth.

Take the story of Raymond, a 52-year-old man who had struggled with alcohol dependence for over two decades. His recovery did not begin with a grand gesture or a dramatic life event. It began with one micro habit: each time he felt the urge to drink, he would text a trusted friend. This small action, repeated consistently, created a new neural association: discomfort led to connection rather than escapism. Over time, that one habit snowballed into others—daily walks, journaling, volunteering. Each action reinforced the next, rewiring not only his brain but his self-concept. He was no longer a man resisting temptation—he was a man building a life worth being present for.

Such stories remind us that habit formation is not merely a clinical process, but a deeply human one. It is grounded in biology, yes, but it is also animated by meaning, identity, and the quiet courage to begin again. The science offers tools and frameworks; it demystifies the mechanisms at play. But the motivation to apply that science—to build a new routine, to resist an old trigger, to celebrate a small win—comes from something far more personal. It comes from the recognition that change is not beyond our reach. It is embedded in our brains, waiting to be activated by choice and repetition.

As we continue through this book, we will explore the strategies that make these changes easier to implement. But never lose sight of this truth: your brain is not working against you. It is working exactly as it was designed to. Its systems are not flawed—they are efficient. And when you understand how they operate, you gain the ability to harness them for your benefit. Habits are not destiny—they are design. And you hold the blueprint.

Why Small Matters

In a culture enamoured with speed and spectacle, the notion of starting small can seem counterintuitive—perhaps even disappointing. Popular narratives of transformation tend to focus on grand gestures: dramatic weight loss, overnight business success, or radical lifestyle shifts. Yet beneath these stories often lies a quieter, more powerful truth—real, lasting change is most often the result of small, consistent actions repeated over time. This is not a philosophical proposition; it is a behavioural and neurological fact. Micro habits—those tiny actions that may take just a minute or two—possess an outsized capacity to initiate meaningful change because they bypass resistance and reduce the mental burden that derails most efforts at self-improvement.

To understand why small matters, we must first consider the psychological phenomenon of *mental resistance.* Whenever we contemplate a new behaviour—starting a fitness regime, adopting a mindfulness practice, launching a creative project—we are met not only by the logistical challenge of time and energy, but also by an invisible internal wall. This resistance manifests as procrastination, self-doubt, or inertia. The brain, designed to conserve energy and minimise perceived threat, reacts to unfamiliar or demanding tasks with hesitation. Even when a goal is important, the sheer scale of the change can activate a subtle fear response, prompting avoidance rather than action.

This resistance is not a moral failing. It is the mind's default mechanism for managing cognitive overload and emotional discomfort. However, it poses a serious obstacle to behavioural change—particularly when the desired change is perceived as complex, effortful, or time-consuming. Herein lies the brilliance of micro habits. By reducing the entry point to something so simple that it hardly feels worth resisting, we lower the threshold for action. The habit becomes easier to start than to avoid.

Imagine someone who wants to develop a regular writing practice. Telling themselves to "write for an hour each day" may trigger a cascade of resistance—worries about time, doubts about quality, and a general sense of pressure. But shifting the initial commitment to "write one sentence" removes the friction. The task becomes so manageable that the brain's protective defences don't engage. More often than not, writing a sentence leads to a paragraph, and sometimes even to a page. But the brilliance lies in the fact that even if it doesn't, the habit has still been honoured. The streak continues. The identity of "writer" is reinforced.

This phenomenon has been echoed across countless domains. Consider the simple act of flossing. Dental professionals have long struggled to encourage patients to make flossing a daily habit. But when people are told they only need to floss *one tooth*, compliance increases dramatically. Once the floss is in hand and the first tooth is done, most people continue. The behaviour gains momentum through initiation, not willpower. The initial micro action becomes a gateway, not a limitation.

What makes this approach so effective is its alignment with the principle of *cognitive ease*. When the brain evaluates a task as easy and familiar, it is more likely to engage. Micro habits create this sense of ease by removing ambiguity and limiting the cognitive load required to begin. Instead of having to plan, strategise, or debate internally, the behaviour is defined, immediate, and unthreatening. This clears a path for action to take place before resistance can gather force.

A closely related concept is that of *decision fatigue*. Each day, we make thousands of decisions—some trivial, others consequential. Over time, the cumulative burden of choice wears down our mental resources. This phenomenon explains why people struggle to make good decisions in the evening, or why even simple tasks feel overwhelming after a long day. When behaviour change depends on making another decision—"Should I go for a run?" "Do I feel like meditating?"—the answer often becomes no, simply because the mind is tired. Micro habits circumvent this trap by pre-deciding the action in advance and embedding it into a consistent routine. They function not as choices, but as defaults.

Consider the example of Elina, a busy solicitor who wanted to incorporate physical activity into her workday but found herself perpetually exhausted and unmotivated. Traditional advice—"go to the gym three times a week"—felt unrealistic. Instead, she committed to doing a single minute of stretching as soon as she arrived home. The simplicity of the action meant she rarely skipped it. Over time, the habit grew organically: one minute became three, then ten. But more importantly, the act of arriving home began to trigger a positive behavioural loop. She now associates the end of the workday with movement and renewal rather than collapse. The initial micro habit didn't just create physical change—it altered the psychological script that had kept her stuck.

This principle extends far beyond health. Micro habits can be applied to productivity, creativity, emotional regulation, and relationship-building. Writing one line of gratitude each evening can rewire attention towards the positive. Making eye contact and offering a genuine greeting each morning can strengthen a family dynamic. Saving a small amount of money daily—an amount so small it seems negligible—can lead to larger financial discipline. The power of these actions lies not in their immediate impact, but in their cumulative effect and the sense of control they instil.

Another reason micro habits are so effective is that they align with how the brain encodes behaviour. As discussed in previous sections, the basal ganglia automate repeated actions, allowing us to execute them without deliberate thought. For a habit to reach this level of automaticity, it must first be practised consistently. This is where many well-intentioned efforts falter. People set goals that require large investments of time and energy—investments they cannot always sustain. As a result, the behaviour is executed sporadically, never gaining enough traction to become a habit. Micro habits, by contrast, are sustainable. Their small size ensures they can be performed even on the busiest days, maintaining the repetition necessary for neural embedding.

It's also worth noting that micro habits are not static. While their strength lies in their simplicity, they are designed to grow. This concept is referred to as *habit scaling*. Once a micro habit is established and automatic, it becomes a foundation upon which larger behaviours can be built. You may begin with a two-minute breathing exercise and eventually find yourself practising twenty minutes of meditation daily. The key is that the expansion feels natural, not forced. The identity has shifted, the context is familiar, and the resistance has been eroded through practice.

Some critics argue that small habits are too insignificant to matter. This misses the point entirely. The goal of a micro habit is not to achieve a result on day one—it is to build the capacity for action. It is to establish a behavioural anchor that endures, even when motivation wavers or life becomes unpredictable. And it is to build trust in oneself—a belief that action is possible, that progress is underway, and that change is within reach.

This psychological shift—what could be called *self-efficacy through simplicity*—is one of the most powerful benefits of micro habits. When we complete a small action that aligns with our goals, we experience a subtle but meaningful boost in confidence. We are no longer someone who *wants* to read more—we are someone who *did* read today. We are not waiting for the right moment to begin—we have already begun. This sense of agency, repeated daily, becomes a self-fulfilling prophecy.

Ultimately, what micro habits offer is a new narrative about change. They replace the outdated model of transformation as upheaval with one of continuous evolution. They teach us that excellence is not born from occasional brilliance but from consistent commitment. And they remind us that our lives are not defined by the scale of our actions but by their direction. Each small act is a vote cast for the person we wish to become.

Why do small steps matter? Because they are the only steps we can take when we are tired, afraid, uncertain, or overwhelmed. And those are the moments that define whether a habit survives or dies. Micro habits are resilient because they are realistic. They meet us where we are, ask little, and offer much. They are the quiet scaffolding of a life well lived—built not on bursts of energy, but on the steady beat of tiny, repeated choices.

In the chapters ahead, we will delve further into how to construct these habits effectively, how to integrate them into different areas of life, and how to use them as levers for larger transformations. But let this be your foundation: when in doubt, start smaller than you think you need to. The human brain does not change through intention alone—it changes through behaviour. And the best behaviour to adopt is the one you'll actually do. Repeatedly. Effortlessly. Even when life is at its most chaotic.

Because change doesn't require a revolution. It requires one small act—repeated with care and purpose—until it becomes who you are.

The Myth of Motivation

Motivation, in popular discourse, has acquired an almost mythical status. It is portrayed as the secret ingredient behind every act of greatness, the spark that separates the high-achievers from the rest, and the wellspring from which all sustained effort is drawn. It is often visualised in cinematic montages—where protagonists rise early, push themselves to extremes, and defy all odds with a ferocious inner drive. In this narrative, motivation is king. If you succeed, it's because you were motivated; if you fail, you simply didn't want it badly enough. But while this view is intoxicating, it is deeply flawed. The idea that motivation alone drives behaviour, and that its absence explains our failures, is not just misleading—it is actively harmful.

Motivation is, by its nature, fickle. It fluctuates according to mood, context, physical state, and environment. You may feel highly driven one day and utterly apathetic the next, even if your goals haven't changed. It is influenced by sleep quality, stress levels, nutrition, hormones, and dozens of intangible factors beyond our conscious control. Relying on motivation to guide consistent action is akin to depending on the weather for your commute: you might make it some days, but there will be plenty of days when you stay home simply because the conditions aren't ideal. Building meaningful habits, therefore, requires a more stable foundation—one that doesn't depend on how enthusiastic you happen to feel at any given moment.

To move beyond the illusion of motivation, we must examine what actually sustains behaviour over time. The answer is not inspiration—it is structure. Behavioural consistency is far more a function of design than desire. What enables someone to go to the gym every morning isn't that they *feel like it*—it's that they have a system that makes it easier to go than to skip. The environment supports the action, the cue is present, the routine is simple, and the friction is low. When habits are embedded into our surroundings and anchored to predictable cues, they begin to function with minimal effort. In contrast, when everything relies on internal resolve, behaviour becomes fragile—easily derailed by distraction, discomfort, or a shift in mood.

This understanding aligns with decades of behavioural research. Psychologists have long noted that willpower is a finite resource. In a phenomenon known as "ego depletion," individuals who exercise self-control in one area tend to struggle with it later in the day. For example, someone who spends the afternoon resisting snacks may be more likely to skip their workout or lash out in frustration that evening. Willpower is not a well we can draw from endlessly—it is more like a muscle that tires with use. When we construct our habits around willpower, we are asking that muscle to work constantly, without rest. It is no wonder so many self-improvement efforts collapse under their own weight.

The alternative lies in creating systems that reduce the need for constant self-regulation. This begins with crafting an environment that makes desired behaviours easy, automatic, and rewarding. Take, for instance, the act of reading before bed. If the book is on your nightstand, a light is easily accessible, and your phone is out of reach, you are far more likely to read than if you need to rummage through a bag, get up to find a charger, or fight the temptation of notifications. The action becomes part of the landscape, not a task to be negotiated.

Real-life examples of this principle abound. Consider the case of Harish, a software engineer who wanted to establish a habit of running in the morning. For months, he told himself he needed to be more motivated. He followed fitness influencers, watched motivational videos, and even posted public goals for accountability. None of it worked for long. What eventually made the difference was laying out his running clothes the night before, preparing his water bottle, and setting his shoes by the door. These micro adjustments didn't make him more inspired—they made the behaviour frictionless. He no longer had to *choose* to run. It simply became what he did after waking. Motivation became irrelevant.

What Harish discovered is echoed by many high-performing individuals: the secret to consistency is not a deeper emotional commitment, but a more intelligent behavioural scaffold. Olympic athletes, for example, don't wake up every morning brimming with motivation. They often face exhaustion, self-doubt, or emotional strain. What keeps them training is not inspiration—it is routine. Their schedules, coaches, and environments are deliberately engineered to minimise decision-making and maximise execution. They don't have to psych themselves up for each session because the habit is already embedded into their lifestyle.

The same logic applies to mundane habits. Brushing your teeth, for most adults, is not something you debate each day. You don't require motivational speeches or affirmations to do it. The action is automatic, triggered by context, reinforced by identity. You brush because that's what people like you do. This is where habits become most powerful—not when they are tasks on a to-do list, but when they are expressions of identity. And identity, once reinforced through action, becomes far more stable than transient motivation.

Another crucial element that replaces motivation is *momentum*. When a habit is easy to start and yields some form of positive feedback, however small, it creates a reinforcing loop. The brain enjoys completion. It enjoys checking a box, closing a loop, or seeing a chain of progress. Habit tracking, visual cues, and micro rewards all serve to generate this sense of motion. Even if the action is minimal—stretching for one minute, writing a single line, meditating for thirty seconds—it signals to the brain that something valuable has been done. This sense of progress can become self-sustaining, especially when anchored to a broader narrative of who you are becoming.

Importantly, the myth of motivation can also trap people in cycles of self-blame. When individuals fail to follow through on their goals, they often assume they simply lack discipline or passion. This internal narrative is corrosive. It erodes confidence and discourages future attempts. But when viewed through the lens of behavioural design, the same failure appears in a very different light: not as a character flaw, but as a system flaw. The question shifts from "Why can't I do this?" to "What structural change would make this easier?" This reframing is empowering. It transforms failure into feedback and invites experimentation over judgment.

This perspective is particularly valuable in contexts of high stress or low energy. When life becomes chaotic—due to work pressure, illness, parenting demands, or emotional upheaval—motivation tends to vanish. This is when most habits are abandoned. But when those habits are small enough, and supported by context, they can survive even the hardest days. A micro habit, such as putting on your trainers or sitting on your meditation cushion, requires so little energy that it can often be performed even when everything else feels overwhelming. These moments of action, however minor, preserve continuity. They send a signal: I may be struggling, but I haven't stopped.

There is also a hidden psychological dividend in choosing action over waiting for motivation. Each time you do something you don't feel like doing—but do it anyway—you reinforce your sense of agency. You learn that you are not at the mercy of your emotions, that your behaviour is not dictated solely by internal weather patterns. Over time, this builds resilience. You come to trust yourself—not because you always feel ready, but because you act regardless. This trust is far more valuable than any fleeting sense of motivation, because it is built on evidence, not emotion.

This is not to suggest that motivation is entirely irrelevant. It has its place. It can serve as a spark, a catalyst, or an accelerant. But it is not the fuel. It is not the foundation. If anything, motivation should be treated as a bonus—pleasant when it appears, but never required. The real work of habit formation lies in the unglamorous, uncelebrated consistency of small actions performed on autopilot. And that consistency is far more achievable when habits are grounded in environment, structure, and identity—not inspiration.

So, if you've been waiting to feel more motivated before starting something important—stop waiting. Instead, ask a more useful question: What is the smallest version of this behaviour I can start today? What context would make it easier? What cue can I attach it to? What reward will keep me coming back? These are the questions that create habits. These are the questions that change lives.

Because the truth is this: you don't need to feel ready. You just need to begin. And once you do, you'll find that action often generates the very motivation you thought you needed beforehand. Not the other way around.

Chapter 2
The Science Behind Micro Habits

When people speak of transformation, they often leap to images of sweeping changes—drastic resolutions, bold life pivots, or epiphanies that promise overnight reinvention. There's something seductively cinematic about the idea. But real change? The kind that lasts? It tends to move in subtler rhythms. Quiet, steady, sometimes so gradual it's barely perceptible until you look back. This is where micro habits come into their own. These small, deliberately chosen behaviours, repeated with regularity, have the capacity to snowball into extraordinary change over time. And this isn't mere speculation; the science behind it is both robust and fascinating.

One of the central ideas underpinning micro habits is that of marginal gains. If the phrase rings a bell, it might be because of its origins in elite sport—specifically, British Cycling under Sir Dave Brailsford's stewardship. His philosophy was disarmingly simple: if you can improve every component of performance by just one percent, the overall effect will be dramatic. Adjust the saddle height. Refine the diet. Optimise sleep. Each change, on its own, hardly worth noting. But collectively? They delivered a revolution. The same logic applies to personal development. A one percent improvement each day may seem inconsequential in the moment, but it doesn't yield linear progress—it compounds. And that compounding, when sustained, alters the trajectory of a life.

This concept is not merely a motivational metaphor; it's firmly rooted in the biology of the brain. Neuroplasticity—the brain's remarkable capacity to rewire itself in response to experience—offers the physiological foundation. We used to believe, rather arrogantly, that after a certain age the brain stopped changing. That view, fortunately, has been left behind. The brain remains adaptable throughout life. Every time we engage in a behaviour, corresponding neural pathways are lit up. Do it again, and the signal strengthens. Keep going, and the pathway becomes a sort of neurological motorway—quicker, more efficient, automatic. Micro habits take advantage of this process by encouraging repeated behaviours that don't tax the brain's finite energy reserves.

Take mindfulness, for instance. Many people are drawn to meditation but struggle to make it a daily practice. A full thirty-minute session sounds admirable—and intimidating. Instead, beginning with two minutes of deep, intentional breathing does something far more achievable: it activates neural networks associated with attention and emotional control. You do it again the next day. And the next. The circuits get stronger. The brain begins to expect the practice. Eventually, the habit becomes less of a chore and more of a default.

One of the reasons this approach works so well is that it doesn't provoke the inner defences that often sabotage change. Human psychology, as behavioural economists have long pointed out, is riddled with biases that trip us up. Chief among them is loss aversion—we're wired to fear loss more than we value gain. A major lifestyle overhaul may promise benefits, but it also threatens to unsettle the familiar. That sense of disruption triggers resistance. Micro habits, being so small and non-intrusive, bypass that alarm system. They don't feel risky. They feel doable, even on a bad day.

There's also the matter of anchoring. Our decisions and behaviours tend to latch onto whatever comes first in a sequence. Use that tendency wisely, and it becomes a powerful tool. For example, writing a single line in a journal before opening your inbox creates a behavioural anchor. It's a small act, but it establishes a rhythm. Likewise, what we consider the "default" often wins by mere ease. If a journal is already open on your desk, or if your gym clothes are in plain sight, you're far more likely to follow through. The behaviour becomes frictionless.

These aren't just theoretical constructs. They show up in the texture of real life. Take Leena, a professional overwhelmed by meetings, deadlines, and the general chaos of the workday. She knew she needed to drink more water, but reminders weren't working. Instead, she began placing a glass of water on her desk before logging in each morning. That simple act changed everything. The cue was visible. The action required no deliberation. And within weeks, drinking water throughout the day had become second nature. The habit had taken root—not through willpower, but through subtle design.

What keeps such behaviours alive beneath the surface is the brain's reward system. Dopamine, a key player here, isn't only released when we succeed—it surges in anticipation of success. That means the brain starts to look forward to certain behaviours when it learns they're followed by something pleasurable or satisfying. It's why checking a box on a habit tracker can feel oddly gratifying. The act itself is minor. The neurological impact is not. Those small victories reinforce the habit loop, making repetition more likely.

And something deeper begins to shift. The transformation isn't limited to behaviour—it touches identity. This is perhaps the most elegant aspect of micro habits: they shape not just what you do, but who you believe yourself to be. Writing one paragraph a day doesn't just produce content; it nurtures the identity of a writer. Taking a brief walk after dinner isn't just exercise; it's a declaration, however quiet, that you are someone who takes care of your health. Each act is a kind of vote for the person you wish to become. And those votes accumulate.

Identity, after all, is a powerful anchor for behaviour. Once we see ourselves in a certain light, we tend to act in ways that affirm that self-image. Micro habits give us a practical route to reshape that image—not by force, but by evidence. Each small action is a whisper: "This is who I am." And because the habit is so modest, it doesn't provoke the resistance or anxiety that often accompanies larger ambitions. It's a gentle nudge, not a shove.

This is why micro habits shouldn't be mistaken for minor life hacks or productivity tricks. They offer something more enduring—a method of self-authorship. Through them, we can revise not only our routines but our sense of self. And they do so without the drama of radical change. No need to overhaul everything at once. No reliance on elusive bursts of motivation. Just a handful of consistent, low-resistance actions aligned with what matters to you.

In the pages ahead, we'll examine these mechanisms in more detail: the power of incremental gains, the flexibility of the brain through neuroplasticity, and how behavioural biases can be harnessed rather than feared. We'll explore how dopamine links emotion to learning, and how habits—even tiny ones—can evolve into identity-defining practices.

Where the first chapter gave us the rationale for focusing on habits, this one goes further. It lays out the mechanics—not in the dry sense of tips and tricks, but through a deeper understanding of why these things actually work. With this perspective, you won't just know *how* to build micro habits—you'll understand *why* they matter, how they alter the mind, and what it means to make them part of who you are becoming.

The Power of Tiny Gains

When people reflect on meaningful change, they often imagine it in dramatic terms—a sudden breakthrough, a bold decision, or an extraordinary effort that turns everything around. Yet, more often than not, real transformation does not arrive as a single event but accumulates through a quiet process of consistent, incremental improvement. This is the essence of *tiny gains*, the cumulative advantage that arises when we focus on getting just a little better, a little more often. The idea may appear deceptively simple, but its scientific, psychological, and practical implications are profound. Tiny gains, though small in scale, create exponential change over time.

The concept of marginal gains gained global prominence through the work of Sir Dave Brailsford, performance director for British Cycling. Faced with a national team that had achieved little on the world stage, Brailsford introduced an approach built not on revolution, but on refinement. He believed that if every aspect of performance could be improved by just one percent—nutrition, recovery, posture, gear, mindset—the results would compound. It sounded modest. But within five years, British cyclists began dominating international competitions, winning Tour de France titles and Olympic golds in unprecedented numbers. Brailsford's marginal gains philosophy did not rely on heroic efforts. It relied on the mathematics of compound improvement.

This same principle can be applied to everyday life with equal effectiveness. If you improve by one percent each day, the effect is not additive, it's exponential. A one percent improvement repeated consistently does not result in being thirty-seven percent better after thirty-seven days—it yields results that are vastly more significant due to the compounding effect. Just as compound interest grows wealth over time, small improvements accumulate and amplify, reshaping outcomes in ways that feel almost magical in hindsight.

Yet despite its efficacy, the notion of small gains often struggles to capture attention. In a world driven by immediacy and spectacle, slow progress feels unrewarding. The incremental nature of tiny gains can seem too subtle, even invisible, in the short term. People abandon new routines because they don't yield immediate results, overlooking the fact that the most meaningful change is often the slowest to reveal itself. Going to the gym once doesn't transform your health. Saving five pounds doesn't alter your financial status. Writing a single paragraph doesn't finish a novel. But repeated daily, these actions become the foundation for transformative outcomes. Over time, they reshape not just what you do, but who you become.

One of the core psychological challenges in embracing tiny gains is overcoming our bias toward *event-based thinking*. We are conditioned to believe that change must be tied to significant events—a new year, a milestone birthday, a crisis, or a deadline. But effective habit formation requires a shift to *process-based thinking*, where progress is measured not by grand moments but by sustained action. This shift is empowering. It means we don't need to wait for the perfect time or an ideal circumstance to begin improving. We can begin today, with whatever resources and energy we have, because the scale of the action matters far less than the consistency of the effort.

This perspective also encourages a different relationship with success and failure. When we think in terms of marginal gains, a lapse or setback is not catastrophic—it's a temporary dip in an otherwise upward trajectory. If improvement is cumulative, then missing a day or falling short is simply part of the process. What matters most is the trend over time, not any single moment. This mindset fosters resilience. It helps people stay committed through the inevitable fluctuations of motivation, mood, and life's unpredictability.

Consider the case of Priya, a mother of two and a full-time employee, who wanted to reclaim her health after years of neglect. With limited time and energy, she began walking for five minutes during her lunch break. It felt embarrassingly small at first, especially compared to the hour-long workouts she used to do in her twenties. But she persisted. Over several weeks, the walks extended to ten minutes. Then fifteen. Eventually, they became daily rituals that improved her mood, lowered her stress, and rekindled a sense of agency. She later added healthier snacks, short stretches in the morning, and better sleep routines. None of these habits were impressive on their own—but collectively, they transformed her well-being. The power of her progress lay not in intensity, but in accumulation.

The elegance of tiny gains is that they are accessible to everyone. Regardless of your starting point—whether you feel stuck, overwhelmed, or discouraged—there is always a small step you can take. You don't need talent, privilege, or perfect conditions. You need only a commitment to start, however humbly. That is what makes the concept so democratic and empowering. It removes the intimidation from change and replaces it with something far more manageable: deliberate, consistent effort.

From a neurological perspective, this approach also aligns with how the brain learns and adapts. Repetition is the key to encoding behaviours in the brain's neural circuits. The more a behaviour is repeated, the more efficient and automatic it becomes. But for repetition to occur, the behaviour must be sustainable. Large, ambitious changes often fail because they require too much effort to be repeated consistently. Micro habits, by contrast, succeed precisely because they are small enough to be repeated without resistance. This repetition strengthens the relevant neural pathways, gradually shifting the behaviour from effortful to effortless.

Tiny gains also shift the narrative of self-perception. Each time we follow through on a small commitment, we reinforce the identity of someone who takes action, who honours their goals, who follows through. These micro signals matter. They shape how we see ourselves, and that identity feeds back into behaviour. If you consistently do five minutes of yoga each morning, you begin to think of yourself as someone who takes care of their body. If you read one page each evening, you reinforce the identity of a reader. This identity shift, though subtle at first, becomes the fuel for deeper, more enduring change.

There is also a philosophical dimension to the power of small gains. In a world that prizes extremes—faster, louder, more impressive—the discipline of quiet, continuous improvement becomes an act of resistance. It is a return to the idea that excellence is forged not in bursts of effort but in the steady refinement of daily habits. It invites us to value consistency over novelty, depth over spectacle, and patience over perfectionism.

To apply this principle effectively, we must embrace two key truths. First, that small does not mean insignificant. Second, that change is not something we wait for—it is something we build, layer by layer, through our actions. This is why a two-minute habit matters. It is not the result that counts at first; it is the act of showing up, of beginning, of building momentum. And once that momentum is established, it becomes a powerful force of its own.

It is easy to overlook the significance of a single choice. But choices are never isolated—they are cumulative. Every time you take the stairs, read a paragraph, resist a distraction, or practise a moment of gratitude, you are casting a vote for the person you wish to become. And with enough votes, that person takes shape—not through force, but through frequency. Not through grand declarations, but through quiet repetitions.

Tiny gains teach us to fall in love with the process, to find satisfaction not only in results but in progress itself. They remind us that growth is not linear, but exponential, and that the most meaningful transformations are those that emerge slowly, naturally, and enduringly. In the same way a single drop of water wears away stone over time, small habits shape the architecture of our lives—not overnight, but inevitably.

The power of tiny gains lies in their reliability. They don't rely on motivation, they don't demand perfection, and they don't require heroics. What they do require is consistency—and faith in the compound effect of your own effort. If you can commit to getting just a little better, day by day, you may find yourself achieving far more than you ever imagined—without the struggle, without the drama, and without the need for sudden epiphanies.

The great paradox of growth is that the smallest actions often create the biggest differences—eventually. Tiny gains don't announce themselves. They whisper. But those who listen, who show up, and who trust the process, find that they are not just changing their behaviour—they are changing their trajectory. And that makes all the difference.

Neuroplasticity in Action

The human brain, once considered a rigid organ with limited capacity for change, is now known to be exquisitely adaptable. This adaptability, known as *neuroplasticity*, refers to the brain's remarkable ability to rewire itself in response to experience, learning, and behaviour. Every thought we have, every movement we make, and every habit we repeat leaves a trace in the neural architecture of our brain. Over time, those traces can become deeply embedded pathways that guide our automatic behaviours and perceptions. When we speak of building micro habits, we are not simply discussing behaviour change—we are speaking of reshaping the very structure of the brain.

At the core of neuroplasticity is the idea that neurons—nerve cells in the brain—can form new connections and strengthen existing ones. This happens in response to repeated stimulation. As the neuroscientific adage goes, "neurons that fire together, wire together." When two neurons are activated simultaneously, the connection between them strengthens, making it more likely that they will activate together again in future. Repetition consolidates this wiring, making certain behaviours and thoughts more automatic. The more often you perform a behaviour, the more your brain refines and reinforces the neural circuit responsible for it, streamlining its execution.

Micro habits, because of their simplicity and consistency, are particularly well-suited to leverage this biological principle. When a habit is small and easy to repeat, it is more likely to be performed regularly. This consistency is what gives the habit a neurological foothold. Whether it's drinking a glass of water upon waking, taking three deep breaths before a meeting, or writing one sentence each day, these actions may seem insignificant in isolation. Yet with repetition, they become the scaffolding for new neural circuits—ones that support the behaviours we want to see more of in our lives.

Consider the case of Amal, a software developer who struggled with anxiety and poor concentration. On the advice of a coach, she began a micro habit of mindful breathing each morning—just sixty seconds of attention to her breath before opening her laptop. It felt trivial at first, but within weeks, Amal noticed a change. She became more grounded before meetings, more patient in problem-solving, and less reactive when things went wrong. What had happened was not just psychological—it was neurobiological. Repeated practice had strengthened the networks in her brain responsible for attention regulation and emotional control. Her micro habit was not just calming her—it was rewiring her.

What makes neuroplasticity so powerful is that it is continuous. It does not stop after childhood or adolescence; it persists throughout life. This has profound implications for how we think about growth and change. We are not fixed. Our brains are not static. We carry within us the capacity to adapt and evolve through deliberate practice and repeated action. This means that micro habits are not mere behavioural tweaks—they are tools for neurological transformation.

This understanding is especially helpful when trying to change long-standing habits or thought patterns. Many people believe they are simply "not wired" to be disciplined, creative, calm, or confident. But these traits are not immutable—they are shaped by repeated experiences and reinforced behaviours. If someone has spent years avoiding difficult conversations, for instance, their brain has become efficient at activating circuits associated with avoidance and fear. By introducing a micro habit—perhaps rehearsing one assertive sentence in private each day—they begin to activate different circuits. With time, repetition, and reinforcement, the brain shifts. The trait that once felt innate becomes malleable.

The impact of neuroplasticity is not limited to psychological states or behaviours; it is also evident in physical and cognitive skills. Studies of musicians, athletes, and polyglots consistently show that those who practise frequently—even in small, regular intervals—develop measurable changes in brain regions associated with their skill. This research has demonstrated that sustained, focused practice can enlarge the hippocampus (involved in memory), thicken the motor cortex (controlling movement), and increase connectivity between hemispheres. Importantly, it is not the length of practice that drives these changes—it is the frequency and repetition.

Micro habits align beautifully with this requirement. Because they are sustainable, they ensure that the behaviour gets rehearsed often enough to effect neurological change. A writer who crafts a single paragraph daily may not notice immediate results, but they are fine-tuning the circuits of language, focus, and creative processing. A musician who practises one scale each day is reinforcing motor skills and auditory sensitivity. These incremental adaptations are quiet but potent—and over time, they reshape what is possible.

It is worth emphasising that neuroplasticity is a double-edged sword. The brain does not differentiate between productive and unproductive habits; it simply strengthens what is repeated. This is why unwanted behaviours can become so entrenched. If you routinely respond to stress by scrolling through your phone or avoiding tasks, those behaviours become deeply encoded. The brain becomes increasingly efficient at performing them, reducing the energy required to engage in them again. This is why breaking a habit can feel like swimming upstream—it is not merely a question of choice, but of neurological inertia.

However, even entrenched circuits can be weakened and replaced. Neuroplasticity allows for what is known as *synaptic pruning*—the gradual weakening and elimination of connections that are no longer used. When a habit is interrupted or replaced consistently, the brain begins to redirect resources. Old patterns fade, and new ones take their place. This is where the consistency of micro habits becomes vital. A small, daily behaviour that reinforces a desired outcome has the potential to override a stronger but less consistent pattern.

Real-world application of this principle can be seen in cognitive behavioural therapy, which often employs repeated exposure and reframing techniques to alter thought patterns. For instance, someone with social anxiety might be encouraged to initiate brief interactions daily, even something as small as making eye contact and saying hello. Though minimal, these actions begin to activate neural networks associated with safety and social connection rather than avoidance and fear. Over time, the anxiety response diminishes—not through willpower, but through rewiring.

Micro habits also have a unique role to play in reinforcing *positive feedback loops*. When an action is followed by a positive emotional or functional outcome, the brain registers it as worthwhile. This reinforces the neural pathway and increases the likelihood of repetition. A person who begins their day with a two-minute stretch may feel slightly more energised or clear-headed. That mild reward, registered by the brain's dopaminergic system, strengthens the association between the cue and the behaviour. If the behaviour is repeated consistently, the reward becomes expected, and the action becomes habitual.

What distinguishes micro habits from larger behavioural changes is not just their size, but their strategic fit with how the brain learns. Large changes often fail because they activate stress responses in the brain. They feel unsafe, overwhelming, or unsustainable. Micro habits, by contrast, operate below the threshold of resistance. They feel doable—even enjoyable—and thus avoid triggering the brain's fight-or-flight mechanisms. This makes them ideal vehicles for harnessing neuroplasticity, because they allow for consistent, low-stress repetition. And repetition, not intensity, is what rewires the brain.

Perhaps one of the most profound implications of neuroplasticity is that it restores agency. Many people feel trapped by their past behaviours, their current limitations, or their perceived lack of potential. But the brain is always listening. It is always adapting. Every action we take, however small, is a signal to the brain about what matters, what is useful, and what should be strengthened. Micro habits provide a powerful way to direct that signal. They give us a mechanism to influence our mental architecture, one action at a time.

This understanding also encourages patience. Neuroplastic change is not instantaneous. It unfolds slowly, often invisibly, over weeks and months. There is no flash of insight or sudden shift. But then, one day, the behaviour feels easier. The response feels natural. The identity feels authentic. And that is the moment when effort gives way to embodiment—when the habit is no longer something you do, but something you *are*.

The scientific reality of neuroplasticity supports the most encouraging message in behavioural change: you are not stuck. Your brain is not fixed. Through consistent, intentional micro habits, you can retrain your mind, alter your emotional responses, and build the capacities you once thought were out of reach. Change is not a matter of trying harder—it is a matter of training smarter. And when the training is gentle, consistent, and strategically aligned with how the brain learns, the results can be profound.

Neuroplasticity is not only a scientific principle; it is a philosophy of possibility. It tells us that who we are is not a static truth but an ongoing construction. Micro habits give us the tools to participate actively in that construction—to become, quite literally, the architects of our own minds. And that is not merely inspiring—it is empowering.

Behavioural Economics and Habit Formation

At first glance, habit formation may appear to be a matter of discipline and repetition—a simple sequence of doing the right thing often enough until it becomes automatic. While repetition is indeed a cornerstone of habit development, this view omits a powerful and often overlooked dimension: the cognitive biases and psychological shortcuts that shape our behaviour beneath the surface. This is where the field of behavioural economics offers invaluable insight. By examining how real people make decisions—imperfectly, emotionally, and within context—it becomes clear that habit formation is as much about design as it is about desire.

Understanding principles like loss aversion, anchoring, and default bias allows us to engineer habits that work *with* our natural inclinations, rather than against them.

One of the most compelling concepts in behavioural economics is *loss aversion.* First identified by psychologists Daniel Kahneman and Amos Tversky, loss aversion refers to the tendency for individuals to feel the pain of loss more acutely than the pleasure of equivalent gain. In other words, losing £50 feels significantly worse than gaining £50 feels good. This asymmetry in emotional impact has profound implications for how we build and maintain habits. People are far more likely to take action to avoid a perceived loss than to achieve a potential benefit.

In practical terms, this means that habits framed as a means to *prevent* loss are often more motivating than those framed as opportunities for gain. For instance, telling someone that skipping their evening walk will undo their recent progress may be more compelling than highlighting the benefits of cardiovascular health. Similarly, apps that use financial stakes—such as forfeiting money if a habit is not completed—leverage loss aversion to drive consistency. While this approach must be used judiciously to avoid negative stress, it illustrates how understanding cognitive bias can increase the likelihood of follow-through.

Loss aversion also explains why people struggle to let go of existing habits, even when they are counterproductive. Giving up late-night screen time, excessive caffeine, or impulse shopping feels like a loss—not only of the behaviour itself but of the comfort or escape it provides. When the reward tied to an existing habit is immediate and pleasurable, the idea of relinquishing it triggers psychological resistance. Effective habit change, therefore, must offer an alternative that satisfies the same psychological need, reducing the sense of loss and increasing the attractiveness of the new behaviour.

Another principle from behavioural economics that influences habit formation is *anchoring.* Anchoring describes our tendency to rely heavily on the first piece of information presented to us when making decisions. This bias can affect how we perceive value, set goals, and judge progress. In the context of habits, anchoring plays a critical role in determining what we consider a reasonable or effective starting point. If someone believes that "real" meditation requires thirty minutes of silence in a cross-legged position, they may never begin. The anchor—the exaggerated standard—creates an all-or-nothing mindset that undermines initiation.

This is where micro habits offer a strategic advantage. By deliberately setting the anchor low—two minutes of meditation, one paragraph of writing, one minute of stretching—we redefine what success looks like. These low anchors reduce intimidation, create early wins, and build momentum. Over time, the behaviour often expands naturally, but it does so from a place of confidence rather than coercion. In this way, anchoring is not just a cognitive bias to be mitigated—it is a psychological tool to be wielded with intention.

Anchoring also influences how we track our progress. People often set unrealistic expectations, and when their progress fails to meet the original benchmark, they feel demoralised. Consider the example of someone trying to get fit. If their anchor is the image of a sculpted athlete training for two hours a day, their own modest 15-minute workouts may feel inadequate. Yet these consistent efforts are precisely what lead to sustainable results. Adjusting the anchor—by comparing oneself not to idealised outcomes but to one's past self—can dramatically improve motivation and reduce the risk of abandoning the habit altogether.

A third behavioural concept crucial to understanding habit formation is the *default bias*, the tendency for people to stick with the pre-set option or status quo. This bias is not rooted in laziness but in cognitive efficiency. Making decisions requires mental effort, and our brains are constantly looking for ways to conserve energy. As a result, we tend to choose the path of least resistance, especially when we are busy, tired, or distracted. The implication for habit design is clear: the easier a behaviour is to execute, and the more it resembles a default, the more likely it is to occur.

This is why environmental design is such a powerful strategy in behaviour change. If healthy snacks are visible and within reach while unhealthy ones are hidden, the brain's natural tendency to go with the default option nudges us toward better choices. Similarly, if a journal is left open on the desk or exercise clothes are placed next to the bed, the action they support is more likely to feel automatic. The goal is to design friction *out* of the habits we want to build and *into* the ones we wish to eliminate. The more seamless the desired behaviour becomes, the less it requires willpower.

Digital platforms have long exploited default bias. Streaming services auto-play the next episode, social media apps provide endless scrolling, and subscription models renew automatically. These defaults are not neutral—they guide behaviour. The same principles can be used constructively. Habit-building apps that automatically log progress, smart devices that remind users to stand or breathe, and planners that start each day with a habit checklist all utilise default bias to promote consistency. When good behaviour becomes the default—something we must *opt out of* rather than *opt into*—it becomes significantly easier to maintain.

These behavioural economics principles are especially powerful when combined. Imagine a workplace initiative designed to increase reading among employees. If the programme offers a visible tracker (anchoring success to small daily reading goals), includes a financial incentive that is lost if goals are missed (leveraging loss aversion), and provides pre-loaded digital reading materials each morning (capitalising on default bias), the likelihood of consistent engagement increases significantly. Each component addresses a different dimension of human decision-making, creating a holistic system that supports the desired habit.

What emerges from this analysis is a broader truth: habit formation is not just about internal strength or personal ambition. It is about working with the cognitive architecture of the human mind. Behavioural economics does not diminish the role of intention or motivation, but it reminds us that intentions often falter unless they are supported by smart design. The most successful habits are not those fuelled by Herculean willpower, but those embedded into daily life through cues, anchors, and effortless defaults.

For individuals, this means taking a different approach to self-improvement. Instead of asking, "How can I be more disciplined?" a more productive question might be, "How can I design this habit so that it's easier to follow than to avoid?" This shift moves the focus from internal struggle to external support—from trying harder to setting smarter defaults.

It also encourages a more compassionate relationship with oneself. Behaviour that appears lazy or inconsistent may, in fact, be entirely rational within the constraints of our cognitive biases. When we understand how factors like loss aversion, anchoring, and default bias shape our choices, we can stop blaming ourselves for not doing more—and instead, begin designing conditions that make doing better the natural outcome.

Behavioural economics thus offers not just explanation but strategy. It equips us with the tools to decode why we behave as we do and, more importantly, how we might behave differently. By incorporating these insights into the design of micro habits, we create routines that align with the reality of human psychology. The result is not only more sustainable behaviour change but a deeper understanding of what it truly means to act intentionally within a world of mental shortcuts.

In the end, habit formation is not about fighting against our biases, but about embracing them—and using them to our advantage. When we understand the unseen forces that guide our decisions, we become better equipped to build habits that last, not through effort alone, but through intelligent design. And that is the foundation upon which real, enduring change is built.

The Role of Dopamine

At the heart of habit formation lies a neurochemical messenger that plays a subtle yet profound role in shaping human behaviour—*dopamine.* Often oversimplified as the brain's "pleasure chemical," dopamine is far more complex than a simple feel-good molecule. It operates within an intricate reward system that guides motivation, reinforces learning, and strengthens habits. Understanding dopamine's role is essential to grasp why small wins matter, why consistency trumps intensity, and why micro habits are so effective in creating lasting behavioural change.

Dopamine is a neurotransmitter—a chemical signal that transmits messages between nerve cells. It is produced in several areas of the brain, but the most important for behaviour change is the *mesolimbic pathway*, often referred to as the reward pathway. This network includes key structures such as the *ventral tegmental area* (VTA) and the *nucleus accumbens*, both of which play central roles in the brain's response to rewarding stimuli. When we engage in an activity that the brain deems valuable—eating, socialising, accomplishing a task—dopamine is released, reinforcing the behaviour and increasing the likelihood that we will repeat it.

Contrary to popular belief, dopamine is not merely a response to pleasure. It is deeply involved in *anticipation* and *motivation*. The neurotransmitter spikes not only when we receive a reward, but also in response to cues that signal a reward is coming. This anticipation is what drives goal-directed behaviour. When you receive a notification on your phone, the slight surge of dopamine does not come from reading the message—it comes from the expectation that the message will bring something rewarding. This is a crucial distinction. Dopamine fuels desire and pursuit; it energises effort and anchors behaviours to outcomes.

This mechanism is fundamental to how habits are formed. In the cue-routine-reward loop, dopamine is released when the brain recognises a cue that has previously led to a rewarding experience. The spike in dopamine motivates the behaviour (routine), and when the expected reward follows, the brain strengthens the association. Over time, the habit becomes more ingrained, not because the behaviour is inherently valuable, but because the brain has learned that it *predictably* leads to a dopamine-driven sense of satisfaction.

This is where *small wins* become incredibly powerful. Each time we complete a micro habit—whether it's writing a sentence, drinking a glass of water, or stretching for two minutes—the brain registers a successful action and often provides a modest but meaningful hit of dopamine. This response reinforces the behaviour, creating a loop that rewards consistency over scale. It's not the magnitude of the action that matters most; it's the reliability of the outcome. When the brain learns that a small behaviour consistently leads to a positive feeling—however slight—it becomes more eager to initiate that behaviour again.

The importance of this consistency cannot be overstated. In habit formation, unpredictability is the enemy of reinforcement. If a behaviour sometimes feels good and sometimes does not, the brain becomes less committed to it. But if it consistently produces a reward—even a small one—the brain begins to automate the sequence. This is why habits that feel satisfying in the moment are far more likely to stick. It's also why framing behaviours in a way that highlights progress, closure, or completion can significantly enhance adherence.

For example, many productivity systems incorporate some form of visual feedback—habit trackers, progress bars, or checklists. These tools may seem trivial, but they are strategically powerful because they tap into dopamine's response to completion. Ticking a box or filling a tracker provides a tangible reward, a momentary signal to the brain that the effort was worthwhile. This is why people feel a sense of gratification when they cross something off a to-do list. The behaviour itself may be minor—sending an email or drinking a cup of tea—but the completed act triggers a neurochemical reward that encourages repetition.

To understand the implications of this, consider a real-world example. James, an overworked teacher, struggled to maintain a daily writing habit. He set ambitious goals but repeatedly failed to meet them, feeling demoralised by the gap between intention and execution. Eventually, he adopted a micro habit approach: write one sentence a day, and track it on a simple calendar. The act of writing the sentence took less than two minutes, but each completion gave him a small rush of satisfaction. Over time, the behaviour expanded naturally. More importantly, the consistency transformed his self-perception—from someone who *wanted* to write, to someone who *did* write. Dopamine played a central role in that transformation, not through pleasure alone, but through anticipation, repetition, and reinforcement.

This neurological mechanism also explains why habits anchored to immediate rewards are more successful than those offering delayed benefits. The human brain is notoriously present-biased; it prioritises short-term gratification over long-term gain. This is a survival mechanism—it helped our ancestors focus on immediate resources and threats—but in modern life, it can undermine our aspirations. Eating a doughnut, skipping a workout, or procrastinating may offer immediate relief or pleasure, while the long-term consequences remain abstract. Habits that reverse this imbalance—offering some form of immediate satisfaction, even symbolic—can help tip the scales toward better choices.

Designing habits to include these small, satisfying moments can be as simple as pairing the behaviour with something enjoyable, acknowledging the completion with a gesture or phrase, or using tools that make progress visible. These tactics are not gimmicks; they are grounded in a deep understanding of how the reward system shapes behaviour. When the brain receives a dopamine signal that a behaviour is complete and satisfying, it files that information away as a pattern worth repeating.

Interestingly, dopamine also plays a role in *habit anticipation*. Once a habit is well established, the mere thought or cue associated with the behaviour can trigger a dopamine release. This anticipatory effect means that the body and mind are preparing for the reward before the behaviour even begins. For a habitual runner, putting on running shoes can start to feel energising. For a daily meditator, hearing the timer sound may evoke calm even before the session begins. These conditioned responses deepen the behavioural groove, making the habit feel more natural and automatic over time.

However, dopamine is not infallible. It can also reinforce unhelpful habits—those that produce short-term pleasure at long-term cost. This is why habits like gambling, overeating, or compulsive phone use are so hard to break. They create powerful reward loops, flooding the brain with dopamine in response to cues and behaviours that offer immediate stimulation. The brain, wired for survival and efficiency, prioritises what is rewarding now, not what is beneficial later.

To counteract these patterns, one effective strategy is to *reengineer* the habit loop—by identifying alternative behaviours that can deliver similar rewards in healthier ways. For instance, replacing a late-night snack with a warm herbal tea and a relaxing routine may not match the dopamine surge of sugar or salt, but with consistency, it can become its own source of comfort and reward. Over time, the brain adjusts. The new behaviour, if repeated and positively reinforced, begins to generate its own dopamine-driven anticipation.

There is also a powerful psychological benefit in understanding the role of dopamine. It demystifies motivation. Many people berate themselves for lacking willpower, failing to realise that their habits are often products of neurochemical conditioning. Once we grasp how dopamine drives repetition, we can shift from self-blame to system design. We can start asking better questions: How can I make this habit more rewarding? How can I create a sense of completion? How can I generate a small win that will keep the behaviour going?

These questions are not just strategic—they are transformative. They invite a more compassionate and scientifically grounded approach to personal growth. They acknowledge that human behaviour is not merely a matter of moral fortitude, but of biological feedback loops that can be adjusted and refined. And they reinforce the idea that change, even profound change, can begin with something as small as a single tick on a checklist or a two-minute task completed with satisfaction.

Dopamine, then, is not simply the fuel of pleasure—it is the engine of reinforcement. It shapes what we seek, how we act, and what we repeat. When we understand its role in behaviour, we gain a powerful ally in the work of habit formation. We learn to design actions that feel good to do, not just good to have done. We learn to trust in the value of small wins. And we begin to see that the real architecture of change is built not with monumental effort, but with quiet, consistent rewards—one dopamine signal at a time.

The Habit-Identity Connection

One of the most overlooked, yet profoundly transformative aspects of habit formation is the subtle but powerful relationship between our behaviours and our sense of self. Beneath the surface of every repeated action lies a narrative we construct about who we are. When we speak of habits, we tend to focus on *what* we do—our routines, patterns, and outcomes. But to understand lasting change, we must ask a deeper question: *who are we becoming through what we repeatedly do?* This is the essence of the habit-identity connection. Micro habits, seemingly minor in isolation, can gradually and convincingly reshape how we perceive ourselves, and in doing so, redefine the trajectory of our lives.

Identity is not fixed. While we may hold onto certain enduring characteristics, much of our identity is fluid, context-dependent, and constantly being reinforced or challenged by our behaviour. Psychologists have long understood that the self is, in part, a social and behavioural construct—we come to understand who we are through what we do, and how others respond to what we do. When a person regularly shows kindness, they begin to internalise the identity of being a kind person. When someone consistently completes creative work, no matter how small, they start to see themselves as a creative individual. The reverse is equally true: when behaviours are inconsistent with desired identities, a dissonance arises, often leading to doubt, frustration, or disengagement.

This is where micro habits wield their greatest power. Because they are small and achievable, they provide daily evidence that supports and reinforces a new identity. They allow us to cast what James Clear aptly calls "votes for the kind of person we want to become." These votes don't need to be dramatic or impressive. What matters is consistency. Each time we follow through on a micro habit, we provide our brain with a subtle signal: *this is what someone like me does.* Over time, these signals accumulate, forming a new self-concept that is grounded in action rather than abstract aspiration.

Consider the example of Priya, a corporate professional who always wanted to become someone who read regularly. She admired readers, bought books, and set ambitious reading goals—yet struggled to follow through. Each failure reinforced an internal narrative: "I'm not really a reader." Frustrated, she decided to scale back her expectations and start with one page a day. The new habit was so small it felt almost silly—but it was also easy to maintain. She kept it up for weeks, eventually reading several pages each day without pressure. More importantly, she began to see herself differently. Her identity shifted from someone who *wanted* to be a reader to someone who *was* a reader. That change in self-perception became the catalyst for a richer reading life—not because her environment or motivation changed, but because her sense of self did.

This phenomenon aligns with what psychologists refer to as *self-perception theory*, which suggests that people come to understand themselves by observing their own behaviour. If I notice that I keep showing up to write, even for just two minutes a day, I start to believe that I must be a writer. If I observe that I meditate regularly, I come to see myself as someone who values mindfulness. The behaviour doesn't just reflect the identity—it shapes it.

It's important to note that identity-based habits differ from outcome-based goals. When people focus solely on outcomes—"I want to lose 10 kilograms," "I want to get promoted," "I want to save £5,000"—they place their identity on the far side of an achievement. This can be motivating in the short term, but it also carries a risk: if progress stalls, motivation wanes. The identity remains external, conditional on results. With micro habits, however, the focus shifts inward. It becomes less about what you *achieve* and more about who you *become*. You begin to live as the person you aspire to be, even before the tangible outcomes arrive.

This is not merely a semantic distinction—it has behavioural consequences. When identity leads the process, habits become easier to sustain because they feel aligned with how we see ourselves. Rather than asking, "Should I go for a run today?" we ask, "What would a healthy person do?" If we see ourselves as healthy, the behaviour feels congruent. If not, the behaviour feels like an effortful attempt to change, often met with resistance. This is why habit change must begin with self-concept. When our habits and our identities are aligned, change feels natural, even inevitable.

Of course, identity shifts are rarely instantaneous. They emerge through repeated evidence. And this is where micro habits are uniquely positioned to facilitate the process. Because they are small, they are less likely to encounter resistance. Because they are consistent, they provide reliable data to the brain. Because they are achievable, they build momentum. And because they are action-oriented, they bypass the traps of overthinking, procrastination, and perfectionism.

For instance, a person who struggles with confidence in public speaking may begin with a micro habit of practising one line in front of a mirror each day. On its own, this act won't turn them into a keynote speaker—but it begins to shift the narrative from "I'm terrible at public speaking" to "I'm someone who practises speaking." Over time, that small identity shift may open the door to more ambitious behaviours—volunteering to lead a team meeting, joining a local speaking group, or presenting at a workshop. But the foundation is laid not through grand actions, but through consistent reinforcement of a new identity.

This approach also invites a more compassionate and sustainable form of self-development. Rather than swinging between extremes of ambition and shame, people can build habits that support a steady evolution of the self. There is no need to wait until you "feel ready" to become the person you want to be. You can begin now, with small, intentional actions that are aligned with the identity you wish to inhabit. These actions, repeated consistently, will do more than create habits—they will reshape your character.

Another important aspect of the habit-identity connection is its role in building resilience. When identity is rooted in behaviour, rather than outcomes, setbacks become less threatening. Missing a workout doesn't mean you're no longer healthy. Skipping a writing session doesn't mean you're not a writer. Temporary lapses do not undermine the identity, because the identity is built on a broad foundation of consistent action. This allows people to recover from setbacks without spiralling into self-doubt or self-sabotage.

Consider the experience of Daniel, a freelance designer who wanted to cultivate more discipline in his creative practice. He started with a micro habit of sketching one object every morning before checking his email. Over time, this habit grew, and so did his confidence. He began to see himself not just as a freelancer, but as a *working artist.* When a major project was delayed and he lost motivation, he still returned to his morning sketches. The identity was anchored not to external validation but to daily practice. That anchor helped him weather the disruption and return to deeper work when the time was right.

This dynamic interplay between habit and identity also has social implications. As we begin to see ourselves differently, we show up differently in relationships, workplaces, and communities. A person who begins to identify as disciplined may hold clearer boundaries. Someone who sees themselves as compassionate may offer support more freely. Identity shapes behaviour, and behaviour, in turn, reinforces identity. The relationship is cyclical, self-sustaining, and, when harnessed wisely, transformational.

In the broader context of micro habits, the identity shift is often the most meaningful outcome. While goals may be achieved and routines may change, the internal story we tell about who we are remains. And when that story is grounded in evidence—actions we've taken, habits we've maintained—it becomes more resilient, more credible, and more empowering.

Ultimately, the question is not merely "What habits should I build?" but "Who am I becoming through these habits?" When we start to answer that question, habit formation ceases to be a superficial attempt at behavioural control. It becomes a form of self-authorship—a deliberate and thoughtful process of becoming the person we aspire to be. And in that process, micro habits are not just practical tools—they are the brushstrokes of identity, slowly painting a new picture of who we are.

Chapter 3
Designing Your Micro Habits for Success

Failure to change, for most of us, doesn't stem from laziness or a lack of desire. It's not a question of motivation or resolve. The stumbling block tends to be more subtle: we misjudge scale and timing. We aim for too much, too soon—and in doing so, we miss the power of showing up, steadily, day after day. Set yourself a grand target—completing a marathon, writing a novel, transforming your health—and the urge is to charge at it. But the 'go big or go home' mentality, while dramatic, often collapses under its own weight. Ambition, unchecked, has a knack for turning on us.

But what if we flipped the script? What if, instead of obsessing over dramatic action, we began with the gentlest possible version of progress? What if success, far from being about exerting more effort, was about embracing less—less pressure, less perfectionism—applied more consistently?

That's the proposition behind micro habits. Don't be misled by the name—they're not diluted versions of "real" habits, but rather the structural underpinnings of sustainable change. They bypass resistance, lower the entry barrier, and build rhythm where previously there was only intention. In this chapter, we're diving into how to build these habits in a way that aligns with how people actually behave—not how they wish they behaved on an ideal day. We'll unpack everything from the deceptively powerful two-minute rule to habit stacking and the use of subtle environmental cues that nudge us forward without fanfare.

The first order of business? Rethinking goals. Traditional goal-setting tends to obsess over the finish line: lose ten kilograms, land that promotion, publish that book. These outcomes are seductive, sure—but they're also abstract, often detached from daily life. It's all very well to dream of writing a novel; it's another matter entirely to sit down at 8 p.m. on a Thursday, laptop open, energy flagging. The better approach, perhaps counterintuitively, is to narrow your focus—to stop gazing at the summit and concentrate on the next foothold.

This shift leads us to micro behaviours: tiny actions that serve as gateways to bigger change. If you want to meditate regularly, don't begin with a thirty-minute session—begin with a single minute of mindful breathing after brushing your teeth. Thinking about going to the gym? Start with changing into workout clothes and doing five push-ups. These miniature forms of the habit aren't concessions—they're tactical moves. They ease the mind's defences, reduce friction, and generate small wins that build psychological momentum.

Enter the two-minute rule. It's one of those ideas that sounds too simple to matter, yet works because of precisely that simplicity. The idea, widely popularised by behavioural science, is straightforward: any habit should begin with an action that takes under two minutes to complete. If it's that short, it doesn't require much in the way of willpower, planning, or energy. Starting becomes the habit. And here's the rub—once you begin, you often keep going. Lacing up your trainers for a quick step outside might turn into a fifteen-minute walk. But even if it doesn't, you've shown up. That counts.

The beauty lies in the nuance: micro habits don't suggest you shrink your aspirations. You still aim high. But you initiate low. It's not about limiting who you want to become—it's about easing the journey to becoming that person. Over time, what begins as a micro habit may well grow in scope, but the point is, you didn't force it. You let the habit mature at its own pace, with repetition as its quiet scaffolding.

To bolster these habits further, consider habit stacking—a technique that involves latching a new behaviour onto something you already do without thinking. It's a clever bit of behavioural piggybacking. Our brains love predictability; they rely on cues to know what comes next. So if you always brew coffee in the morning, that's a ready-made prompt for reviewing your calendar or stretching for a minute. By nesting a new action inside an established routine, you reduce decision fatigue and increase the odds of it sticking.

Of course, not every anchor works equally well. Habit stacking is most effective when your chosen cue is stable—something that happens daily—and the new behaviour is brief. Let's say you brush your teeth every morning (one would hope); attach to that the habit of jotting down a quick gratitude note or doing a wall sit. Take your daily train commute—why not spend it learning vocabulary on a language app or reading a single page? The trick is to build a seamless behavioural chain where one act smoothly nudges the next.

Still, even the most ingenious stacking method won't rescue a habit from poor design. Which brings us to an underrated but crucial principle: simplicity. The habits that survive aren't the ones that look impressive on paper. They're the ones that are easy to grasp, easy to do, and, perhaps most importantly, easy to repeat. Simplicity is the antidote to friction. Complexity, on the other hand, is a trap—it introduces mental clutter, doubt, and a higher likelihood of opting out entirely.

Clear beats clever. Say you want to be more reflective. Don't resolve vaguely to "think deeply every day." Instead, define a specific behaviour: "write one sentence in my journal after breakfast." Your brain knows what to do. It doesn't have to negotiate. Vague intentions invite procrastination; specific micro habits remove ambiguity and make action feel automatic.

And then there's the visual element—another quiet force in sustaining change. Human beings are astonishingly responsive to what they see. A habit tracker, a wall calendar, a simple checklist—these aren't childish gimmicks. They're powerful tools of reinforcement. The act of marking a box or logging a win releases a small but meaningful shot of satisfaction. Over time, these visual cues help maintain streaks, build pride, and, perhaps more surprisingly, create a feedback loop that drives consistency.

Tracking, even in its simplest form, also fosters a kind of personal accountability. You begin to see patterns. You notice where you're consistent and where you fall off. That awareness becomes a lever for adjustment. And when you inevitably miss a day (as all humans do), having a record softens the guilt and helps you reset with clarity rather than shame.

Consider Andrew, a software engineer recovering from a long stretch of physical inactivity. He didn't join a gym or buy fancy equipment. He started with five squats each morning after brushing his teeth. That's it. A tiny, daily act. Each completed habit earned a green dot on his calendar. Five squats soon became ten. Then twenty. He didn't change the cue—brushing his teeth remained the anchor—but the behaviour scaled as it became familiar. The green dots served as both progress marker and quiet cheerleader. The habit stuck, not because it was heroic, but because it was smart, and small, and designed to last.

Which brings us to a deeper truth: designing micro habits isn't about summoning discipline. It's about building architecture. You're not dragging yourself towards change—you're crafting an environment where change feels natural. This system comprises cues, actions, feedback, and identity. It's scaffolded by clarity, held up by simplicity, and powered by repetition. And underneath it all is a simple but profound question: who are you becoming?

In the rest of this chapter, we'll work through how to build these micro habits into your own life—carefully, intentionally, and without romanticising the process. You'll find that the most meaningful changes rarely announce themselves with drama. They emerge through quiet, consistent action. Over time, these tiny behaviours don't just shape what you do—they shape how you see yourself. And that, in the end, is where real transformation begins.

Start Small, Think Big

Ambition is a double-edged sword. On one hand, it inspires people to strive, to grow, and to stretch beyond their current limits. On the other, it can quickly become overwhelming. Grand goals often come wrapped in complexity, uncertainty, and unrealistic timelines. The bigger the vision, the more resistance it tends to provoke. Yet the problem isn't with ambition itself—it's with the way we approach it. Rather than leaping toward monumental change in a single bound, a far more effective strategy is to start small while keeping your vision expansive. This principle—start small, think big—is the linchpin of sustainable personal transformation. It allows us to preserve the scale of our aspirations while reducing the psychological and logistical friction that so often prevents progress.

Human beings are not wired to operate in huge conceptual leaps. Our brains crave clarity, structure, and tangible next steps. When we are presented with a large goal—say, writing a novel or running a marathon—our immediate reaction is often not excitement but paralysis. The sheer volume of effort required seems daunting, and the lack of a clear starting point makes the first step feel ambiguous. In this state, many people delay action, convinced that they need more time, better conditions, or a stronger burst of motivation before they begin. But the truth is, action breeds clarity. The only way to make a grand objective feel less intimidating is to break it down into something so small it can be executed today, even in the midst of chaos, fatigue, or uncertainty.

Take the example of Mira, a university lecturer who had long wanted to write a book. Each year, she added it to her list of resolutions, and each year it went untouched. The idea of writing 70,000 words felt Herculean amidst her professional and family responsibilities. Eventually, she adopted the strategy of starting with a micro commitment: write for two minutes a day, no more. At first, the goal seemed almost trivial. But within weeks, those two minutes became five, then ten. The act of starting created momentum. More importantly, it reshaped her identity—from someone who wanted to write, to someone who *did* write, every day. Eighteen months later, her manuscript was complete. The success wasn't born from a heroic effort, but from a humble and consistent one.

The effectiveness of this approach is grounded in both psychological and behavioural science. Large goals typically reside in the domain of the prefrontal cortex—the rational, analytical part of the brain that is involved in planning and abstraction. But when the prefrontal cortex is taxed by stress, fatigue, or competing demands, its ability to prioritise and initiate complex tasks diminishes. That's when people resort to avoidance, procrastination, or self-justification. By contrast, small, specific actions engage simpler neural pathways. They require less cognitive effort, produce quicker rewards, and are far more likely to become repeatable. This is not about lowering your standards; it's about reducing the activation energy required to initiate behaviour.

In physics, activation energy is the minimum energy needed to start a reaction. The same principle applies to human behaviour. A task that requires 45 minutes, deep focus, and a perfectly quiet environment has a high activation energy. A task that takes two minutes and can be performed anywhere has a low one. When you consistently lower the threshold for action, you increase the likelihood of showing up. And when you show up, day after day, your efforts compound. What starts as a small step becomes a ritual, and what starts as a ritual becomes a deeply ingrained part of your life.

There is a misconception that small actions are only suitable for beginners or those with low confidence. In fact, this method is used by top performers across disciplines. Elite athletes start their training sessions with basic drills. Acclaimed authors have daily minimums that are often modest. Successful entrepreneurs block out short, focused bursts for creative thinking. The small start is not a compromise—it is a strategy. It conserves energy, builds mastery, and establishes the consistency needed for high achievement.

This method is also remarkably versatile. Whether your goal is to improve your health, deepen relationships, develop a new skill, or manage finances more wisely, it can be deconstructed into micro behaviours that are easy to initiate and sustain. If you want to get fitter, start with a daily five-minute walk. If you want to be more present with your family, begin by putting your phone away for the first ten minutes after arriving home. If you're looking to build mindfulness, start with one mindful breath when you wake up. These actions might seem too small to matter—but they are the raw material from which larger change is built. Each repetition strengthens a habit loop: cue, routine, reward. Over time, this loop becomes embedded in your neural circuitry, reducing reliance on willpower and increasing automaticity.

It's also worth noting that starting small protects you from the most common saboteurs of self-improvement: perfectionism and all-or-nothing thinking. When people set large goals, they often attach perfectionist expectations to them. If they miss a workout or fail to write for a day, they feel they've failed entirely. This mindset creates brittleness. By contrast, micro habits are anti-fragile. They are designed to survive the messiness of real life. If your goal is to floss one tooth, there is no excuse not to do it. And once you do, you're likely to do more. But even if you don't, you've still succeeded. This consistency builds confidence and momentum far more reliably than occasional intensity.

Furthermore, beginning small encourages a feedback-rich environment. With each small win, you gain a sense of progress. This sense of forward motion is critical to motivation. The brain's reward system, especially the release of dopamine, is not solely activated by outcomes, but by the *anticipation* and *perception* of progress. When you see yourself moving, however incrementally, your brain reinforces the behaviour. This feedback loop turns action into habit, and habit into identity.

Let's return to the case of Tariq, an aspiring artist who hadn't picked up a pencil in years. He dreamed of illustrating a graphic novel but felt disconnected from his creative self. Instead of setting a goal to draw for an hour each day, he committed to sketching one line every evening. That's it—just one line. The simplicity of the task removed all resistance. Over time, the act of picking up the pencil became second nature. Most nights, he drew more than one line, but even when he didn't, he maintained the habit. Within six months, he had filled two sketchbooks and felt more creatively alive than he had in a decade. Starting small didn't constrain his vision—it revived it.

The magic of this approach is that it makes the first step feel safe, achievable, and immediate. And once the first step is taken, the second becomes easier. Starting small doesn't mean thinking small. The ultimate vision can remain vast—run that marathon, build that business, master that skill. But instead of charging at it, you lay a brick each day, one deliberate act at a time. Eventually, those bricks form a foundation strong enough to support any ambition.

To apply this principle effectively, it helps to begin each goal with a clarifying question: *What is the smallest possible action I can take today that moves me in the direction of this goal?* The answer should feel almost laughably easy. That's a good sign. If it doesn't feel too small, it's probably too big. And if it feels easy enough to do even on your worst day, you've found a sustainable entry point.

Starting small also teaches humility and respect for process. It reminds us that meaningful change is not made in grand declarations but in quiet repetitions. That greatness is less about talent or passion and more about perseverance and patience. That even the most extraordinary outcomes begin with an ordinary act—a minute of focus, a stretch, a breath, a sentence, a step.

In the end, the idea is not to diminish your ambition but to build the scaffolding needed to sustain it. Big thinking needs small doing. Vision needs ritual. Change needs traction. And traction begins when we reduce the distance between where we are and where we start. By learning to think expansively while acting incrementally, we unlock the secret not just to starting—but to continuing, evolving, and ultimately succeeding.

Start small. Think big. Then keep going. The scale of your success will be determined not by how loudly you begin, but by how quietly and consistently you continue.

The Two-Minute Rule in Practice

One of the most pervasive misconceptions about habit formation is the assumption that effective change must be effortful and time-consuming. People often believe that unless a behaviour is substantial—twenty-minute workouts, hour-long writing sessions, elaborate meditation routines—it is unlikely to produce meaningful results. This belief is not only inaccurate; it is deeply counterproductive. It places unnecessary pressure on the individual to begin with intensity, thereby increasing the likelihood of resistance, delay, or eventual abandonment. The alternative, rooted in behavioural science and practical wisdom, is startlingly simple: start so small that it takes less than two minutes. This is the essence of the two-minute rule.

The two-minute rule is more than a productivity hack. It is a strategic method for overcoming inertia and establishing behavioural consistency. The premise is straightforward—any new habit should take less than two minutes to perform at the outset. The logic behind this approach rests on a fundamental truth about human behaviour:

the most difficult part of any habit is not finishing it, but starting it. By making the initiation of the habit so simple that it barely registers as effort, we drastically increase the likelihood of beginning. And once a behaviour is started, it often continues beyond the initial micro-commitment.

Consider someone who wants to develop a regular reading habit. Instead of aiming to read a chapter a day, they begin with the commitment to read one sentence. This takes less than two minutes, feels entirely manageable, and yet retains the essence of the desired identity: "I am someone who reads." Over time, one sentence becomes one page, one page becomes five, and soon the habit expands naturally, without force. The real victory lies not in how much is read each day, but in the consistency of the reading. Habits, after all, are forged through frequency, not intensity.

Practical examples of the two-minute rule abound across all areas of life. A person seeking better fitness might start with the habit of putting on their running shoes and stepping outside. They don't commit to a workout—just the act of gearing up and opening the door. Often, the resistance dissipates once the threshold is crossed, and the walk or run happens organically. But even if it doesn't, the habit has been honoured. The streak is alive. The identity is reinforced. Similarly, someone who wishes to practise gratitude may begin by writing down one word or one line in a journal each night. The effort is minimal, yet the emotional payoff can be substantial, particularly when sustained over time.

The genius of the two-minute rule lies in its ability to outmanoeuvre the mental barriers that stall behaviour. Our brains are wired to avoid perceived effort. When a task feels big, it activates our internal defence mechanisms—procrastination, rationalisation, avoidance. But a task that feels quick and easy slips past these defences. It is mentally framed not as a challenge, but as a triviality—something barely worth resisting. This reframing is crucial. Once the behaviour begins, momentum takes over. The principle of behavioural activation comes into play: action precedes motivation. We feel more inclined to continue once we are already in motion.

This principle was clearly illustrated in the case of Anya, a full-time caregiver who wanted to incorporate mindfulness into her overwhelmed daily routine. Rather than attempting a 15-minute meditation, she began with a two-minute pause each morning, simply sitting with her eyes closed and breathing slowly. The habit was so unobtrusive that it blended effortlessly into her day. Within a few weeks, the brief pause became something she looked forward to. Eventually, it extended to five minutes, then occasionally to ten. But even on the most difficult days, she honoured the original two-minute commitment. The practice grounded her, not because of its length, but because of its reliability.

Another compelling application of the rule is in creative work. Many aspiring writers, artists, or musicians find themselves paralysed by perfectionism and the fear of producing something substandard. The two-minute rule provides a way to bypass this internal censor. For instance, a writer might commit to writing one sentence or opening their document and typing a single word. The act of opening the document itself becomes the habit. Once the first sentence is written, the mind typically wants to complete the thought. This approach not only breaks the paralysis of the blank page but builds the muscle of showing up, which is arguably the most important part of any creative practice.

The two-minute rule also plays a vital role in reshaping self-perception. Each time we complete a micro habit, no matter how trivial it seems, we cast a vote for the identity we are trying to build. A person who brushes one tooth is still reinforcing the identity of someone who takes care of their hygiene. A person who declutters one item reinforces the identity of someone who maintains an organised space. These micro commitments compound over time, not just in results, but in how we see ourselves. And once identity shifts, behaviour follows more easily. We act in alignment with who we believe we are.

There is also a broader societal value in this concept. Many people feel chronically time-poor, overextended, and overwhelmed by competing responsibilities. The two-minute rule acknowledges this reality. It offers a model of change that fits into real life, not an idealised version of it. It meets people where they are—at the end of a long day, amidst the chaos of parenting, in the margins of a busy work schedule—and says: *you can begin here.* You don't need to overhaul your life to make progress. You need only two minutes of deliberate action.

Of course, critics may argue that two minutes is too insignificant to matter. But this view misunderstands the nature of compounding behaviour. The purpose of the two-minute rule is not to stay at two minutes forever. It is to initiate a behaviour that, once started, often continues. But even if it doesn't, the real value lies in the consistency. The person who meditates for two minutes a day will, over time, accumulate far more practice than the person who meditates for twenty minutes once a week—or not at all because they are waiting for the perfect moment.

Moreover, the two-minute habit creates what psychologists call a *keystone behaviour*—a small action that leads to other positive behaviours. For example, someone who spends two minutes preparing a healthy snack is more likely to eat well throughout the day. Someone who organises their desk for two minutes may find themselves diving into focused work. The initial behaviour sets a tone, activates a mindset, and opens the door to further action. In this way, the two-minute habit becomes the spark for a larger behavioural cascade.

To sustain this approach, it's helpful to apply two complementary strategies: anchoring and tracking. Anchoring involves tying the new habit to an existing routine, making it easier to remember and perform. For instance, stretching for two minutes after brushing your teeth or writing a journal line right after making your morning coffee. Tracking, on the other hand, introduces visual reinforcement—using a calendar, app, or notebook to mark each successful habit execution. The visual proof of consistency creates its own form of motivation, tapping into the brain's love for completion and progress.

The key, however, is to honour the commitment. If the habit is defined as taking two minutes, then doing more is optional, not required. This protects the integrity of the habit. On tough days, the micro version still gets done, preserving the streak and reinforcing the identity. On better days, the habit may expand naturally. But expansion is a bonus, not a baseline. The psychological safety of this rule—its lack of pressure—is what gives it such enduring power.

Ultimately, the two-minute rule is a reorientation of how we think about change. It teaches us that meaningful transformation does not require grand gestures or bursts of willpower. It requires reliability. It requires starting. It requires showing up. Two minutes may seem like nothing, but it is everything when it becomes a doorway through which consistency, confidence, and identity are built.

By making habits small enough to succeed and easy enough to repeat, we create a sustainable path to self-improvement that fits into the texture of daily life. The real value of the two-minute rule is not in what gets accomplished in two minutes—but in what it initiates. The habit. The momentum. The shift in self-perception. And that is the architecture of enduring change.

Habit Stacking

One of the greatest challenges in building new habits is not the behaviour itself, but remembering to perform it. We may have every intention of stretching in the morning, drinking more water, or writing a gratitude entry each night, but intentions are fragile. Life is filled with distractions, interruptions, and cognitive overload, all of which erode our ability to reliably act on new behavioural goals. What's needed is not just a plan but an anchor—something consistent in our daily lives that can serve as a prompt for the new habit to emerge. This is the psychological logic behind *habit stacking*, a deceptively simple yet remarkably effective strategy for creating durable, automatic behavioural routines.

Habit stacking involves linking a new habit to an existing one, so that the current behaviour serves as a trigger for the new one. It works by exploiting the predictability of our established routines, transforming them into launch pads for new practices. When done correctly, this approach bypasses many of the obstacles associated with habit formation—particularly forgetfulness and lack of context—by embedding new actions within the fabric of what we already do. Rather than relying on willpower or reminders, we build habits into the flow of life, making them more intuitive, automatic, and resilient.

The idea finds its roots in behavioural psychology, particularly in the principle of cue-based habit formation. As discussed earlier in the context of the habit loop, every habitual behaviour is initiated by a cue—a time of day, a location, an emotional state, or another preceding behaviour. By consciously choosing to pair a desired habit with a reliable cue—often an action we already perform consistently—we harness the brain's existing wiring rather than trying to forge an entirely new path from scratch. The mental effort required to initiate the new habit is reduced significantly, increasing the likelihood that it will stick.

Consider the example of Rajiv, a software developer who wanted to begin practising mindfulness but struggled to find the time or remember to meditate. After reflecting on his daily routine, he realised that he brewed coffee each morning without fail. He decided to add a simple breath-focused meditation while the coffee steeped. By anchoring his new habit to a pre-existing behaviour, he created a dependable cue-action sequence. Within weeks, the meditation became as natural to him as the coffee itself—not because he had superior discipline, but because he had designed a system that removed the need for conscious decision-making.

What makes habit stacking so powerful is that it transforms abstract intentions into concrete, situational behaviours. Rather than vaguely committing to "read more," you decide to read one page after brushing your teeth each night. Instead of hoping to practise gratitude, you write down one thing you're thankful for right after closing your laptop for the day. These small but intentional links tether the desired behaviour to a specific moment in your existing schedule, removing ambiguity and increasing clarity. And clarity, as behavioural research repeatedly shows, is one of the most important factors in habit adherence.

The strategy also works across various domains of life—physical health, mental well-being, productivity, relationships, and more. For someone trying to build a hydration habit, they might drink a glass of water immediately after going to the toilet. A person working on strength might do five squats after checking their phone in the morning. A professional aiming to improve communication might send a message of appreciation to a colleague each time they finish a meeting. These pairings may seem minor, even trivial, but their power lies in consistency and context. When new habits are consistently embedded within reliable routines, they are far more likely to endure.

It is worth noting that not all pairings are created equal. The success of habit stacking depends on choosing the *right* anchor behaviour—something that is already deeply ingrained, occurs regularly, and requires minimal thought to initiate. The more consistent the anchor, the more dependable the cue. For example, brushing your teeth, turning on the kettle, or opening your laptop can serve as excellent anchors because they happen predictably in specific contexts. By contrast, events that occur sporadically or behaviours that are themselves unstable are poor choices for stacking.

Another key aspect of successful habit stacking is specificity. The more precisely you define the behaviour and its placement in time, the easier it becomes to execute. Ambiguous plans like "I'll stretch more often" or "I'll journal when I have time" are vulnerable to distraction and delay. But when you commit to "I'll stretch for two minutes after I put on my pyjamas" or "I'll write one sentence in my journal after turning off my desk lamp," the decision has already been made. You are not negotiating with yourself in the moment—you are following a clear sequence that has already been mentally rehearsed.

This structured sequencing has a cascading effect on behaviour. Once a habit is embedded and reliably performed, it opens the door for additional habits to be added to the stack. This concept, sometimes referred to as behavioural chaining, allows complex routines to be built incrementally. What begins as a two-minute meditation after pouring tea can eventually evolve into a morning ritual of breathing, stretching, journaling, and planning—all initiated by the simple act of boiling water. Each link in the chain strengthens the next, creating a rhythm of behaviours that support and reinforce one another.

Importantly, habit stacking also reduces the reliance on motivation, which is notoriously unreliable over the long term. When behaviour becomes contextual rather than emotional—triggered by a routine rather than a mood—it becomes more stable. This is particularly helpful during stressful or low-energy periods, when motivation tends to falter. If your stretching routine is tied to brushing your teeth, you're more likely to do it even when you're tired. If your daily gratitude entry is linked to shutting down your computer, you're less likely to forget it on busy days. The system carries you through the fluctuations of willpower because it is not dependent on willpower to function.

One of the most elegant features of habit stacking is that it supports identity formation. Each time you follow through on the sequence, you reinforce a sense of who you are. If you journal after brushing your teeth every night, you start to see yourself as reflective. If you review your goals after making your morning coffee, you begin to feel purposeful. These identity cues are subtle but powerful. They do not require loud affirmations or dramatic declarations—just small, consistent actions tied to your existing life.

Take, for instance, Nia, a young lawyer who wanted to develop better posture and body awareness. She committed to doing a 30-second posture check after every video call. This new habit was perfectly anchored to an activity that occurred multiple times a day and required no additional scheduling or reminders. Over time, Nia found herself naturally standing taller, breathing more deeply, and even moving with greater confidence. The effect was not just physical—it influenced how she viewed herself: as someone who was composed, grounded, and attentive to detail. Her habit stack became a subtle, structural support for her evolving identity.

There is also an emotional elegance to habit stacking. Because the behaviour is embedded within something familiar, it feels safe and manageable. This familiarity breeds a sense of calm and predictability, which can be especially valuable in chaotic or high-pressure environments. Rather than disrupting your day, the new habit becomes part of its fabric. It feels like a natural extension of what you already do, not an intrusive addition demanding attention.

However, like any behavioural tool, habit stacking is not immune to disruption. Life circumstances change, routines are interrupted, and anchors may shift. The key to maintaining the habit stack in such scenarios is adaptability. When the original anchor disappears—such as a change in schedule or a relocation—it's important to reassess and relink the habit to a new, stable behaviour. The flexibility to re-anchor ensures continuity without starting from scratch.

In applying habit stacking to your own life, begin by identifying a reliable routine that already occurs daily without fail. Choose a habit that supports your broader values or goals and define it in clear, actionable terms. Then test the stack for a few days. If it feels too forced or awkward, revise the timing or the behaviour itself. The aim is not perfection but fit—finding a pattern that feels natural enough to repeat without strain.

Over time, these modest sequences will compound into meaningful change. The habit of placing your shoes by the door after tidying the kitchen can lead to regular walks. The act of reviewing your finances after your weekly grocery trip can build long-term fiscal discipline. None of these shifts require dramatic effort. They require a thoughtful pairing of behaviours and the patience to let small, daily actions shape your future.

Habit stacking reminds us that behaviour change need not be revolutionary. It can be rhythmic, contextual, and quietly powerful. By linking new habits to the anchors that already hold our days together, we create behavioural structures that support consistency, reduce friction, and honour the identity we are working to embody. And that is how lasting transformation is not forced into life—but woven seamlessly into it.

The Art of Simplicity

In an age that often glorifies complexity and overachievement, simplicity can feel countercultural—almost too modest to be effective. Yet when it comes to behavioural change and the development of sustainable habits, simplicity is not only beneficial; it is essential. The art of simplicity is the strategic design of behaviours that are so clear, frictionless, and manageable that they become virtually immune to resistance. It is about creating habits that are easy to begin, easy to maintain, and ultimately hard to abandon—not because of discipline or motivation, but because their design naturally supports sustainability.

Simplicity works because the human brain, for all its cognitive sophistication, is remarkably conservative when it comes to expending energy. Our cognitive systems are designed to economise effort. Faced with a complex or ambiguous task, the brain instinctively delays, avoids, or delegates it to future-you—an imagined version of yourself who somehow has more time, energy, and willpower. Simplicity short-circuits this hesitation. It reduces decision points, eliminates ambiguity, and lowers the psychological cost of action. A habit that takes little thought or preparation has a far greater chance of being executed consistently than one that demands elaborate planning or self-negotiation.

This principle is clearly evident in the work of behavioural scientists such as BJ Fogg and James Clear, who both emphasise the value of scaling behaviours down to their simplest possible form. When a habit feels too difficult, the solution is not to summon more willpower, but to redesign the behaviour so that it feels effortless to initiate. The easier it is to start, the more likely it is to be repeated. And repetition, as we know, is the linchpin of habit formation.

Take, for example, the case of Sophie, a financial analyst who aspired to incorporate regular stretching into her sedentary workday. Her initial goal—attend a 60-minute yoga class three times a week—was admirable but unrealistic given her workload and energy levels. After several failed attempts and growing frustration, she reframed her habit through the lens of simplicity. She began with one stretch for one minute every morning before checking her emails. This minor adjustment transformed her experience. The habit no longer felt burdensome or disruptive. It became part of her daily rhythm. Within weeks, she was stretching longer and more frequently, not because she forced herself to do more, but because the initial behaviour had become deeply embedded and enjoyable.

What Sophie's experience illustrates is that simplicity does not mean thinking small; it means *starting* small and removing unnecessary friction. Friction, in behavioural terms, refers to anything that makes a habit harder to perform—time constraints, environmental clutter, unclear next steps, or cognitive overload. When habits are too elaborate or demand multiple decisions, friction accumulates. Each additional step or point of uncertainty becomes a hurdle. Eventually, these hurdles wear down resolve, leading to avoidance or inconsistency.

This is why the most sustainable habits are those that require minimal setup, minimal tools, and minimal cognitive effort. Think of the difference between deciding to read one page of a book left on your pillow versus finding a book, choosing a chapter, and settling into a specific reading chair. The second routine might feel more "complete," but the first is far more likely to happen regularly. Simplicity wins not by offering the perfect experience but by offering a *repeatable* one.

Simplicity also enhances flexibility. Life is unpredictable. Schedules change, moods fluctuate, obligations arise. Habits that are too rigid or resource-intensive tend to collapse under the weight of real-world variability. But simple habits can bend without breaking. They can adapt to different contexts and survive low-motivation days. If your journaling habit is defined as "write one sentence" rather than "write for 20 minutes in complete silence," it can survive a noisy household, a late night, or an emotionally taxing day. You can still do the habit, and doing the habit—even at its most basic level—reinforces the identity and continuity that keep you engaged over the long term.

Another powerful aspect of simplicity is its ability to build psychological momentum. When a habit is easy to complete, it creates a sense of success and closure. This success triggers a small reward response in the brain, releasing dopamine and reinforcing the behaviour. Over time, the association between the cue and the habit becomes more deeply encoded, requiring less conscious effort to perform. Eventually, the habit feels automatic—not because it is monumental, but because it is effortless and satisfying to repeat.

This simplicity-driven momentum also has a compounding effect. A single simple habit often becomes the anchor for additional behaviours. A person who begins by flossing one tooth may naturally floss them all. Someone who opens their writing app to type one line may end up writing a paragraph. These expansions are not required—they are welcomed, because they arise from a place of readiness and rhythm rather than pressure. The key is that the base behaviour remains simple enough to never feel intimidating.

Simplicity also fosters clarity, which is vital for habit initiation. Vague intentions like "eat healthier" or "be more organised" are nearly impossible to act on consistently because they lack a defined starting point. But when habits are simplified into concrete, visible actions—"eat a piece of fruit with breakfast" or "clear one item off my desk before starting work"—they become actionable. The brain doesn't have to wonder what to do. It just does it.

Real-world applications of simplicity abound. In professional environments, simplifying workflows and reducing decision fatigue often leads to higher productivity. In education, breaking down tasks into clear, bite-sized steps increases student engagement. In health, simple actions like putting a water bottle on your desk or taking the stairs instead of the lift build movement into the day without requiring formal exercise time. The cumulative impact of these small, simple behaviours is far greater than sporadic bursts of complex effort.

Yet perhaps the most overlooked benefit of simplicity is its psychological grace. It liberates us from the tyranny of perfectionism and the constant comparison to idealised versions of who we think we should be. Simplicity allows us to begin where we are, with what we have. It strips away the pressure to optimise, impress, or perform, and replaces it with the gentle discipline of repetition. It whispers that consistency matters more than ambition, and that progress is more about rhythm than revolution.

This doesn't mean that complexity should always be avoided. There is a time and place for challenging routines, deep work, and intensive goals. But these should be built *on top of* a foundation of simplicity. They should emerge from habits that are already stable, reliable, and frictionless. In this way, simplicity becomes the soil from which more ambitious behaviours can grow—not by forcing them, but by creating the right conditions for them to flourish.

In habit formation, less truly is more. When we remove the unnecessary, we reveal the essential. When we simplify, we create space for consistency, for identity, and for growth. And when we honour the art of simplicity—not as a constraint but as a strategy—we discover that the most enduring changes often begin with the smallest, most effortless acts.

Simplicity is not the absence of sophistication. It is its highest form. In designing habits that are elegantly minimal, we invite them to endure not because they are grand, but because they are *doable.* Every day. Without exception. That is the art—and the power—of simplicity.

Tracking for Success

In the architecture of habit formation, one element consistently proves to be more powerful than it first appears: visual tracking. While it may seem like a modest tool—nothing more than marking a calendar, checking a box, or filling in a digital log—the practice of tracking habits provides psychological structure, emotional reinforcement, and strategic clarity. It transforms fleeting intentions into tangible data, turning subjective efforts into objective records. More importantly, it creates a visible narrative of consistency, which sustains motivation long after the initial enthusiasm has faded.

The human brain is hardwired to respond to progress. We crave closure, completion, and evidence of movement towards something meaningful. When progress is visible, even in its smallest forms, it triggers a rewarding dopamine response that strengthens behavioural patterns. This neurological mechanism is central to why tracking works. Each time we mark a completed habit—whether by drawing an 'X' on a calendar or logging a workout in an app—we experience a subtle but powerful sense of achievement. This moment of completion reinforces the behaviour and increases the likelihood of repetition.

Consider the case of Leah, a university student who struggled to maintain a study routine amidst a packed schedule and fluctuating energy levels. After several failed attempts to stick with complex planners and digital reminders, she created a simple habit tracker using a grid on her bedroom wall. Every evening she coloured one square for each study session completed. The act of colouring became a mini ritual, one that not only helped her visualise her consistency but also gave her a quiet sense of satisfaction. Over time, the visual accumulation of progress motivated her to avoid breaking the chain. The tracker turned her effort into evidence—a subtle, daily reminder that she was the kind of person who followed through.

This visibility is crucial. Without it, habits often operate in a vacuum. We perform them, forget them, and fail to recognise their cumulative impact. Visual tracking reintroduces awareness. It allows us to witness the continuity of our actions, giving form to what is otherwise intangible. Whether it's a calendar with ticks, a notebook with coloured bars, or a digital dashboard showing progress graphs, the presence of a visual cue helps bridge the psychological gap between effort and reward.

There's also an important behavioural principle at play here: what gets measured gets managed. When we track a habit, we're not just recording outcomes—we're paying attention. And attention alters behaviour. This is not surveillance; it's self-stewardship. By keeping a visual log of our habits, we increase our mindfulness around them. We start to notice patterns—when we're most consistent, when we lapse, and what tends to interfere. This feedback loop enables intelligent adaptation. Rather than abandoning a habit when life becomes busy or progress stalls, we can make informed adjustments. We become more strategic, not just more disciplined.

This approach is particularly valuable for those pursuing long-term or delayed-return goals. Many meaningful habits—like exercising, reading, saving, or meditating—do not offer immediate results. They accumulate benefits slowly, almost imperceptibly. Without a tracking system, it's easy to lose sight of this accumulation and feel as though the effort isn't worth it. A habit tracker makes the invisible visible.

It tells a story of progress, not through transformation, but through repetition.

For example, James, a small business owner trying to reduce his screen time in the evening, began tracking the number of nights he put his phone away by 9 p.m. At first, the habit itself felt inconsequential—sometimes even frustrating, as the urge to check notifications remained strong. But his tracker began to fill, and as the chain of consecutive days grew longer, so did his sense of control and satisfaction. The streak became a form of accountability. He didn't want to break it, not because of guilt, but because of the pride he felt in maintaining it. The tracker had turned a small behavioural shift into a source of personal credibility.

The psychological weight of streaks cannot be underestimated. They play into our intrinsic desire for consistency and integrity. Once we have completed a habit several days in a row, we begin to view ourselves as someone who does this thing regularly. That identity is precious, and most people will go out of their way to protect it. This is why people are reluctant to break a streak—even if the habit itself only takes a minute. The act of tracking creates emotional investment in the behaviour, which then deepens the identity reinforcement loop. The longer the streak, the stronger the identity. And the stronger the identity, the easier it is to act in alignment with it.

Interestingly, even when streaks are broken—as they inevitably are—the presence of a tracker offers a structured way to reflect and restart. Rather than interpreting a missed day as failure, the tracker allows for perspective. You see that you've completed the habit 25 out of 30 days, not failed five times. This shift in framing protects motivation and encourages resilience. It transforms setbacks from catastrophes into data points. With a clear view of your overall pattern, it's easier to get back on track rather than spiral into discouragement.

This principle is especially valuable in the context of micro habits, which may seem too minor to matter on their own. When you write one line in your journal, drink a glass of water, or do five squats, the immediate payoff may be subtle. But tracking these small acts gives them weight. It elevates the experience from something forgettable to something worth noting. And as the days pass, what looked insignificant becomes a record of steady engagement—a physical manifestation of internal discipline.

From a design perspective, the best tracking systems are the simplest. They must be easy to use, quick to update, and immediately visible. Complexity undermines consistency. If tracking a habit takes longer than performing it, resistance builds. A paper calendar, a wall chart, or a minimalist app can be more effective than sophisticated tools packed with features. The goal is not to analyse your habits obsessively, but to give them a visual presence in your daily life—a gentle nudge that reinforces commitment.

Moreover, visual cues are not limited to trackers. Placing objects in your environment that remind you of your habits can serve a similar function. A yoga mat unrolled by the bedside, a book placed on your pillow, a filled water bottle on your desk—these visual markers speak to the brain in a language it understands. They reduce friction, reinforce context, and trigger behaviour without conscious thought. Like trackers, they make the desired action feel close at hand, not abstract or demanding.

Importantly, tracking should not become punitive. It is not a system for self-criticism or performance anxiety. Rather, it is a compassionate tool for reflection and encouragement. If used correctly, it fosters a sense of agency and continuity. It becomes a visual affirmation that change is possible—not through radical overhaul, but through consistent, visible effort. It is a reminder that even small acts, repeated often enough, can build something meaningful.

This shift—from pressure to presence, from perfection to pattern—is what makes tracking so effective. It reframes behaviour as part of a long arc of self-alignment, rather than a test of willpower. By recording the action, we honour it. We recognise that the habit matters—not because it impresses others, but because it reinforces our values, our aspirations, and our evolving identity.

In the landscape of habit design, tracking is not a mere accessory—it is an anchor. It grounds our efforts in evidence. It tells the truth about what we are doing, not what we wish we were doing. And in doing so, it gives us the clarity to stay the course or adjust as needed. Tracking does not create discipline, but it reveals it. It offers us the chance to see our consistency, to celebrate our progress, and to understand ourselves a little better through the patterns we leave behind.

In this way, a habit tracker is more than a tool. It is a mirror, a compass, and a quiet form of self-respect. And when used wisely, it becomes one of the most powerful allies in the pursuit of meaningful, lasting change.

Chapter 4
Creating a Habit-Friendly Environment

Success in building lasting habits is often chalked up to elusive traits like discipline, motivation, or sheer force of will. And while those certainly have their place, the real driver of consistent behaviour is often hiding in plain sight: our environment. The spaces we move through, the objects we encounter, the people we surround ourselves with—these quiet, ever-present elements exert more influence on our actions than we care to admit. In fact, they frequently shape what we do before we've even had a chance to make a conscious decision. Set the stage well, and good behaviour can feel almost effortless. But if your environment is working against you, even the best intentions tend to buckle.

Designing an environment that supports your habits isn't about controlling every variable, nor is it about sterile perfection. Rather, it's about being deliberate. It's about creating conditions where the path of least resistance gently shepherds you toward the behaviours you want to reinforce. Good habits, when framed properly, can become the easiest option. Bad ones? A bit more of a hassle. That subtle reorientation can make all the difference.

At the heart of this approach lie environmental cues—those little nudges, often visual or tactile, that prompt action before we've consciously decided to act. A pair of trainers visible by the door. A book left on your pillow. A sticky note at eye-level on the fridge. These cues don't shout—they whisper. And their power lies in that subtlety. When integrated into existing routines, they quietly encourage repetition. You don't need to summon resolve to drink more water if there's already a glass filled and waiting on your desk. You don't need to strain to remember a habit that's embedded in your surroundings.

Take Dev, a sales consultant who struggled to drink enough water during hectic workdays. He didn't download a flashy app or set hourly reminders. Instead, he began each morning by placing a full glass of water beside his computer. That's it. The simplicity of the gesture was its genius. The glass became a silent cue—persistent, visible, hard to ignore. Eventually, hydration became automatic, not because Dev became more disciplined, but because the environment stopped requiring discipline in the first place.

Of course, this dynamic runs in both directions. The same environments that support good habits can just as easily promote those we'd rather avoid. Think of snacks left in plain sight, phones vibrating constantly with notifications, or the remote lounging within easy reach. These features don't just invite distraction—they all but guarantee it. The solution? Not greater restraint, but less temptation. Not internal policing, but external redesign. If you want to avoid scrolling mindlessly, remove the app. If you're trying to curb sugar cravings, don't keep biscuits on the counter. Introduce friction, even the smallest kind, and the behaviour becomes just inconvenient enough to give you pause. And sometimes, a pause is all you need.

This notion—of friction as a behavioural lever—isn't a hack, but a principle. Friction makes difficult things harder and easy things easier. To encourage a habit, remove the steps that slow you down. Want to work out? Lay out your gear the night before. Want to eat well? Prepare your lunch ahead of time. The fewer the obstacles, the less effort it takes to follow through. The less effort, the more consistent you become.

On the flip side, adding friction can disarm undesirable habits with surprising elegance. Disable autoplay on your streaming service. Put your phone in another room after 9 p.m. Hide the sweets on the highest shelf you have. The goal isn't to outlaw pleasure or deny comfort, but to break the unconscious loop. That small interruption creates space. And in that space, you get to choose, rather than react.

But environments aren't just physical—they're social. Perhaps even more than objects and cues, other people shape how we behave. We mimic, mirror, and adapt to those around us, often without realising we're doing it. It's not weakness; it's human nature. If your team takes walking breaks, you'll probably join in. If your mates go to the gym regularly, it feels normal to exercise. But if your circle normalises burnout, bingeing, or self-neglect, going against the grain can start to feel like resistance.

That's where intentionality becomes crucial. Crafting a supportive social environment isn't about cutting ties with everyone who doesn't meditate or meal prep. It's about introducing voices that echo your values, so your goals don't feel like solitary pursuits. A friend who checks in on your writing habit. A local running group that meets twice a week. A Slack channel for freelancers who share progress. These aren't trivial; they're anchors. They expand your environment beyond the walls of your home or office and into something relational and reinforcing.

Jaya, a freelance illustrator, is a case in point. For years, she struggled to maintain a regular drawing routine. Talent wasn't the issue—loneliness was. Her breakthrough didn't come through productivity hacks, but from joining an online sketching community. The difference was immediate. No longer isolated, her creative habit became social, shared, witnessed. The habit wasn't just hers anymore—it belonged to a larger rhythm, and that changed everything.

It bears repeating: effective environmental design doesn't require a complete overhaul. It thrives on the small, deliberate tweaks. A mantra on the mirror. A calendar in plain view. Dumbbells near the sofa. These things may seem inconsequential, even a little quaint. But they stack. They send a message—not only to your conscious mind but to your subconscious—that this space, this life, is aligned with your intentions. You're not just thinking about change. You're inviting it in.

And therein lies a deeper reward. When your environment begins to reflect your aspirations, there's a subtle but powerful sense of integrity. Your surroundings stop being neutral or chaotic. They become coherent. And that coherence eases the burden of change. It creates flow. It steadies you. You start to feel like your daily actions match the story you're trying to write about who you are.

Will it be perfect? Of course not. Environments are dynamic. They get messy. Social influences clash. Friction returns. Some days you'll fall out of sync. But perfection was never the point. The more you shape your surroundings with care, the less you have to battle your impulses. It's not about having more control over yourself; it's about engineering the world around you to offer a little less resistance.

In the end, curating a habit-supportive environment is both a practical move and a moral one. It says: I recognise that change is hard, and I'm going to make it just a little bit easier. It's a nod to the reality that motivation comes and goes, but structure can stay. And it's a quiet refusal to let your surroundings shape you by accident. Every small shift in your space becomes a vote—for the habits you want, the life you envision, and the self you're becoming.

The Power of Environment Design

Much of what we attribute to discipline is, in fact, the product of design. While personal willpower is commonly praised as the hallmark of successful people, a growing body of behavioural science suggests that our physical and social environments shape our actions far more than we like to admit. Our surroundings, often in subtle and imperceptible ways, guide our decisions, cue our habits, and determine the ease or difficulty with which we pursue our goals. If willpower is a muscle that fatigues with overuse, then environment is the scaffolding that holds behaviour in place when motivation falters.

This realisation is not new. The psychologist Kurt Lewin, one of the founders of modern social psychology, proposed that behaviour is a function of the person and their environment. In his famous equation, $B = f(P,E)$, he recognised that even the most capable individual would behave differently under altered circumstances. A motivated student might struggle to study in a noisy room, just as a habitual snacker might unconsciously reach for crisps when a bowl is always within arm's reach. These are not failures of character but outcomes of context.

Environment design, therefore, is not about controlling every aspect of your surroundings, but about intentionally shaping them to support the behaviours you want to cultivate. It is the practice of aligning your physical and social settings with your goals so that desired habits become the path of least resistance. When your environment is structured well, the behaviour you want to perform becomes easier, more intuitive, and more automatic. This removes the burden from your willpower and builds reliability into your routines.

One of the most compelling examples of this principle comes from public health research. In the early 2000s, a cafeteria at a university hospital in the United States redesigned its layout to promote healthier eating. By placing bottled water at eye level in multiple locations and making sugary drinks less accessible, they dramatically increased water purchases and decreased soda consumption. Importantly, there were no lectures, no posters, and no appeals to motivation—just a shift in how the environment presented choices. This small change in context yielded measurable changes in behaviour without requiring any additional effort from the individuals involved.

This experiment reflects a broader truth: our actions are highly susceptible to cues in our immediate surroundings. If we want to write more, a laptop on a clean desk is more inviting than one buried under papers. If we want to eat better, a fruit bowl on the counter beats a fridge full of convenience food. If we hope to move more, keeping running shoes visible and accessible is far more effective than storing them in a cupboard under the stairs. These are not acts of chance; they are acts of design. They create a behavioural default that works *for* us, rather than against us.

Of course, environmental cues can just as easily foster undesirable behaviours. The smartphone on the bedside table that triggers mindless scrolling. The snack drawer at arm's length in the office that encourages frequent grazing. The television remote placed prominently on the coffee table that makes binge-watching the default post-dinner activity. These arrangements are not neutral; they are actively nudging us toward behaviours that may not align with our values. Recognising these influences allows us to make conscious adjustments, however modest, that begin to shift our default behaviours toward something more constructive.

One of the most effective strategies in environment design is to *reduce friction* for desired behaviours and *increase friction* for undesired ones. Friction, in this context, refers to any small obstacle that adds effort, time, or complexity to an action. Even minor inconveniences—such as needing to dig through a drawer or log into a separate app—can be enough to derail a habit. By contrast, when the behaviour is made seamless and easy to initiate, it becomes more likely to occur.

Take the case of Rahul, an accountant who wanted to start journalling at night. He initially left his journal in a drawer, often forgetting about it or feeling too tired to retrieve it at the end of the day. After re-evaluating his setup, he placed the journal and pen directly on his pillow each morning. That one change reframed the habit from an effortful task to a natural part of his nightly routine. The environment did the prompting, not his memory or willpower.

The power of environmental nudges has also been harnessed in workplace settings. Open-plan offices that include standing desks and breakout spaces tend to encourage mobility and informal collaboration. When healthy snacks are made freely available while processed ones are hidden or require effort to access, people naturally gravitate toward the healthier option. Similarly, digital environments can be designed for or against productivity. A desktop free of distracting icons, with applications set to launch directly into focused work mode, can significantly improve concentration.

It's important to understand that environment design is not a one-size-fits-all concept. The effectiveness of any cue or setup depends on individual tendencies, lifestyle constraints, and personal associations. For some, a clutter-free minimalist desk is inspiring; for others, it feels sterile. The goal is not to replicate an idealised version of order, but to craft a setting that feels supportive and congruent with your own rhythms. This requires some experimentation and reflection—testing different setups and observing which ones lead to greater consistency and ease.

Social environments are equally, if not more, influential. Our behaviours are continuously shaped by the people around us—what they normalise, encourage, and reward. The expectations of family members, friends, colleagues, and communities create a kind of behavioural gravity that can either lift us up or weigh us down. If you spend time with people who value curiosity, you're more likely to read. If your peers prioritise exercise, you'll likely move more. Conversely, if your circle is steeped in negativity, avoidance, or excess, resisting that influence takes considerable effort.

Being intentional about your social environment doesn't mean isolating yourself or seeking perfection in others. It means paying attention to who influences your habits and how. It may mean choosing to spend more time with those who share your values, or initiating new groups—such as writing meetups, walking clubs, or shared accountability circles—that reinforce the habits you wish to cultivate. When your environment includes people who expect and encourage you to show up for yourself, consistency becomes less of a solo struggle and more of a shared norm.

Digital environments, too, deserve scrutiny. The apps we install, the notifications we allow, the websites we bookmark—all of these elements constitute a digital landscape that either supports or sabotages our focus and intention. Curating this environment by turning off alerts, arranging your phone home screen around productivity tools, or using website blockers during work hours can yield substantial behavioural dividends. Here again, success lies not in increasing internal resistance, but in reducing external triggers.

When people hear about environment design, they sometimes imagine it requires a complete overhaul of their life or living space. But small, deliberate changes are usually more effective. A light sensor in the hallway that prompts you to stretch. A notebook placed next to the kettle to encourage morning gratitude. A playlist queued up and ready for the gym. These adjustments may seem minor, but their influence compounds. Over time, they create an environment that supports the identity you are working to embody.

What makes this approach particularly empowering is that it moves the locus of control from willpower—a fickle and depletable resource—to strategy. It acknowledges that human behaviour is shaped as much by the path we walk through as by the direction we intend to go. If the path is clear, well-lit, and inviting, we're more likely to move forward. If it's cluttered with obstacles and distractions, we'll hesitate, detour, or stop altogether.

Ultimately, the power of environment design lies in its subtlety. It doesn't demand discipline; it invites ease. It doesn't shout instructions; it whispers suggestions. And over time, those suggestions shape routines, those routines build habits, and those habits become the architecture of a meaningful and intentional life.

By designing our surroundings with care and purpose, we honour the truth that behaviour is context-driven. We position ourselves to succeed not by trying harder, but by making the right behaviours easier. In doing so, we create a world—our own little microcosm—that quietly, continuously, and reliably supports the person we wish to become.

Cues and Triggers

Every habit begins with a prompt. Whether we're aware of it or not, our actions are typically preceded by some form of signal—an environmental cue, a time-based reminder, a physical sensation, or an emotional state. These cues are the invisible levers of behaviour, quietly shaping our routines and responses. The science of behaviour change, particularly as outlined in the cue-routine-reward model, underscores the importance of recognising and designing effective triggers if we are to cultivate lasting, meaningful habits. Without a cue, even the most well-intentioned habit remains dormant. With the right cue, a desired behaviour can become not only automatic but effortless.

Cues are powerful because they operate beneath the surface of consciousness. They are not commands but suggestions—subtle prompts that invite a particular behaviour. Over time, repeated exposure to a specific cue linked with a particular action strengthens the neurological pathway between them. This process, known as associative learning, is what makes habits feel second nature. The brain, ever efficient, learns to connect certain stimuli with certain responses, enabling us to act with minimal deliberation. This automaticity is what makes habits sustainable. But for a habit to become automatic, it must first be triggered reliably. That's where cue design comes into play.

One of the most common mistakes people make when attempting to form a new habit is relying solely on motivation or willpower. They assume that if the desire is strong enough, the action will follow. Yet, without a reliable cue, the intention lacks a foothold in daily life. The behaviour never finds a consistent home. Designing effective cues is, therefore, not an optional part of habit formation—it is foundational. The cue is the habit's entry point into the real world.

Effective cues have several key qualities. They are specific, consistent, and easily observable. A vague intention like "I'll go for a run later" is unlikely to materialise because it lacks a clear cue. There's no specific time, place, or prompt to initiate the behaviour. By contrast, a cue such as "I will put on my running shoes immediately after I brush my teeth in the morning" ties the behaviour to a fixed anchor in your existing routine. This type of cue is known as a temporal or sequential cue—it uses something you already do as a springboard for the new habit. Because the anchor is reliable, the new behaviour becomes easier to remember and execute.

This strategy was crucial for Mina, a freelance copywriter who wanted to build a consistent reading habit. Despite her love for books, she rarely made time to read during the day. After some reflection, she decided to link reading with her lunch break. She placed a novel on her dining table and committed to reading one page before eating. The cue—sitting down to eat—was already ingrained in her day. By associating reading with this established routine, she made the habit frictionless. What began as a one-page commitment gradually expanded, but the consistency came from the reliability of the cue.

Environmental cues are another effective category. Our surroundings are filled with triggers that influence our behaviour—sometimes positively, often unconsciously. A kettlebell in the middle of the living room may prompt you to stretch or do a few reps. A meditation cushion in plain view may remind you to pause and breathe. The layout of your space can serve as a behavioural map, nudging you toward or away from particular actions. When designing cues, placement matters. If the cue is out of sight, it may as well not exist. Visibility enhances salience, and salience increases the probability of action.

This principle is employed masterfully in retail and marketing environments. Grocery stores place high-margin products at eye level, cafes place pastries under glass domes near the register, and mobile apps use red badges to prompt user engagement. These are all engineered cues—deliberate stimuli meant to drive behaviour. In our personal lives, we can use the same logic, but with greater intentionality. We can design our environments not to sell us something, but to support the kind of person we wish to become.

Sensory cues—such as smells, sounds, and tactile sensations—can also be remarkably effective. The scent of peppermint oil may prompt a moment of focused breathing. The sound of a particular playlist might initiate a writing session. These sensory associations can be powerful once established, but they require repetition and consistency. By pairing a sensory experience with a specific behaviour over time, the cue becomes a behavioural trigger.

Emotional cues are more complex. They occur when certain feelings or mental states prompt specific behaviours. Stress, boredom, anxiety, or even celebration can become cues for action. For instance, someone might reach for their phone when feeling anxious, or open a snack cupboard when bored. These emotional-behavioural loops often underpin habits we wish to change. Recognising the emotional triggers of unwanted habits is the first step in redesigning them. If anxiety leads to scrolling social media, for example, one could replace that loop with a healthier response, such as writing in a journal or doing deep breathing. But the substitution will only stick if the emotional cue remains consistent and the new behaviour is easily accessible.

Time-based cues also play a role. These are habits tied to a specific time of day—such as brushing your teeth at 7 a.m. or stretching before bed. While time alone is less powerful than event-based or location-based cues, it can be reinforced through the structure of a daily schedule. Digital tools like alarms and calendar reminders can act as surrogate cues, though they are most effective when tied to a behaviour you already perform. An alarm prompting you to stand every hour may be ignored unless it coincides with an activity like refilling your water bottle or walking to the printer.

The key to creating effective cues is predictability. The more reliably a cue appears in your day, the stronger its association with the desired behaviour. Random or inconsistent triggers lead to erratic execution. Consistency is the breeding ground of automaticity. Over time, the repeated pairing of cue and behaviour becomes so ingrained that the action feels almost inevitable. You don't decide whether to do it—you simply do it.

One of the most elegant applications of cue-based design is the habit stacking technique, where new habits are attached to existing ones. This leverages the strength of routines already encoded in your neurological architecture. If you already make coffee every morning, that behaviour becomes a reliable anchor for another habit—perhaps reviewing your goals, writing one line in a journal, or reading a paragraph of a non-fiction book. The coffee is the cue; the behaviour is the response. This sequence becomes the loop.

However, cues can also backfire if not designed with care. If the anchor habit is inconsistent, the new habit may never take hold. If the cue is associated with multiple behaviours—some of which are undesirable—it can lead to confusion or conflict. For example, if you try to meditate every time you sit on your sofa, but the sofa is also where you binge-watch television, the cue lacks clarity. In such cases, creating a dedicated space or choosing a different cue may be necessary.

Contextual clarity is essential. A cue should prompt *one* action, not many. It should be as unambiguous as possible. The strength of a cue lies not in its intensity, but in its reliability and specificity. Over time, a well-designed cue becomes less of a prompt and more of a switch. It tells your brain, "now we do this," and your brain obliges with minimal friction.

This dynamic explains why successful habits often feel easy—not because they are effortless by nature, but because the effort of decision-making has been outsourced to design. The cue handles the initiation. The behaviour flows from that initiation. The loop strengthens with repetition. Eventually, the behaviour becomes less a task to complete and more a part of your operating system.

Designing effective cues, then, is not a trivial detail—it is a fundamental practice in behavioural architecture. It is about crafting an environment, both external and internal, that makes the behaviour you want not only likely, but automatic. By embedding clear, consistent, and contextual cues into the rhythm of your day, you reduce the need for willpower, increase your capacity for consistency, and bring your habits into alignment with the life you intend to live. With cues designed for ease, the hard part isn't doing the behaviour—it's *not* doing it. That's when you know your system is working.

Removing Friction

When people struggle to form new habits, they often blame a lack of discipline, time, or motivation. While these factors can certainly contribute to behavioural inconsistencies, they are rarely the root cause. More often than not, the true culprit is friction—the small, often invisible obstacles that make a habit more difficult than it needs to be. Friction doesn't necessarily stop us outright; it simply makes taking action feel inconvenient, effortful, or cognitively taxing. Over time, this resistance builds, gradually wearing down our consistency. To cultivate lasting habits, then, we must learn not just to work harder, but to work *smarter*—by identifying and removing friction wherever it arises.

Friction takes many forms. Sometimes it's physical: your running shoes are buried in the cupboard, your notebook is nowhere to be found, or your healthy food is stored behind processed snacks. Sometimes it's logistical: the gym is far from home, the meal plan requires obscure ingredients, or the app is cumbersome to use. Other times, it's psychological: the task feels overwhelming, the process is unclear, or there's no immediate payoff. Each instance of friction adds a layer of resistance between you and your intention. Even when the resistance is mild, it creates just enough hesitation to derail the habit before it begins.

The good news is that friction is modifiable. It is not a fixed barrier but a variable one—something that can be decreased for positive habits and increased for negative ones. This is not about making habits more virtuous, but about making them *easier*. Likewise, for the behaviours we want to reduce or eliminate, we don't necessarily need to use force or self-denial; we need only to make those behaviours more cumbersome to perform. Friction, when understood and applied strategically, becomes one of the most powerful tools in the architecture of behaviour change.

Start by observing where friction arises in your current routines. It often shows up as the micro-delays that precede action—the pause before a workout, the scroll before opening a document, the reluctance to cook because ingredients need chopping. These moments are opportunities for intervention. The key is to streamline the initiation phase of the habit, because once you've started, momentum tends to carry you forward. Therefore, one of the most effective strategies is to prepare your environment in advance, removing the need to make decisions at the moment of action.

This was the breakthrough for Ravi, a client who wanted to begin exercising in the morning but never managed to do so. Each day, he would wake up and then decide whether to work out, what to wear, and which routine to follow. By the time he'd finished deliberating, the window of opportunity had passed. After a habit audit, he began setting out his clothes the night before, choosing his workout ahead of time, and placing his yoga mat beside his bed. The change was subtle, but the impact was significant. By reducing the number of decisions required in the morning, he lowered the friction and made the habit far easier to maintain.

This approach—removing steps, decisions, or sources of delay—is widely applicable. If you want to eat more healthily, wash and prep vegetables as soon as you buy them. If you aim to drink more water, keep a filled bottle within reach at all times. If you're trying to write regularly, leave your manuscript open on your desktop so you can resume immediately. These adjustments might seem minor, but they shift the behavioural cost-benefit equation. They remove the early hesitation that often prevents action, replacing it with a clear and frictionless path forward.

Conversely, when dealing with negative habits, the goal is to *add* friction. This doesn't require deprivation or punishment; it requires intelligent design. If you want to reduce screen time, sign out of social media apps or delete them from your home screen. If you tend to snack mindlessly, keep less healthy options out of immediate sight or in hard-to-reach places. If late-night television keeps you from sleeping, unplug the TV or remove the remote batteries at the end of the evening. These interventions don't prevent the behaviour outright—they simply insert a pause, a moment of reflection that creates an opportunity to choose differently.

This principle of increasing friction was employed with great success by Nina, a high school teacher who found herself repeatedly distracted by her phone during work hours. Rather than attempting to use sheer willpower, she began storing her phone in a drawer across the room and enabling "do not disturb" mode. This created a small, but meaningful, barrier. Checking her phone now required standing up and crossing the room—a break in flow that prompted her to question whether it was worth it. As a result, her phone use declined dramatically, and her ability to focus improved without any increase in effort or motivation.

It's important to understand that friction is not purely logistical; it can also be emotional or cognitive. For example, if a habit is associated with uncertainty—like not knowing how to start meditating or what to eat for breakfast—this ambiguity creates friction. The brain resists uncertainty because it demands cognitive processing. To reduce this form of friction, create scripts, templates, or routines that clarify what to do. Instead of aiming to "meditate for 10 minutes," use a guided app and sit at the same time and place each day. Instead of "eat a healthy breakfast," prepare a shortlist of go-to meals you enjoy and can prepare quickly. These strategies reduce decision fatigue and promote habitual execution.

Another form of cognitive friction is lack of closure. When a habit doesn't have a clear endpoint, it feels harder to start. This is why open-ended goals—like "write more" or "be more active"—are less effective than specific ones such as "write 100 words" or "walk for ten minutes." Defining the end helps to define the start. You know when you're finished, which makes beginning feel less daunting.

An often-overlooked contributor to friction is the misalignment between environment and habit. Trying to focus in a cluttered space, relax in a noisy room, or exercise in an area lacking privacy introduces layers of friction that drain mental energy. In such cases, the solution is not just to adjust the habit, but to adjust the setting. Create a space that cues and supports the behaviour you want. Even symbolic cues—a candle for reflection, a playlist for focus, a chair for reading—can reduce the internal resistance by signalling that "this is where this behaviour happens."

Social friction also plays a role. If your environment includes people who undermine your habits—by mocking, dismissing, or inadvertently sabotaging your efforts—the resistance can be substantial. Navigating this requires tact, but also clarity. You may need to explain your goals, set boundaries, or find allies who reinforce rather than erode your commitments. Social alignment reduces the psychological friction of going against the norm and makes sticking with your habits feel less like swimming upstream.

All of this underscores a larger truth: successful habit formation is not just about building discipline—it's about building systems. When your environment is designed with care and the friction is intelligently managed, habits can develop with a sense of ease and inevitability. They require less deliberation, less inner negotiation, and less emotional drag. Behaviour becomes a product of structure rather than sheer will.

This does not mean that every habit will always feel easy. There will still be days of resistance, fatigue, or competing demands. But a low-friction habit is far more resilient to these fluctuations than one that relies on daily inspiration. It's also more adaptable. When circumstances change, the habit can be recalibrated by identifying new sources of friction and addressing them directly. This makes the practice of habit maintenance as dynamic as the lives we lead.

Removing friction, then, is not about eliminating all effort—it is about eliminating *unnecessary* effort. It's about clearing the runway so your behaviours can take off without constant troubleshooting. It is the quiet, often invisible discipline of smoothing the path so that what matters most can happen with the least resistance.

When we reduce the friction around our desired behaviours and increase it around those we wish to avoid, we shift the behavioural equation in our favour. We make consistency more natural, more reliable, and more deeply embedded in the routines of everyday life. And with every layer of resistance we remove, we come closer to creating a system where action is not something we fight for—but something that flows.

The Influence of Social Circles

Human behaviour is never entirely individual. Despite our self-conception as autonomous beings, our decisions, actions, and habits are profoundly shaped by the people we spend time with. Social circles act as silent architects of our behavioural norms. They reinforce what is acceptable, desirable, and typical—often without explicit instruction. This influence operates with such subtlety that we seldom notice it, yet its power is pervasive. When it comes to habit formation, the role of peer environments cannot be overstated. Our social context can serve as either scaffolding for growth or quicksand that pulls us back into inertia and inconsistency.

Much of this dynamic rests on our evolutionary wiring. Humans evolved in tightly-knit groups where belonging was essential for survival. As a result, we developed acute social sensitivity—a radar finely tuned to cues of acceptance, rejection, and conformity. Even today, in our modern, more individualistic societies, that instinct persists. We mirror the behaviours, language, postures, and even emotional responses of those around us. The psychological term for this is "social contagion"—the phenomenon by which attitudes and behaviours spread within groups, sometimes as rapidly as a virus.

When the people around us embody the habits we aspire to adopt, their presence becomes a powerful motivational and structural force. A group of friends who exercise regularly will make movement feel normal. Colleagues who take punctuality seriously will subtly encourage promptness. A book club that meets every week will reinforce a reading habit that might otherwise be sporadic. The group doesn't have to explicitly demand anything; its collective expectations and routines shape the behaviour of individuals through ambient pressure.

This was the case for Shreya, a medical student who had long struggled to maintain focus during long study sessions. She began attending a campus study group not because she expected it to revolutionise her learning, but because she was tired of working alone. What she discovered, however, was that the shared silence and focused atmosphere of the group dramatically improved her productivity. The act of being surrounded by people engaged in the same behaviour helped her maintain attention and consistency. Her environment did not shout for her attention—it modelled a rhythm she could follow.

Importantly, social support doesn't always have to come from those pursuing the *same* goals. It can also come from people who simply respect and encourage your efforts. A partner who honours your early morning exercise routine, a housemate who refrains from offering you a cigarette, or a manager who accommodates your meditation break—these allies create a permissive, supportive environment where habits are more likely to take root. They reduce resistance not by pushing you forward, but by not holding you back.

Yet the opposite is also true. When our social environment dismisses, mocks, or undermines our habits, those behaviours become more difficult to sustain. Peer pressure may not be overt, but it can be corrosive. Sarcastic comments about your healthy eating, passive resistance to your new sleep schedule, or subtle disinterest in your creative ambitions—all of these create psychological drag. The behaviour feels like a deviation from the group norm, which triggers internal conflict. Conformity, often unconscious, begins to erode the habit.

Consider Raj, a junior associate at a consultancy firm. After reading about the benefits of deep work, he began blocking off two hours each morning for uninterrupted focus. Initially, he found the routine energising and productive. But when his team members began making jokes about him "disappearing" or questioned why he wasn't immediately responsive on chat, he started feeling guilty. Without direct opposition, the ambient social signals were enough to derail his routine. Eventually, he returned to the default of constant availability—not because the habit failed him, but because his environment did.

The good news is that awareness of social influence allows for strategic intervention. We may not always choose our colleagues or family members, but we *can* choose who we seek out for reinforcement. This is where the idea of identity-based communities becomes powerful. Whether it's a running club, a co-working space for writers, or a mindfulness retreat, joining a group where your desired habit is the norm creates an atmosphere of implicit accountability. You begin to see yourself not just as someone *trying* to build a habit, but as someone who *belongs* to a community where that habit is valued.

This sense of belonging is transformative. When habits are supported by identity—"I'm part of a group that does this"—they gain emotional depth. The behaviour becomes not just a task to tick off, but an expression of shared values. You feel connected to something larger than yourself. This connection reduces the psychological cost of the habit and strengthens your commitment through social affirmation.

Technology can also be leveraged to amplify positive social influence. Online forums, habit-tracking communities, and challenge-based apps provide a sense of collective momentum. While virtual relationships may lack some of the intimacy of in-person support, they still offer validation, encouragement, and a visible standard of consistency. Even a simple comment of encouragement from a stranger who understands your goal can provide a surprising surge of motivation.

However, not all social accountability is created equal. The tone matters. Public shaming or punitive feedback can backfire, triggering defensiveness and disengagement. True support is empathetic, not evaluative. It meets people where they are, celebrates effort, and creates psychological safety. This is why it's important to surround yourself not just with high performers, but with compassionate ones—people who inspire you without making you feel inadequate.

Equally important is the role we play in other people's habit formation. Just as we are shaped by those around us, we also shape them. Our habits broadcast signals—about what's possible, what's desirable, and what's acceptable. When you wake up early to run, someone notices. When you choose not to drink at a party, someone observes. When you carry a book instead of your phone, someone registers the choice. These subtle acts create a ripple effect. They plant the idea that alternatives exist, that habits can change, that identity is fluid.

Understanding this reciprocal nature of influence adds a layer of responsibility, but also opportunity. By modelling consistency, resilience, and curiosity, we become silent allies in other people's transformation. We contribute not just to our own behavioural ecosystem, but to the collective one.

There are also cultural dynamics at play. In some environments, conformity is strongly encouraged and deviation is frowned upon. In others, individuality is prized and experimentation is welcomed. Recognising the broader social values in your workplace, family, or community helps you anticipate where support will be abundant and where resistance may emerge. This knowledge allows you to prepare, adapt, and seek out supplementary support where needed.

Finally, it's worth reflecting on your internalised social scripts. Sometimes, the voices of our past—parents, teachers, peers—continue to influence our habits long after the social context has changed. These internalised critics or expectations can shape behaviour as powerfully as current relationships. Bringing these influences to light allows for conscious renegotiation. You get to choose which voices you continue to listen to, and which you leave behind.

Social influence is not inherently positive or negative—it is simply *powerful.* Its direction depends on awareness and design. By surrounding yourself with people who reflect the habits and values you aspire to embody, you make growth feel natural. You remove the friction of isolation and replace it with the ease of alignment. Your habits become supported, not just by intention, but by interaction.

As we move through life, our habits become the scripts we live by—and our social circles, the co-authors of those scripts. Choosing your collaborators wisely, and understanding your role in theirs, transforms habit formation from a solitary endeavour into a relational one. And in doing so, it elevates change from something you work on *alone* to something you build *together*.

Micro Adjustments for Macro Impact

The idea that small changes can lead to significant results is a concept that, while often invoked, is rarely understood in its full behavioural context. When applied with care, micro adjustments—subtle tweaks in our daily environments—can dramatically reshape the course of our habits. These adjustments do not require grand gestures, nor do they demand a complete overhaul of lifestyle. Instead, they rely on the art of strategic modification: identifying and refining the conditions under which our behaviour occurs. When our surroundings are slightly reoriented to support our intentions, the outcomes can be surprisingly profound.

Modern behavioural psychology, particularly the research around habit formation, suggests that our choices are more a product of our context than of conscious deliberation. We may believe we are rational actors, making decisions based on logic and willpower, but most of what we do is driven by the immediate cues and conditions around us. Our environment acts as a behavioural script, subtly guiding our actions through design, placement, and accessibility. Understanding this allows us to engage with our surroundings not passively, but as co-authors in shaping behaviour.

Micro adjustments function on the principle of cumulative advantage. A tiny edge—doing something one per cent better, one minute earlier, or one step closer—multiplies over time. The aim is not to revolutionise how we live but to calibrate the details. These minor environmental shifts don't just increase the likelihood of initiating a desired habit; they also make the behaviour more sustainable because they minimise friction and decision fatigue.

Consider the case of Ashwin, a lawyer who wanted to build a reading habit amidst his demanding schedule. He didn't create a new reading routine from scratch. Instead, he made two minor adjustments: he placed a paperback on the cushion of his favourite chair each evening, and he put his phone charger across the room rather than on the bedside table. These tiny changes disrupted his default tendency to scroll and replaced it with an inviting cue to read. Within weeks, the chair became his reading spot, and the book became part of his wind-down ritual. The habit grew not because of more time or motivation, but because of a small shift in physical context.

Micro adjustments work because they lower the cognitive and emotional resistance associated with change. Starting something new often feels daunting—not because the behaviour itself is difficult, but because our environment hasn't been primed to support it. When everything around us signals the old routine, the new one feels intrusive or fragile. But when the context begins to shift—even slightly—our behaviour follows with far less effort. These contextual nudges have the power to transform "I should" into "I did."

For those trying to integrate exercise into a sedentary lifestyle, one micro adjustment might be laying out workout clothes the night before or setting a specific pair of trainers by the door. For someone aiming to drink more water, placing a bottle on the desk in clear view makes the habit almost reflexive. These actions take seconds but create a persistent visual cue. The brain, attuned to its environment, gradually learns to associate these cues with the new behaviour. Over time, repetition forges a loop, and the habit becomes less dependent on intention and more a matter of default.

It's easy to underestimate the influence of our physical environment because we adapt to it so quickly. What seems like background noise actually plays a starring role in shaping our patterns. The design of your kitchen can influence how you eat. The layout of your workspace affects how you think and focus. The position of your digital devices shapes your attention span. These settings are not neutral—they are active participants in your daily behaviour. A few centimetres in layout, a shift in lighting, or a change in storage can either invite or obstruct the habits we hope to maintain.

This was exemplified in the life of Karen, a graphic designer working from home. Struggling with procrastination, she found herself constantly distracted by clutter and visual noise in her workspace. Rather than making dramatic lifestyle changes, she introduced a series of micro adjustments. She removed all non-essential items from her desk, designated a single tray for her phone and unrelated papers, and lit a specific candle when she began focused work. These tweaks reduced sensory overload and gave her brain a cue that it was time to engage. Her productivity improved not because she suddenly became more disciplined, but because her environment quietly removed the need for extra self-regulation.

What makes micro adjustments especially effective is their adaptability. They allow for immediate feedback and fine-tuning. Unlike major lifestyle changes—which can be emotionally disruptive and logistically difficult—micro adjustments are easy to implement and reverse. This flexibility encourages experimentation. You might try moving your meditation cushion to a sunnier spot, setting your journal on top of your laptop, or shifting your desk to face a quieter direction. If it works, keep it. If not, try something else. Behavioural design is iterative. The goal is not perfection but optimisation.

It's also important to recognise that micro adjustments are not limited to physical objects or space. They apply equally to digital environments, routines, and even social settings. A person trying to reduce screen time might move their most distracting apps off the home screen. Someone looking to focus more deeply might disable notifications during certain hours or set specific browser restrictions. These are digital equivalents of rearranging furniture—adjustments that reduce distraction and increase intentionality. Again, the magnitude of effort is small, but the behavioural return can be substantial.

Social micro adjustments are equally powerful. If your habit is being subtly undermined by your social context, changing how or when you interact can yield significant results. A subtle boundary, such as wearing headphones in a shared space to signal focus, or politely declining to discuss certain topics at certain times, can help reinforce behavioural boundaries. You're not cutting people off—you're reshaping your interaction in a way that better supports your habits and wellbeing.

One of the core strengths of micro adjustments is their ability to reduce decision fatigue. When we're forced to make repeated decisions throughout the day—what to wear, when to exercise, what to eat—our cognitive resources are depleted. This makes it harder to resist temptation and maintain new behaviours. Micro adjustments resolve this by scripting certain choices in advance. When your environment is already aligned with your goals, fewer decisions are required. You don't wonder whether to read or scroll; the book is already open. You don't debate whether to stretch; your mat is unrolled. This simplicity fosters sustainability.

Moreover, micro adjustments build confidence. When you succeed in implementing a small change, you signal to yourself that you are capable of adaptation. This creates a sense of progress, which enhances motivation. These wins may seem insignificant at first glance, but their psychological weight accumulates. They provide evidence that change is possible, manageable, and repeatable. This growing sense of agency becomes a foundation for further development.

This was the experience of Omar, a university lecturer who wanted to improve his mental health through regular reflection. Grand journalling ambitions had repeatedly failed. But one day, he simply placed a small notepad on his pillow with a pen resting atop. The act of moving the pen to lie down became the cue to write a single sentence. Over weeks, that sentence became a few. Sometimes it didn't, and that was fine too. But the habit endured—not because of its scale, but because the context supported its continuation. A pen. A pad. A quiet moment. That was enough.

What emerges from these examples is a deeper truth about behavioural design: large results often do not require large interventions. They require precise ones. Changing your context by just a few degrees in the right direction can, over time, alter your trajectory dramatically. Much like the course of an aircraft is determined by slight alterations early in the flight, our habits follow the paths shaped by early conditions. When those conditions are aligned with our values and goals, the outcomes speak for themselves.

In the pursuit of behavioural change, there is a temptation to go big—to set ambitious targets, make bold declarations, and imagine overnight transformation. But real change tends to unfold quietly, incrementally, and in response to subtle signals. The power of micro adjustments lies in their humility. They ask little but deliver much. They don't demand radical motivation; they provide gentle direction. And over time, they accumulate into a life that feels more aligned, more intentional, and more resilient.

The task, then, is not to overhaul your life but to observe it. To notice where friction occurs, where support is lacking, and where your environment might be gently nudged in your favour. It is to design a world—however small, however local—that works *with* your habits, not against them. In doing so, you don't just change your behaviour. You shape the conditions that allow better behaviour to flourish.

Micro adjustments are not a shortcut to change. They are the foundation of it. And when embraced with thoughtfulness and curiosity, they become the most sustainable and empowering way to build a life of consistent, meaningful action.

Chapter 5
Overcoming Resistance and Staying Consistent

There's something intoxicating about the decision to change. In those first few moments—perhaps hours, even days—we're carried by a wave of intention: wake up earlier, commit to writing, fit in regular workouts, meditate before bed. The vision is crisp, the energy is high. But then, as it always does, life intervenes. That initial charge dulls, resistance sets in, and before we know it, our shiny new routine begins to wobble. We delay, rationalise, abandon. Not because we've forgotten what we want—but because repetition, frankly, is hard.

The behaviour itself is rarely the real hurdle. It's the friction—internal and external—that makes sticking with it so punishing. Mental static, emotional weariness, mounting pressures from the day... These undercurrents quietly sabotage our resolve. If habit formation boiled down to simply *knowing* what to do, we'd all be ticking off our goals with mechanical precision. But of course, we're not machines.

This chapter steps directly into that gritty terrain. It doesn't sugar-coat the process, nor does it wallow in defeatism. Instead, it attempts something more useful: a dissection of resistance itself—why it surfaces, how it disrupts us, and what can be done when it inevitably reappears. Because building habits is not a test of willpower. It's a dance between intention and reality, and like any dance, it helps to know the steps.

Let's begin with one of resistance's most familiar faces: procrastination. On the surface, it presents as laziness, as if we simply can't be bothered. But underneath that lazy disguise often lies something more vulnerable—avoidance born of discomfort. We delay not because we don't care, but because we expect the task to be unpleasant or taxing or—worst of all—a reflection of our limitations. The effort feels heavy before it's even begun.

Yet here's the rub: procrastination doesn't actually make us feel better. It buys us temporary relief, yes, but the cost is steep—anxiety, guilt, that gnawing feeling of falling short. Recognising this emotional loop is crucial. And then comes the practical move: shrink the task. Drastically. Write one sentence. Do a two-minute sketch. Stretch for thirty seconds. The goal isn't to finish—it's to begin. Because once in motion, the resistance often loses its grip.

Then there's perfectionism, procrastination's uptight cousin. It dresses itself up as high standards but, more often than not, it's just fear in a tuxedo. Perfectionism builds a rigid framework where anything less than 100% feels like failure. If there's no time for a full gym session, we skip it entirely. If we can't meditate for twenty minutes, we don't bother. It's an exhausting way to live. And worse—it keeps us from building habits at all. The way forward here is reframing. Half a session still counts. Five minutes on the mat is not nothing. Perfection is not the price of progress.

Lurking behind both procrastination and perfectionism is a deeper, more insidious force: fear of failure. This one doesn't always announce itself. It masquerades as "busyness" or "bad timing." But at its heart is the same truth: not trying feels safer than trying and coming up short. So we hedge. We dabble. We plan instead of doing. And we miss the growth that comes from effort.

The antidote? Exposure. Not in the dramatic, throw-yourself-into-the-deep-end sense, but through consistent, low-pressure repetition. Engage with the habit in ways that don't threaten your self-worth. Messy, imperfect, incomplete—doesn't matter. What you're building isn't a performance. It's tolerance. Over time, the fear shrinks. You learn that missteps aren't verdicts. They're just part of the rhythm.

But the deepest resistance often comes from within—not from fear, but from inner conflict. This is where self-sabotage enters the frame. You want to eat better, but some part of you clings to the belief that you don't deserve to feel good. You crave discipline, yet associate routine with loss of freedom. These are not minor mental quirks. They're old narratives, stitched into our identity. And until they're unearthed, they'll keep hijacking our best efforts.

There's no neat fix here. But awareness changes the equation. Writing things down, reflecting in quiet moments, speaking with someone who can hold space—these acts shine light on the scripts we've inherited or absorbed. And in that light, we begin to choose which stories we still want to live by.

Of course, insight alone doesn't create change. For that, we need tools. Not grand systems or life overhauls, but small, practical nudges. Visual cues are a classic example—a note on your mirror, a calendar on the fridge, a phone lock screen that reminds you why you started. These cues aren't magic, but they help cut through the noise. They keep your intentions visible, especially on days when focus is scarce.

Another tool in the box: commitment devices. These aren't about locking yourself into rigid contracts but creating gentle pressure that bridges today's good intentions with tomorrow's temptations. Tell a friend. Book a class in advance. Set up a small reward for consistency. The power here lies in externalising the habit—not hiding it in your head but anchoring it in shared reality. We're social beings. We like to follow through when others are watching—not out of shame, but connection.

Still, let's not pretend that even the best-laid plans don't go awry. Setbacks happen. They always do. The crucial difference is in how we meet them. Those who maintain habits over the long haul aren't the ones who never miss a day. They're the ones who know how to return after they do. They don't spiral into self-blame or abandon the whole project. They pause. They ask, "What knocked me off track? What could I do differently next time?" Curiosity over criticism. That's the pivot point.

And then—perhaps the most underrated strategy of all—comes celebration. Yes, celebration. Not fireworks or fanfare, but the quiet act of acknowledging that you showed up. That you did what you said you would. Tick the box. Say it aloud. Give yourself a nod in the mirror. These micro-rewards send a clear message to the brain: this matters. And what the brain perceives as meaningful, it begins to crave. Over time, that craving turns into rhythm. That rhythm becomes habit.

Our culture tends to lionise breakthroughs, but real change is made in moments so small they're easy to dismiss. A breath taken with intention. A few words written when you could have scrolled. A stretch instead of a snooze. These are the units of transformation. Stack enough of them, and the path reshapes itself beneath your feet.

Resistance, then, is not the villain of this story. It's the terrain. Understand it, navigate it, and you gain something better than perfection—you gain resilience. Which is all habit really asks of us. Not that we get it right every time, but that we return. Again and again, however clumsily, until the returning itself becomes second nature.

So as you move through this chapter, expect friction. Expect setbacks. But also expect insight. Expect to meet yourself anew, with a bit more generosity, a bit more grit. Because consistency isn't about never wavering. It's about what you do the day after you do. And that—quietly, stubbornly—is how habits are made.

Identifying Common Barriers

The desire for personal transformation is nearly universal. Whether it's building a fitness routine, adopting a mindfulness practice, or developing a writing habit, many people earnestly begin the process of change with genuine intent. Yet, despite this desire, progress often falters. Habits are formed not in the moment of decision but in the repetition of small actions—and sustaining that repetition is where many fall short. What holds people back is not always a lack of clarity or resources, but rather the hidden psychological barriers that interfere with consistency. Among the most pervasive of these are procrastination, perfectionism, and fear of failure. Each operates differently, but all have the power to quietly unravel even the best-laid plans.

Procrastination is often mistaken for laziness, but in reality, it is more a mechanism of avoidance than apathy. At its core, procrastination is an emotional regulation strategy. We postpone tasks not because we don't value them, but because we want to avoid the uncomfortable feelings associated with them—uncertainty, effort, risk of inadequacy, or simply the prospect of not knowing where to start. In this sense, procrastination is not a problem of productivity; it is a symptom of emotional resistance.

The problem arises when we defer action long enough that the discomfort we sought to avoid becomes amplified. Guilt, stress, and diminished self-worth begin to accumulate, further entrenching the cycle. The key to disrupting this pattern lies in recognising the emotional undertones of delay. Rather than labelling oneself as unmotivated or weak, one might ask, "What emotion am I trying to escape by not doing this now?" That question alone can surface important insights and allow a more compassionate, constructive response.

For example, Sarah, a teacher who aspired to write a novel, found herself endlessly reorganising her notes rather than beginning the actual draft. The task felt monumental, and she feared starting without a perfect plan. The longer she avoided writing, the more pressure she felt to make the eventual effort "worth it." Her procrastination wasn't about laziness—it was rooted in self-doubt and a fear of not measuring up. Once she reframed her task from "writing a perfect novel" to "writing a messy first paragraph," she found that starting became much easier. The friction wasn't in the writing—it was in how she *thought* about writing.

Closely linked to procrastination is perfectionism, a barrier that masquerades as a strength but often functions as a constraint. Perfectionists typically set impossibly high standards for themselves, then equate anything less than flawless execution with failure. The outcome is paralysis. The fear of producing substandard work leads to avoidance, and the desire to "get it right" the first time prevents learning through iteration.

Perfectionism thrives on binary thinking. Either you are exceptional, or you are inadequate. There is no middle ground. This mindset leaves no space for gradual improvement, which is the very essence of habit formation. Habits, by nature, are meant to evolve. They are not fixed standards of excellence but processes of becoming. When perfectionism infects the process, it strips habits of their flexibility and replaces progress with pressure.

Take the example of Jamal, a marketing executive trying to build a consistent public speaking habit. He was enthusiastic at first but abandoned his efforts after a few underwhelming practice sessions. Because his performance didn't match his ideal image, he judged his efforts as failures. What he needed was not more talent, but more tolerance—for discomfort, imperfection, and slow progress. Once he gave himself permission to "be bad" before getting better, his confidence—and skill—grew steadily.

Perfectionism is also particularly insidious because it's often reinforced by social and professional environments that reward only high achievement. Individuals may internalise the belief that their worth is tied to outcomes, making any setback feel like a threat to identity. Overcoming this barrier requires more than strategic advice—it calls for a shift in mindset. Recognising that excellence is a *product* of consistent imperfection, not its absence, is critical. Valuing volume over quality in the early stages of a habit—ten rough sketches rather than one masterpiece, five short runs rather than one perfect workout—can help retrain the brain to accept progress over perfection.

Fear of failure, while overlapping with the previous two barriers, deserves distinct attention. This fear can manifest in two paradoxical ways: either through complete avoidance or through over-preparation. In the first case, we avoid starting altogether to shield ourselves from the possibility of failing. In the second, we overthink and overanalyse, believing that more preparation will insulate us from error. Both responses are rooted in the belief that failure is a reflection of the self, rather than a natural part of learning.

At its heart, fear of failure is a threat to self-concept. If you believe that failing at something means you *are* a failure, then of course you will resist taking risks. This is especially potent in adults, who are often conditioned by early schooling or workplace cultures that penalise mistakes. Children, by contrast, are more willing to try, stumble, and try again—not because they are braver, but because their identity is less rigidly defined.

Overcoming fear of failure requires a reconceptualisation of what failure means. It is not a verdict; it is data. A missed day in a habit loop is not a collapse—it is information about what disrupted the routine. A poorly executed project is not shameful—it is a lesson in planning, pacing, or context. When failure is viewed through the lens of learning rather than judgement, it becomes easier to tolerate. And when it is tolerated, action becomes more frequent, and consistency more achievable.

Practical approaches can support this mindset shift. For instance, someone trying to build a habit of daily sketching might deliberately draw something poorly each week, as an act of resistance against perfectionism and failure-avoidance. This inoculation technique—exposing oneself in small doses to what one fears—can gradually reduce anxiety and increase behavioural flexibility.

Realising that these barriers—procrastination, perfectionism, and fear of failure—are normal rather than pathological is itself a liberating insight. They are not flaws to be eradicated, but human tendencies to be understood and worked with. Most people, at some point, encounter them. The difference between those who move forward and those who remain stuck is not the absence of these barriers but the presence of awareness and strategy.

The process of habit formation, then, becomes less about "fixing" oneself and more about navigating these barriers with skill. Instead of seeing resistance as a sign that something is wrong, we can view it as an invitation to go deeper—to ask what emotions, beliefs, or environmental factors are making action feel difficult. By naming these elements, we reduce their power. By adjusting our context, reframing our mindset, and embracing imperfection, we make space for new patterns to take hold.

What matters most is consistency, not intensity. A habit done imperfectly is still a habit. An action taken late is still an action. A disrupted streak is not the end—it is a moment of recalibration. When we understand the psychology of our own resistance, we become better equipped to design lives that support rather than stifle our growth.

In the pages that follow, we will move beyond diagnosis and into practical solutions. But it begins here, with the recognition that the barriers to habit formation are not barriers to who you are. They are signals—pointing to where gentle attention and thoughtful adjustment are needed. When approached with curiosity rather than condemnation, these signals become guides. And through them, sustainable change becomes not only possible but deeply humane.

The Psychology of Self-Sabotage

Few things are as frustrating as knowing exactly what we need to do to improve our lives, yet consistently failing to follow through. Whether it's exercising regularly, eating well, prioritising rest, or setting aside time for personal growth, the benefits of change are often clear—and still, we resist. This internal contradiction is one of the most puzzling and universal features of human behaviour. At its core lies the phenomenon of self-sabotage: a subtle, often unconscious set of behaviours and patterns that undermine our best intentions. Understanding the psychology behind it is not only enlightening—it is essential for building habits that stick.

Self-sabotage is not necessarily dramatic. It doesn't always involve overt acts of destruction or impulsive reversals. More often, it appears in quiet, habitual forms: procrastination, missed deadlines, avoidance of feedback, overcommitting, skipping steps, or quitting just as momentum is building. It is the late-night binge after a week of healthy eating, the delay of an important email, the decision to "start tomorrow" for the seventh day in a row. On the surface, these actions seem trivial. But when repeated, they create patterns of self-defeat that compromise long-term goals.

To understand why people sabotage themselves—even when they know better—we must explore the psychological drivers beneath the surface. One of the most significant is cognitive dissonance: the discomfort that arises when our actions are misaligned with our self-concept or values. When we engage in behaviour that challenges our internal identity—say, taking initiative on a project when we secretly believe we're not leadership material—our mind seeks to resolve the tension. One way to do this is to abandon the behaviour so it no longer contradicts the identity. In this way, the habit is not what's rejected; it's the incongruence it creates.

This is why identity work is so critical in habit formation. If someone still sees themselves as "not a morning person," they will unconsciously resist early wake-ups, even with the best alarm system. If they believe they're inherently disorganised, they'll sabotage efforts to create structure. The underlying identity acts as a ceiling, limiting what feels authentic or possible. The conflict isn't between the goal and the effort—it's between the behaviour and the story we tell ourselves about who we are.

Another powerful psychological driver of self-sabotage is fear—not just fear of failure, but fear of success. Success brings change, and change, even when positive, threatens stability. It disrupts the known patterns of interaction and expectation. If you become more confident, what happens to relationships built on self-deprecation? If you become more productive, will people expect even more from you? These unconscious calculations often result in what psychologists call "upper-limiting"—a term popularised by Gay Hendricks to describe the self-imposed limits people place on their success. When we get close to breaking through a barrier, we pull back. Not because we're incapable, but because we're unsettled by what might come next.

This dynamic was vividly illustrated by Priya, a graphic designer who began freelancing after years in a structured corporate job. Her initial months were marked by incredible creative output, client praise, and increasing revenue. But just as her business began to take off, she found herself missing deadlines, ignoring new inquiries, and doubting her decisions. On the surface, she blamed time management. In reality, she was afraid of scaling her success beyond what she believed she could handle. Subconsciously, she was sabotaging her progress to stay within the bounds of comfort and familiarity.

The inner critic is another central figure in the psychology of self-sabotage. Most people carry internalised voices—echoes of past criticism, unmet expectations, or negative social comparisons. These voices form a running commentary that questions our worth, competence, and capability. When we begin a new habit or attempt a meaningful change, the inner critic often grows louder. It warns us of looking foolish, of wasting time, of aiming too high. To silence it, we retreat. We abandon the new behaviour not because it's failing, but because it makes us feel exposed.

The critic doesn't operate with facts. It operates with familiar scripts, often borrowed from childhood, education, or toxic social dynamics. Overcoming this voice requires more than positive affirmations. It requires active disempowerment—acknowledging the presence of the voice without granting it authority. One effective strategy is externalisation: writing down the criticisms as if spoken by another person and then evaluating them objectively. Would you accept this tone from a friend? If not, why accept it from your own thoughts?

A further factor driving self-sabotage is emotional regulation. Many of us have never been taught how to manage uncomfortable emotions constructively. When stress, anxiety, or uncertainty arise, we look for immediate relief—often in behaviours that compromise our long-term goals. These comfort behaviours may include scrolling, snacking, avoidance, or escapism. They work because they soothe the nervous system, even if they come with consequences later. In this light, self-sabotage is not irrational—it's a coping mechanism. It's the brain's attempt to reduce perceived threat in the moment.

Building emotional literacy is, therefore, a crucial part of overcoming self-sabotage. The ability to name and process feelings allows us to respond rather than react. Mindfulness, breathwork, and journaling are not just wellness trends—they are practical tools that create space between stimulus and response. When we are able to sit with discomfort without fleeing into self-sabotage, we reclaim the agency to act in alignment with our values.

Another often overlooked contributor is the lure of familiarity. Even dysfunctional patterns offer a kind of comfort. They are predictable. They don't require redefinition. This is particularly true in social contexts, where identity is relational. Changing habits may disrupt dynamics with friends, partners, or colleagues who are invested in the "old" version of you. The fear of social dislocation can be powerful enough to keep people tethered to habits they know are harmful. This is why support systems matter. Having at least one person who believes in your capacity for change—and treats your growth as normal—can tip the balance.

It's also essential to examine the broader cultural narratives that reinforce self-sabotage. Many societies promote productivity, performance, and self-worth as tightly linked. In this context, rest feels lazy, vulnerability feels weak, and incremental progress feels insufficient. These norms create an internal pressure cooker where people strive to "prove" themselves through behaviour. When the pressure becomes too intense, sabotage offers an escape. It becomes the release valve. The behaviour that undermines progress is paradoxically what restores a sense of emotional equilibrium.

Counteracting self-sabotage, then, is not about pushing harder. It's about listening more closely. It's about recognising when your resistance is protecting an old identity, buffering against fear, or coping with pain. Rather than override these responses, we can interrogate them. What is this behaviour protecting me from? What belief is it reinforcing? What emotion is it helping me avoid? These questions shift the conversation from shame to curiosity. And curiosity opens the door to change.

Practical interventions must match this nuanced understanding. It's not enough to adopt new behaviours—we must create new internal conditions for those behaviours to flourish. This may involve redefining success not as flawless execution, but as alignment with one's values. It may require creating environments that reduce cognitive load and support regulation. Or it might involve naming and grieving the parts of ourselves that must be left behind in order to grow.

Importantly, the presence of self-sabotage does not mean you are broken or unmotivated. It means you are human, complex, and caught in the friction between competing psychological forces. Change, even positive change, threatens the status quo. And the mind, wired for predictability, resists disruption. But with insight, intention, and compassion, it is entirely possible to move beyond sabotage—not by eradicating resistance, but by working with it.

What ultimately transforms self-sabotage into self-support is awareness. When we understand the deeper reasons behind our resistance, we are no longer captive to it. We can respond with empathy rather than self-reproach. We can design habits that honour our limits as well as our aspirations. And in doing so, we replace patterns of avoidance with patterns of alignment—small, consistent acts that honour who we are *and* who we are becoming.

Micro Strategies for Motivation

Motivation is often misunderstood. People tend to view it as a force that must be summoned, a spark of inspiration that propels them into action. In reality, motivation is more fleeting than we would like to admit. It comes and goes, influenced by sleep, mood, weather, distractions, and the countless micro-pressures of daily life. Relying on motivation alone is like depending on sunshine to power your home without a backup generator. It works beautifully—when it works. But when it doesn't, progress stalls. That's why those who sustain habits over time don't wait for motivation. Instead, they design strategies that keep behaviour going even when motivation lags. These strategies are small, subtle, and highly effective.

Micro strategies for motivation are behavioural tools that lower the friction between intention and action. They don't require you to summon vast reserves of energy or focus; rather, they shape your environment, mindset, and routines so that the desired action becomes more automatic. These strategies can take the form of visual cues, social contracts, external tracking systems, or environmental tweaks. What they all share is their ability to prompt behaviour without needing constant internal effort. They are scaffolding for discipline—not replacements for it, but reliable supports that reduce the likelihood of breakdown.

One of the simplest and most impactful of these strategies is the use of visual reminders. Human attention is highly responsive to visual stimuli. What we see regularly shapes what we do regularly. A calendar with check marks, a sticky note on the bathroom mirror, a whiteboard with your top priorities—these visuals serve as gentle nudges, not mandates. They remind us of what we've committed to and bring our abstract intentions into concrete, visible form.

This was the turning point for Amar, a university student who struggled to revise consistently for exams. Despite setting clear intentions and drafting meticulous study timetables, he would regularly forget or ignore his revision goals in the haze of daily demands. After a conversation with his academic mentor, Amar began placing a large weekly planner on his wall, colour-coding his revision sessions and ticking them off in real-time. The visual presence of the planner transformed his intentions into a persistent, unobtrusive call to action. It not only helped him stay on track but also gave him a small dopamine hit with every ticked box—a psychological reward that reinforced the habit.

Visual cues work best when they are placed in locations that intersect with the intended habit. If you want to practise guitar more regularly, leave it on a stand in your living room instead of packed away in a case. If you want to drink more water, place a filled glass or bottle in your workspace. These adjustments may seem trivial, but they increase what behavioural scientists call "cue salience"—the visibility and relevance of a prompt in the moment you need it most.

Another effective strategy for sustaining motivation is the use of commitment devices. These are pre-commitments we make—either publicly or privately—that help lock us into a future behaviour. The psychology behind this is rooted in the concept of "present bias," the tendency to prioritise immediate gratification over long-term benefit. Commitment devices help us overcome this by creating consequences or incentives that bridge the gap between now and later.

One powerful example of this comes from the world of behavioural economics. A group of researchers working with individuals trying to save money found that when participants agreed to auto-deduct a percentage of their future salary increases into a savings account—rather than from their current pay—they saved significantly more over time. They didn't have to make a decision each month; the system made it for them. That's the genius of commitment devices—they reduce decision fatigue and align short-term behaviour with long-term values.

On a personal level, commitment devices can be as simple as booking a class in advance, scheduling a workout with a friend, or setting a screen lock on distracting apps during your work window. For Rahul, an aspiring novelist, the breakthrough came when he committed to emailing a chapter draft to a friend every Friday. The friend didn't edit or even comment—he simply received it. But the act of knowing someone was expecting it created a light pressure that kept Rahul writing consistently. His motivation didn't stem from inspiration; it stemmed from obligation—and in this case, that obligation served him well.

Accountability partners take the concept of commitment one step further by adding relational dynamics. Humans are social creatures, and our behaviour is shaped not only by internal goals but by the people we trust, admire, and want to be respected by. Accountability taps into this social wiring, allowing our relationships to reinforce our actions.

This doesn't mean hiring a coach or joining a high-performance mastermind group—although those can be useful. It can be as simple as a weekly phone call, a shared spreadsheet, or a WhatsApp message with a friend. What matters is that someone else knows what you've committed to and checks in on your progress. For Maya, a clinical psychologist trying to maintain a daily gratitude practice, it was a mutual agreement with a colleague to share three things they were grateful for every morning via text. Knowing that someone else was waiting for her message made the practice easier to sustain, even on days when she felt distracted or low.

The most effective accountability relationships are reciprocal and non-judgemental. They function not as pressure but as partnership. They offer encouragement without coddling, challenge without criticism. These relationships work not just because they create external stakes, but because they affirm the identity you are trying to reinforce. When someone else sees you as consistent, reliable, or disciplined, you are more likely to behave in ways that confirm that perception.

Importantly, micro strategies for motivation don't replace the deeper work of values clarification and habit design. But they do make the process more resilient. They serve as behavioural "nudges"—a term coined by behavioural economists Richard Thaler and Cass Sunstein to describe subtle design interventions that steer decisions without removing freedom of choice. A nudge doesn't force you to act, but it makes the desired action easier and more likely.

Another often overlooked technique involves reducing the cost of re-entry after a break. Habits don't break from a single missed day; they break when one missed day becomes a pattern. When people fall off track, they often feel a sense of guilt or shame, which ironically reduces motivation further. Designing an easy way back—such as restarting at a simpler level or celebrating a "comeback" streak—keeps the habit resilient. It reframes relapse not as failure, but as interruption, and removes the emotional weight that keeps people stuck.

The art of sustaining motivation lies not in grand declarations, but in daily systems. Systems that are visible, social, and self-reinforcing. Micro strategies work not because they push harder, but because they remove unnecessary resistance. They create cues where there was ambiguity, structure where there was drift, and reminders where there was forgetfulness.

Ultimately, habits that endure are not the result of superhuman effort. They are the product of design—of choosing tools that compensate for our natural inconsistencies and fluctuations in energy. These tools don't eliminate the need for effort, but they reduce the cost of starting and the likelihood of stopping. And in the rhythm of daily life, those two variables—how easily you start and how rarely you stop—make all the difference.

Motivation, then, is not something to chase. It is something to engineer. Through cues, commitments, and connection, we build an environment in which action becomes the path of least resistance. And in doing so, we free ourselves from waiting to feel ready, and begin simply by beginning—again and again, until consistency becomes identity.

Dealing with Setbacks

The path to consistent behavioural change is rarely linear. While books, podcasts, and social media often showcase habit transformation as a clean arc from decision to success, the reality is far more complex—and far more human. Progress comes in fits and starts. Enthusiasm gives way to resistance. Intentions collide with exhaustion. And sooner or later, even the most well-designed habit is interrupted. A missed workout, a skipped writing session, an indulgent weekend after weeks of mindful eating—these are not aberrations; they are inevitable features of long-term change. The question is not whether setbacks will happen, but how we respond when they do.

One of the most common misconceptions about habit formation is that consistency means perfection. This belief sets people up for failure. The first time they lapse, guilt takes over. They tell themselves they've broken the streak, ruined their progress, or proved they never had what it takes to begin with. This kind of all-or-nothing thinking turns a single missed action into a downward spiral. The problem is not the lapse itself—it's the self-punishing narrative that follows.

To build sustainable habits, we must reframe the meaning of a setback. Rather than seeing it as a failure, we need to view it as feedback. Every lapse offers information about the fragility of the habit under certain conditions—information we can use to strengthen it. A habit interrupted by stress, travel, fatigue, or distraction hasn't failed; it has simply encountered friction. That friction tells us something about our systems, routines, and mental models. When approached with curiosity instead of criticism, a setback becomes an inflection point—a moment to adapt rather than abandon.

Consider the example of Nisha, an early-career researcher who began meditating daily to manage anxiety. For the first three weeks, she was consistent, motivated by both personal need and a sense of novelty. But during a particularly demanding week of deadlines and travel, her meditation practice slipped. She felt disheartened and questioned her discipline. Her initial reaction was to abandon the habit entirely, assuming she'd "ruined it." But after speaking with a friend, she took a different approach. She reviewed her week, identified the time constraints and contextual barriers that made meditation less accessible, and created a shortened version of her practice—a five-minute breathing routine she could do from her phone, wherever she was. That single act of adaptation helped her recover quickly and re-establish momentum.

The ability to bounce back from lapses is what separates temporary efforts from lasting behavioural change. Psychologists refer to this as "psychological flexibility"—the capacity to adjust one's behaviour in the face of obstacles without being derailed by internal distress. When people lack this flexibility, they tend to fuse with their emotional reactions. "I feel guilty, so I must be failing." "I didn't do it today, so I probably won't tomorrow." These narratives become self-fulfilling. But when flexibility is present, individuals can hold their emotions lightly, acknowledge them, and still take value-aligned action.

An important part of developing this mindset is learning to detach identity from performance. Missing a workout does not mean you are undisciplined. Forgetting to write one day does not mean you are not a writer. Habits are practices, not verdicts. They are behaviours we return to—not conditions we maintain perfectly. When we define ourselves by our consistency rather than our resilience, we set ourselves up for brittle self-esteem. But when we embrace a growth-oriented identity—"I'm someone who comes back after lapses"—we cultivate confidence that lasts beyond temporary setbacks.

The language we use around setbacks also matters. Words like "falling off the wagon" or "breaking the streak" reinforce a binary mindset. They imply that progress is either intact or destroyed, with no in-between. A more constructive metaphor is that of a detour. You haven't left the path—you've just taken a side road. The destination hasn't changed; you're simply recalibrating. This shift in framing softens the emotional blow and makes it easier to resume action.

There is also value in normalising setbacks by anticipating them. Rather than treating lapses as aberrations, we can build them into our expectations. This does not mean planning to fail, but rather preparing to recover. By asking questions like, "What will I do if I miss a day?" or "How can I re-engage when life gets chaotic?" we remove the element of surprise and equip ourselves with contingency plans. This kind of mental rehearsal is a technique borrowed from cognitive behavioural therapy and used by elite performers in sport and business. It reduces panic when things go wrong and fosters a calm, strategic response.

Another key to dealing with setbacks is tracking. While habit trackers are often used to celebrate streaks, they can also be used to study patterns. If a habit fails to stick, it's useful to record when and why it falters. Was it the time of day? The surrounding environment? Competing priorities? Emotional fatigue? These observations reveal the hidden dynamics at play. Often, what looks like a motivation problem is actually a design flaw. A journaling habit that collapses after work might thrive in the morning. A walking routine that feels burdensome after dark might need to be anchored to lunch breaks instead. The lapse becomes a lens—a way to optimise rather than abandon.

It is also worth reflecting on the stories we carry about failure. Many of us internalised beliefs about productivity and success that equate mistakes with moral weakness. These stories are rarely examined, but they live in our self-talk. "I'm just not good at sticking to things." "I always mess it up eventually." These phrases are not truths—they are habits of thought. And like any habit, they can be changed. By consciously rewriting these narratives—"I'm learning how to adapt," "I prioritised other needs this week, and now I'm returning"—we create a self-concept that supports rather than sabotages habit continuity.

Community can also play a critical role in navigating setbacks. Sharing a lapse with a trusted friend, mentor, or accountability partner can reduce shame and increase perspective. Often, simply saying, "I missed a few days, and I'm trying to get back on track," is enough to break the spiral of isolation and reconnect with purpose. The feedback we receive in these moments can be grounding. Most people are more understanding of our lapses than we are. They remind us that progress is not a straight line and that returning is a mark of maturity, not weakness.

Ultimately, the goal is not to never stumble. The goal is to stumble wisely. To notice, reflect, adjust, and re-engage. This process turns each setback into a site of learning. It teaches us about our limits, our rhythms, and our environments. It sharpens our self-awareness and strengthens our behavioural toolkit. Over time, we begin to trust ourselves—not because we never lapse, but because we always come back.

What emerges from this mindset is a deeper kind of motivation. Not the short-lived boost of novelty, but the enduring commitment to a value-aligned life. Setbacks are no longer threats to our identity or momentum. They are simply part of the landscape of change. And when we treat them as such, we remain free—not to be perfect, but to begin again, as many times as needed.

The Power of Small Wins

There is a quiet yet potent force at the heart of lasting change. It doesn't shout. It doesn't boast. It doesn't demand transformation overnight. Rather, it builds momentum in whispers—in tiny acts repeated consistently, in micro-moments of effort acknowledged and reinforced. This is the power of small wins: the incremental, often overlooked victories that serve as the scaffolding for profound and enduring behavioural change. In the realm of habit formation, small wins are not optional add-ons; they are foundational elements. They are the fuel that sustains the engine of progress when motivation dips and results feel distant.

Psychologically, small wins leverage the brain's natural reward system. Each time we complete a task, however modest, our brain releases a burst of dopamine—a neurotransmitter associated with pleasure, motivation, and learning. This neurological reward reinforces the action, making it more likely that we will repeat it. In this way, small wins create a self-perpetuating loop of behaviour. They offer a sense of completion, however temporary, that satisfies our desire for achievement and fuels our willingness to keep going.

Importantly, small wins shift our focus from distant outcomes to immediate action. When goals are framed exclusively in terms of long-term results—losing ten kilograms, publishing a novel, running a marathon—they can feel intimidating and remote. These outcomes require weeks, months, or even years of sustained effort. Without intermediate markers of progress, the emotional cost of persistence can outweigh the perceived benefit. Small wins mitigate this by offering tangible evidence that something is working, even if the ultimate goal remains far off.

Consider the experience of Anil, a software developer who decided to get back into shape after a long sedentary stretch. Initially, he set a goal of going to the gym four times a week and overhauling his diet. Predictably, his enthusiasm waned after a fortnight. But when he refocused on smaller wins—walking 8,000 steps a day, completing a five-minute stretch routine each morning, choosing water over soda once per day—his mindset shifted. These actions were manageable. They didn't feel like disruptions; they felt like progress. And critically, each success boosted his confidence, which in turn made the next action feel more doable. What began as a set of trivial changes evolved into a robust, self-reinforcing routine.

One of the most compelling insights from behavioural science is that confidence is built not by achieving big goals, but by accumulating small proofs of competence. Every time we show up—whether it's writing a paragraph, preparing a healthy meal, or sitting down to meditate—we send a signal to ourselves: *I'm the kind of person who does this.* Over time, these signals shape our identity. We stop seeing habits as something we're trying to build, and start seeing them as something we *already* embody. This identity shift is subtle, but profound. It replaces friction with flow, self-doubt with quiet assurance.

Small wins also play a critical role in disrupting negative cycles. When people feel stuck, overwhelmed, or discouraged, they often believe they must make a grand gesture to turn things around. But the truth is, momentum is built from the ground up. A small, well-timed win can act as a psychological reset—a way to regain agency and reorient attention toward what is possible. For someone recovering from burnout, this might be making their bed each morning. For someone navigating grief, it might be cooking one nourishing meal. These acts are not trivial. They are anchors in a sea of uncertainty.

Emma, a client of mine recovering from a long period of creative block, exemplified this principle. For months, she had been unable to write, paralysed by the weight of expectations and fear of not producing anything worthwhile. When we reframed her writing goal from "finish a chapter" to "open the document and write one sentence," she experienced a breakthrough. That sentence often led to a few more, and occasionally to an entire page. But even on days when it didn't, the act of showing up counted. It reinforced her sense of commitment and eroded the narrative that she was no longer a writer.

Celebrating small wins is an essential part of this process. It may sound superficial, but acknowledgement matters. When we pause to notice and appreciate our efforts, we mark them as significant. This doesn't require extravagant rewards or public declarations. Often, a brief moment of reflection, a journal entry, or a tick on a habit tracker is enough. The point is not to inflate the importance of the task, but to give the brain a cue: *This mattered. Do it again.*

Neglecting to recognise small wins is a form of psychological self-sabotage. It creates a false narrative that we're not progressing, even when we are. Over time, this erodes motivation and resilience. The paradox is that people who are hardest on themselves often accomplish less, not more. Perfectionism and self-criticism choke momentum, while self-compassion and acknowledgment sustain it. Building the habit of celebrating small wins is a way of practising that self-compassion—not as indulgence, but as strategic reinforcement.

From a neurological perspective, this approach taps into the concept of variable reinforcement. The brain craves novelty and surprise. When we allow ourselves to feel a burst of satisfaction from completing a small task—especially one that was difficult to initiate—we create a feedback loop that keeps us engaged. This is why gamification techniques, such as streak tracking or point systems, can be effective. They turn routine actions into sources of intermittent reward. But even without technology, we can create this dynamic by noticing and appreciating the micro-milestones that accumulate daily.

There is also a cultural angle to this conversation. Many societies glorify the big leap—the dramatic transformation, the overnight success, the sweeping resolution. In doing so, they overlook the quiet heroism of sustained effort. They discount the power of showing up on days when you don't feel like it, of doing the thing even when no one is watching. Small wins may not be newsworthy, but they are the building blocks of every meaningful accomplishment. They are not the story's climax—they are its structure.

To fully harness the power of small wins, it helps to track them. This doesn't mean obsessively measuring every action, but rather maintaining some visible record of effort. This could take the form of a bullet journal, a wall calendar, or a simple note-taking app. The act of recording creates a visual arc of progress—a story of consistency that becomes harder to ignore. When doubt creeps in, as it inevitably will, this record serves as counter-evidence. It says, *Look how far you've come, one step at a time.*

There is also something inherently democratic about small wins. They are available to everyone, regardless of schedule, resources, or starting point. You don't need ideal conditions to complete a two-minute habit. You don't need extraordinary discipline to take one positive action. This accessibility is what makes the concept so powerful. It levels the field and places lasting change within reach, not because it makes it effortless, but because it makes it manageable.

In sum, small wins are the foundation of sustainable behaviour. They create momentum, reinforce identity, interrupt inertia, and build confidence. They are not symbolic gestures. They are practical tools for progress. When we learn to value and celebrate them, we rewire our relationship with effort. We stop waiting for perfect conditions and start finding success in the everyday. And as those successes accumulate, they reveal a truth often obscured by grand ambitions: that meaningful change does not begin with giant leaps, but with a thousand quiet steps, taken with intention, and honoured as they deserve.

Chapter 6
Scaling Micro Habits for Major Transformation

At the core of any true transformation lies a curious paradox: the most profound changes tend not to announce themselves with fanfare, but instead tiptoe in, disguised as the tiniest of actions. In an age so bewitched by speed and sweeping reinvention, it's remarkably easy to discount the quiet power of small, deliberate steps. Yet the brilliance of micro habits rests not just in their manageability, but in their remarkable ability to scale. What begins as an almost forgettable gesture—a minute of focus, a modest decision, a nudge in a new direction—can, when repeated with patience, evolve into something far more consequential. This chapter is a meditation on that metamorphosis: how small beginnings build momentum, intensify their influence, and slowly reconfigure the architecture of our lives.

Momentum, once sparked, has a mind of its own. There's a particular phenomenon—call it behavioural inertia, or the compounding rhythm of repetition—whereby tiny habits, once lodged in place, begin to generate their own propulsion. Think of a snowball tumbling down a slope, quietly accumulating mass and speed. A morning stretch doesn't look like much on day one, but done daily, it begins to weave itself into the fabric of your identity. The gesture itself stays small, but the ease with which you return to it—that shifts. Each repetition chips away at resistance, each success reinforcing a sense of continuity and quiet self-belief. And that, really, is the foundation from which larger practices sprout.

Crucially, this expansion doesn't happen through effortful scaling or brute determination. The human brain is wired to favour efficiency. When a task is repeated, it becomes easier—less conscious, more automatic. Neural networks sharpen; attention reorganises itself. Soon enough, the habit no longer feels bolted on—it feels native. The one-minute breathing pause morphs into a full mindfulness session, not because you forced it, but because it started to feel like the next logical step. Writing a paragraph after dinner turns into finishing chapters. A casual evening stroll? Suddenly, it's the cornerstone of a fitness routine. There's no coercion in this process. It's a kind of behavioural invitation—offered and accepted over time.

This is the power of growing from micro to macro. Habits need not leap to become larger. They unfold, gradually, when given room and rhythm. What begins as a modest routine becomes, with time, a scaffold for more. The key lies in stability. A consistent micro habit builds mental and logistical space—opening the door to expansion without disruption. You're not starting something new; you're extending something familiar. And because of that, it sticks.

Consider Aarav—a copywriter, often overwhelmed, perpetually lamenting his inconsistency with writing. His solution? Write one sentence per day. That's it. Not a page. Not an essay. Just one sentence. Within a few weeks, his hand often kept moving after the sentence was done. A month in, he was writing full paragraphs without resistance. Three months on, the habit had scaled—organically—into a half-hour daily session. His progress wasn't fuelled by ambition, but by consistency. He didn't chase transformation; he let it accrue.

Even so, momentum, like any rhythm, can falter. Most habit journeys encounter a plateau—a strange, often dispiriting lull where the fire dims and progress flattens. It's tempting to interpret this as failure. It's not. It's simply a sign that the current structure has served its purpose and now needs reshaping. Plateaus are invitations—not end points. They ask for attention, a light recalibration, perhaps a tweak in pace or scope. They're a chance to reaffirm what's working and refresh what's not.

One effective way to breathe life back into a stagnant habit is by reintroducing challenge—not in the form of giant leaps, but as subtle increases in intensity. If you've been journaling for five minutes, try a new prompt. If your workouts feel rote, experiment with resistance or variation. These tiny modifications rekindle interest and stimulate the reward mechanisms that drive engagement.

There's also something to be said for changing the backdrop. Habits become stale not just from repetition, but from environmental monotony. Move your practice to a different room, shift it to another time of day, pair it with a new routine. The change may seem trivial, but it can restore a sense of novelty, which—ironically—makes the old habit feel new again.

But where micro habits truly come into their own is in their compounding nature. Much like compound interest, small behaviours repeated over time generate returns that far exceed their initial investment. The early days can feel unrewarding—like tossing coins into a well and hearing no splash. But with patience, those investments deepen. Ten minutes of daily reading may not sound revolutionary, yet give it six months and you'll notice more than a few finished books. You'll also notice sharper concentration, enriched vocabulary, and perhaps even a broader intellectual appetite. One habit—many outcomes.

This is what most people miss: we expect behaviour change to be tidy and linear, but it rarely is. True growth curves upwards, then bends outward. The gym habit improves not only strength but sleep. A meditation practice soothes anxiety and sharpens presence at meetings. Small actions, when practiced consistently, ripple across domains. That is where the real alchemy lies.

Sometimes these ripple effects are obvious. More often, they're pleasantly surprising. A man decides to prioritise his sleep, hoping to feel a bit more rested. Weeks later, he realises his temper has softened; his conversations with his children are calmer. Or take the woman who begins to journal each night, ostensibly to process her thoughts—but soon finds herself making faster, clearer decisions at work. These aren't coincidences. They are emergent effects—the by-product of greater clarity, steadier energy, and more intentional living.

Rohan, a corporate trainer, provides another rich example. His journey began simply: cook dinner at home three nights a week. That was it. No detox plans. No elaborate schedules. But the shift snowballed. Home cooking lowered his stress, improved digestion, nudged him towards better sleep. He drank less. He started reading again. He picked up photography—a hobby he hadn't touched in years. The path wasn't planned. It unfolded because one small change gave him the confidence, and the emotional bandwidth, to explore others.

And that's the beauty of it all. These habits—though modest in appearance—do more than tweak behaviour. They begin to reshape who we think we are. They chip away at limiting beliefs, expand what we consider possible, and slowly redefine our priorities. Change becomes less about striving and more about aligning. Less about force, more about rhythm.

As we move deeper into this chapter, we'll look at practical ways to strengthen and scale these micro habits. But before we get tactical, it's worth pausing to acknowledge something vital: the most enduring transformations don't erupt out of grand realisations. They unfold quietly, often imperceptibly, through repetition. You show up. You keep showing up. And one day, the practice that once felt like effort becomes second nature.

Scaling isn't about doing more for its own sake. It's about investing more deeply in what already works, allowing growth to happen in its own time. When you let go of urgency, and trust in the integrity of small steps, change stops being a distant ideal and starts becoming your lived reality. Not in flashes. But in quiet, continuous motion.

The Momentum Effect

One of the most powerful forces in behaviour change is momentum. When properly harnessed, it transforms modest beginnings into significant outcomes—not through heroic effort, but through steady progression. Momentum explains why a single micro habit, practiced consistently, can evolve into a life-defining routine. It is the unseen propulsion behind sustained change, a self-amplifying cycle in which small victories compound, confidence builds, and new capacities emerge. Understanding how momentum operates—and learning how to cultivate it deliberately—is essential for anyone seeking meaningful, lasting transformation.

Momentum, in the context of habits, refers to the gradual acceleration of behaviour that occurs when action becomes easier, more rewarding, and more embedded in daily life. It begins quietly, often with a two-minute action that feels almost trivial: writing a sentence, drinking a glass of water, completing a brief stretch. Yet over time, these micro behaviours establish a pattern of movement. That movement becomes self-reinforcing. One success makes the next more likely. One repetition lowers the resistance for the next. And before long, what began as an experiment becomes a habit—and then, potentially, an identity.

This effect is not just anecdotal. Research in behavioural science consistently shows that the hardest part of any action is starting. Once initiated, the cognitive load diminishes. The brain shifts from deliberation to execution. That shift is often enough to carry us beyond the minimal threshold and into deeper engagement. A person who sets out to read a single page might find themselves reading ten. Someone who laces up their trainers for a five-minute walk might end up jogging around the block. The initial act serves as a behavioural gateway, unlocking a level of energy and focus that wasn't accessible before movement began.

This phenomenon is illustrated clearly in the story of Aditi, a young architect who found herself creatively blocked and overwhelmed. Her initial plan to rebuild her design portfolio was ambitious, involving long hours of focused work and high-stakes self-assessment. Unsurprisingly, she procrastinated. The expectations were too high. The emotional risk felt too great. So she reframed her approach: every day, she would spend two minutes sketching—no agenda, no outcomes, just movement. Within a week, she found herself sketching for twenty minutes. Within a month, she was completing full-scale concept drafts. The habit, once in motion, gained a rhythm. Her initial sketches weren't spectacular. But they were *something.* And something leads to more.

This is the core insight of the momentum effect: it is easier to keep going than to start again. Each act of follow-through reduces the psychological distance between where you are and where you intend to be. This reduction builds confidence, and that confidence, in turn, fuels action. The pattern repeats, and with each loop, the behaviour becomes more stable, more automatic, and more expansive.

Momentum also changes how we perceive effort. A habit that once felt demanding starts to feel natural. The energy cost diminishes not because the task is objectively easier, but because our relationship to it changes. The neural circuits involved become more efficient. Our body and mind anticipate the behaviour, prepare for it, and execute it with reduced resistance. This is why someone who once struggled to meditate for five minutes can eventually sit for thirty without strain. It's not a matter of willpower; it's a matter of progressive adaptation.

But perhaps the most compelling feature of momentum is that it builds in multiple dimensions. It doesn't just make habits easier; it also makes them more attractive. As progress accumulates, the intrinsic satisfaction of seeing results becomes its own reward. The motivation to continue no longer hinges on external incentives or abstract goals. It arises from within, fuelled by a growing sense of agency and self-efficacy. The behaviour becomes meaningful, not just effective.

Consider the example of Kabir, a high school teacher who struggled with morning fatigue and poor dietary habits. Rather than attempting a complete lifestyle overhaul, he started with a five-minute morning walk. Initially, the impact was minimal. But the walk woke him up just enough to make a better breakfast decision. That decision improved his energy mid-morning, which made him more focused during lessons. The improved performance led him to leave work on time, which freed up mental space for evening reading—something he'd long wanted to prioritise. The habit of walking didn't just create physical momentum; it initiated a cascade of beneficial changes across unrelated areas of his life.

This ripple effect is central to why momentum matters. Habits do not exist in isolation. They interact, amplify, and reinforce one another. A positive behaviour in one domain can improve performance, mood, or energy in another. A consistent writing practice can spill over into better communication skills. Regular sleep hygiene can improve emotional regulation. Gratitude journaling can increase empathy in interpersonal relationships. Each habit carries with it not only direct benefits, but also the capacity to influence other behaviours through shared psychological resources—like attention, willpower, and emotional tone.

However, momentum is fragile in its early stages. It must be protected from overreach. One of the most common mistakes people make is to prematurely escalate a habit when it begins to work. A five-minute practice that feels good is suddenly expanded to an hour. The friction returns. The behaviour becomes demanding again. And without the foundation of consistency, the momentum collapses. Sustainable scaling is gradual, responsive, and intuitive. It allows the habit to grow at the pace of integration, not ambition.

Sustaining momentum also requires managing disruptions. Life is dynamic. Schedules shift, priorities compete, motivation fluctuates. When a habit is interrupted, the key is not to panic but to preserve the pattern of action in some form. A micro version of the habit—even a symbolic one—keeps the behavioural loop intact. If you can't write for thirty minutes, write a sentence. If you can't work out, do five push-ups. These acts may seem insignificant, but they protect the identity being formed. They maintain the sense of continuity that momentum depends upon.

There's also a social dimension to momentum. When others begin to notice your consistency, they often provide reinforcement—comments, support, shared admiration. These social cues further strengthen your commitment. You begin to be seen not only as someone who *does* the behaviour, but as someone who *is* that kind of person. This recognition, even when unspoken, helps anchor the habit in your identity.

In behavioural economics, this feedback loop is known as a positive externality—the unexpected but beneficial side-effect of consistent action. It helps to think of your habits as investments, not just in outcomes, but in reputation, identity, and influence. When you maintain momentum, you're not just building muscle or skills or knowledge. You're building trust—with yourself and others. And that trust is a powerful asset.

The momentum effect, then, is more than a theory of progress. It is a principle of transformation that honours the power of modest beginnings. It reminds us that consistency outperforms intensity, and that movement—no matter how slight—can reshape not only behaviour, but self-perception, confidence, and even worldview.

In cultivating momentum, you are not chasing results. You are building a behavioural ecosystem that sustains itself. One in which each action makes the next easier, each win makes the next more likely, and each repetition draws you closer not just to what you want to *do*, but to who you want to *be*. It is this compounding, integrated, and deeply human process that allows small habits to evolve into powerful expressions of growth—and ultimately, to change lives from the inside out.

From Micro to Macro

The genius of micro habits lies in their unassuming simplicity. They ask little of us, demand no dramatic lifestyle changes, and are designed to bypass the internal resistance that so often derails our best intentions. But while micro habits start small, their true power emerges in their ability to scale. When approached thoughtfully, these modest actions evolve into substantial routines that shape not only what we do, but who we become. The transition from micro to macro is not accidental. It is the product of strategic expansion—of nurturing consistency until it naturally matures into something larger. The key is to scale without overwhelm, allowing momentum and identity to guide the pace of growth.

Scaling micro habits is not a linear process. It doesn't follow a strict formula of doubling effort every few weeks. Rather, it unfolds organically, much like a sapling growing into a tree. Initially fragile, the habit needs consistency to establish roots. Once stable, it begins to branch out, extending its reach and capacity. The shift to a more robust routine happens not through ambition alone, but through a quiet accumulation of readiness. Over time, what once felt effortful becomes second nature—and in that space of familiarity, there is room to stretch.

One of the central reasons micro habits scale so effectively is that they build behavioural fluency. This is the psychological equivalent of muscle memory. Repeated action lowers the cognitive load required to initiate the task. Decision fatigue diminishes. Resistance recedes. The behaviour begins to run on automaticity, freeing up attention and energy to deepen or expand the practice. When this fluency is present, increasing duration, intensity, or complexity no longer feels burdensome. It feels like a natural next step.

Take the example of Neha, a civil servant who wanted to incorporate regular strength training into her week. Initially, she committed to one minute of squats each morning. The act was symbolic more than substantive, but it created a routine. She did it in the same space, at the same time, every day. After a few weeks, she added a plank. Then a set of lunges. By the third month, she was following a full fifteen-minute bodyweight routine without ever consciously deciding to scale up. Her body asked for more because the habit was well-rooted. The growth didn't come from pressure—it came from integration.

This highlights an important distinction in habit design: scaling should follow consistency, not precede it. When people rush to expand a habit before it has become stable, they risk destabilising it entirely. The habit no longer feels effortless; it starts to feel like a demand. And when something feels like a demand, the brain begins to push back. What began as an empowering practice becomes another item on an already crowded to-do list. The result is often burnout or disengagement. To avoid this, scaling should feel optional, not obligatory. The question is not, "How can I do more?" but "Am I ready for more?" That readiness is felt, not forced.

Another factor that facilitates the shift from micro to macro is identity alignment. As habits settle into our daily rhythm, they begin to inform our self-perception. The person who meditates for two minutes each day begins to see themselves as someone who values calm and presence. The person who writes a paragraph every morning begins to feel like a writer. These identity shifts are subtle but profound. They reduce internal conflict and increase behavioural coherence. When the identity is in place, scaling the habit feels less like adding a new task and more like expressing an existing trait. The expansion becomes an extension of the self, not an imposition on it.

This identity-based progression was evident in the case of Julian, a project manager who struggled with confidence and assertiveness in meetings. To build a sense of presence, he started with a two-minute daily practice of standing in front of the mirror and stating one professional affirmation aloud. Over time, he added deep breathing, then visualisation, then short vocal warmups. Eventually, his routine grew into a full morning ritual that helped him enter the workday with poise and clarity. The routine scaled not because he needed it to, but because it aligned with a self-image he was actively constructing. His behaviour was no longer about doing—it was about becoming.

The gradual expansion of habits also benefits from strategic context adjustments. Small shifts in environment or structure can support larger iterations of a habit without introducing overwhelm. For example, moving your writing desk to a quieter part of the house may allow a short writing session to expand into a deeper one. Upgrading from a basic yoga mat to a designated practice area can create the conditions for longer and more focused sessions. These changes are not about buying motivation but about removing friction. They signal to the brain that this behaviour matters and deserves space.

Technology can play a supportive role here as well. For those tracking their progress, apps and habit trackers can offer visual reinforcement. Seeing a streak build, even from two-minute efforts, creates a sense of accountability and pride. Over time, this data becomes motivation in itself. It tells a story of consistency, and that story creates a psychological anchor. As the habit grows, the tracker evolves with it—not by demanding more, but by reflecting more.

However, it's worth noting that not all habits need to scale. Some micro habits are powerful precisely because of their smallness. Their role is to serve as keystones—anchors that stabilise the day, cue other behaviours, or reinforce identity. A single deep breath before opening your laptop. A moment of gratitude before eating. A sentence written before sleep. These may never evolve into hour-long routines, but their impact is cumulative and meaningful. The key is to discern which habits are meant to grow, and which are meant to ground. Scaling is a path, not a rule.

It is also important to manage expectations during this phase of development. Scaling is not always linear, and progress does not always feel smooth. There will be days when the expanded habit feels too much, and the micro version becomes a fallback. That is not regression—it is resilience. The ability to return to a smaller form of the habit ensures continuity without compromising wellbeing. This flexibility is the hallmark of sustainable behaviour. It honours the reality of changing energy levels, competing demands, and emotional cycles.

Over time, what begins as a brief, focused habit may evolve into a cornerstone of one's lifestyle. A two-minute reading habit might become a morning of quiet study. A single gratitude note might lead to deeper relational presence. A short language lesson might open the door to international travel and cultural fluency. These transitions are not driven by willpower alone; they are shaped by patience, context, identity, and rhythm.

Scaling a micro habit into a macro routine, then, is less about discipline and more about design. It requires attention to timing, sensitivity to context, and an appreciation for the psychological foundations of behaviour. It asks us to listen to the signals of readiness and to expand with grace, not urgency. And above all, it reminds us that meaningful change is not measured by how fast we grow, but by how steadily we rise.

By nurturing small habits until they are ready to stretch, we lay the groundwork for expansive, authentic transformation. We move from tentative beginnings to confident expression—not by leap, but by layering. And in doing so, we build routines that are not only bigger, but better—because they are rooted in who we truly are.

Breaking Through Plateaus

There is an unspoken moment in every long-term effort when progress seems to halt. Despite continued effort, the gains become marginal, motivation wanes, and a creeping sense of frustration begins to set in. This moment—commonly referred to as a plateau—is not a failure, but a phase. It is a natural feature of any growth curve, whether in fitness, learning, creativity, or personal development. Yet it remains one of the most misunderstood and mishandled aspects of habit formation. Many abandon their practices at this point, believing they have reached their limit. In truth, they have simply arrived at the point where superficial progress gives way to deeper work.

Understanding plateaus begins with recognising their inevitability. Any system, once stabilised, reaches a point of equilibrium. In the early stages of habit formation, the improvements are dramatic because the starting point is low. The contrast between doing nothing and doing something is stark. A person who goes from no physical activity to walking five minutes a day will feel a surge in energy and mood almost immediately. A writer who begins drafting a paragraph each morning will quickly generate a sense of productivity and purpose. But as the body and mind adapt to these behaviours, the novelty fades and the gains diminish. What was once energising becomes routine. The excitement gives way to predictability, and predictability, if left unaddressed, leads to stagnation.

This is the plateau—not a flatline of effort, but a flattening of perceived reward. It is important to note that during a plateau, meaningful change may still be occurring beneath the surface. Neural pathways are being reinforced, baseline standards are rising, and identity is continuing to solidify. But the lack of visible progress can be disheartening, especially in a culture that prizes continuous improvement and measurable outcomes. The challenge, therefore, is to stay engaged even when progress is not immediately apparent, and to apply specific strategies that can reignite momentum without sacrificing sustainability.

One such strategy is recalibration—reviewing the habit in light of current context and capacity. Often, a habit plateaus not because it has stopped working, but because life circumstances have changed. What was once the ideal time for a workout may now be too rushed. A journaling practice that once felt reflective may now feel repetitive. Recalibrating involves asking: Is this habit still serving me as it once did? Do I need to adjust the timing, the format, or the goal? This form of self-inquiry is not about dismantling the habit, but about evolving it. It allows the practice to remain dynamic, responsive to the realities of a shifting life.

For instance, Amaan, a corporate analyst who had maintained a consistent thirty-minute reading habit for nearly a year, found himself losing interest in his evening sessions. The material felt dry, and the mental fatigue from his job made deep reading a chore rather than a pleasure. Rather than abandoning the habit, he diversified it. He began alternating between fiction, essays, and audiobooks. He moved his reading to the morning, when his mind was fresher. These subtle shifts reignited his curiosity and restored the sense of growth he initially experienced. The habit remained intact—but its shape evolved to match his current state.

Another powerful tool for breaking through plateaus is deliberate challenge. Habits, by nature, thrive on repetition. But repetition, when too predictable, breeds complacency. Introducing controlled difficulty can re-engage the brain and body. This does not mean making the habit harder for its own sake, but making it richer. A person meditating for ten minutes daily might experiment with a new technique. A language learner who has memorised basic vocabulary might start constructing sentences or engaging in conversation. These layers of challenge restore novelty and signal to the brain that learning is still occurring.

Yet challenge must be balanced with attainability. A common mistake is to overcorrect—jumping from a plateau into an overly ambitious upgrade that is unsustainable. The key is to find the edge: the point at which the habit feels slightly demanding but not demoralising. This edge keeps the nervous system engaged and the habit meaningful. It also helps sustain the neurochemical feedback loop that makes behaviour feel rewarding. When the brain detects progress, it releases dopamine—not only when we achieve goals, but when we sense we are moving towards them. Maintaining that sense of progression is essential for motivation.

Variety is another antidote to stagnation. While consistency is the backbone of habit development, variety prevents the onset of boredom and cognitive fatigue. A person who practices yoga every day might rotate styles—vinyasa one day, yin the next, restorative on weekends. A writer might switch from essays to dialogue or poetry. This variety keeps the structure intact while refreshing the experience. It prevents the habit from becoming stale and allows for creative expression within a familiar framework.

Beyond behavioural tweaks, breaking through a plateau also involves addressing mindset. The belief that progress should be constant is not only false—it is harmful. Progress is rarely linear. It is cyclical, iterative, and often imperceptible. Growth includes periods of consolidation, where skills settle into long-term memory, where behaviours become stabilised, and where the nervous system catches up with new demands. These periods are not wasted—they are necessary. But if they are misinterpreted as stagnation, they can lead to self-doubt and disengagement.

This is why it is essential to track not only external outcomes, but internal shifts. A person might not lift heavier weights or write more words, but they may notice greater ease, less hesitation, or deeper presence. These qualitative changes matter. They reflect mastery, not just output. Paying attention to them restores a sense of momentum and reinforces commitment.

It is also helpful to seek reflection from others during plateau phases. A mentor, coach, or peer can offer perspective on subtle progress that we might overlook. They can validate the work being done and suggest refinements that reawaken motivation. These conversations are especially valuable when internal feedback feels flat. External validation, when given constructively, can act as a mirror—showing us where we have grown, even when we cannot feel it ourselves.

The final, and perhaps most vital, strategy for moving beyond a plateau is to reconnect with purpose. When habits lose meaning, they lose energy. Revisiting the original reason for the habit—its emotional, personal, or ethical value—can re-energise the practice. Sometimes, the goal has shifted, or the original motivation no longer resonates. In such cases, the habit must be reanchored in something current, something true. When the purpose is clear, effort feels less burdensome. The habit is no longer about performance—it becomes an act of alignment.

Take Ayesha, a medical student who began journaling during her first year to manage stress. Initially, the practice helped her process her emotions and reflect on her learning. But as exams intensified and time became scarce, the journaling began to feel like a chore. Rather than drop the habit, she reframed its purpose. Instead of writing long reflections, she began jotting down one sentence about what she learned or felt each day. This kept her connected to the original intent—emotional processing and self-awareness—without the pressure of a specific format. The habit endured, not because it was grand, but because it stayed meaningful.

Ultimately, plateaus are invitations, not verdicts. They invite us to deepen, to adjust, to reflect. They remind us that the goal of habit-building is not to race forward endlessly, but to cultivate a rhythm that can be sustained. By responding to stagnation with curiosity rather than criticism, we transform it from a dead-end into a turning point. We learn to see the plateau not as a sign to stop, but as a signal to evolve.

In this way, breaking through a plateau becomes less about pushing harder and more about listening more carefully. It is about tuning into the subtleties of progress, the shifts in energy, the quiet recalibrations that keep our practices alive. And in doing so, we not only move forward—we move deeper into the kind of life we are consciously choosing to build.

The Compounding Power of Consistency

If there is one force in habit formation that is universally underestimated, it is consistency. Not brilliance. Not intensity. Not ambition. Just the quiet, repeated act of showing up—day after day, in small, deliberate ways. While the world celebrates rapid transformations and overnight successes, true progress tends to unfold in a far less dramatic fashion. It creeps forward incrementally, often unnoticed until the accumulation becomes impossible to ignore. This is the compounding power of consistency: the subtle, exponential growth that results from sustained effort over time.

At first glance, the effects of consistency may appear modest, even disappointing. The initial return on investment from small, habitual actions is often invisible. Someone who starts stretching for two minutes each morning may not immediately feel more limber. A person who begins journalling daily may not notice a surge in self-awareness within the first week. And yet, these practices lay down the architecture for transformation. They are the behavioural equivalents of planting seeds—buried beneath the surface, quietly developing root systems before any growth becomes visible.

The mathematics of compounding offers a compelling analogy. Just as a small financial investment, when allowed to grow over decades, can yield extraordinary results through compound interest, so too can minor habits generate significant life changes when compounded consistently. A one percent improvement each day does not sound revolutionary. But over the course of a year, that daily improvement translates into a 37-fold increase in effectiveness. The magic lies not in the size of the effort, but in its repetition. Time amplifies the effects of consistency far beyond what is intuitively obvious.

To appreciate this in practical terms, consider the case of Renu, a customer service manager who decided to improve her communication skills. Rather than signing up for an intensive course or attending weekend seminars, she chose a micro habit: summarising each client interaction in one sentence, noting what went well and what could have been better. Initially, this exercise seemed trivial. It added less than a minute to each call. But after several months, Renu had developed a deep understanding of language tone, pacing, and emotional cues. Her performance reviews improved. Colleagues began seeking her input on difficult cases. What had started as a minor behavioural tweak evolved into a professional asset—built not through sporadic effort, but through daily practice.

Consistency is particularly potent because it transforms not just actions, but identity. Each time we perform a behaviour, we vote for the kind of person we believe ourselves to be. The person who writes daily, even for five minutes, starts to see themselves as a writer. The one who stretches every evening begins to identify as someone who cares for their body. This gradual shift in self-concept creates a reinforcing loop. Identity makes behaviour feel natural. Behaviour, in turn, reinforces identity. The consistency becomes more than habit—it becomes who we are.

This feedback loop is powerful, but it requires patience. In our results-driven culture, we're often conditioned to expect immediate payoffs. If we don't see tangible benefits quickly, we interpret our efforts as ineffective. This short-termism undermines the very principle of compounding. The early stages of consistent effort are deceptive; they are front-loaded with effort and back-loaded with results. If we abandon our practice too soon, we never reach the inflection point where growth accelerates.

Take the example of a novice musician learning the piano. The first few weeks are marked by awkward finger positions and halting rhythms. Progress feels painfully slow. But with consistent daily practice, the brain begins to build and strengthen neural pathways. Muscle memory develops. Patterns become intuitive. After months of persistence, a leap in fluency occurs—not because the practice suddenly became more intense, but because the foundation had finally solidified. Without consistency, that leap would never have happened.

The neurological basis for this lies in a principle known as Hebb's law: "neurons that fire together, wire together." Repeated actions create more efficient pathways in the brain. These pathways reduce the energy cost of performing the behaviour, making it easier to repeat. Consistency, then, is not merely a matter of discipline—it is a matter of biology. Each repetition literally reshapes the brain, embedding the behaviour more deeply into our neural architecture.

Consistency also provides a protective buffer against volatility. Life is unpredictable. Motivation fluctuates. External conditions change. But a well-established habit, practised consistently, acts as a stabilising force. It becomes a reliable anchor in the midst of uncertainty. For someone navigating grief, a daily gratitude practice offers a small island of steadiness. For an entrepreneur facing chaotic workdays, a five-minute planning session each morning provides clarity and control. These habits may not solve every problem, but they reduce cognitive overload and create psychological resilience.

Moreover, consistency creates its own form of motivation. The act of maintaining a streak, however small, generates a sense of accomplishment that fuels future behaviour. This is known as the "success cycle": when we do something well, we feel good. That good feeling increases our likelihood of doing it again. Over time, the behaviour becomes emotionally rewarding, not just rationally desirable. It shifts from something we "should" do to something we "want" to do.

Yet it's crucial to understand that consistency does not mean rigidity. Life requires adaptability. A consistent practice can include variability in intensity or format. A person committed to daily movement may alternate between walking, stretching, and strength training. A committed reader might switch between fiction, non-fiction, and audiobooks. The consistency lies in the commitment to the practice, not the uniformity of its expression. This flexibility prevents burnout and ensures sustainability.

Another advantage of consistent action is that it reveals patterns. By doing something regularly, we gather data about what works, what doesn't, and why. This feedback allows us to fine-tune our approach. A person who writes every day will notice which times of day yield the most creative output. Someone tracking their meals will become aware of emotional eating triggers. This self-knowledge is invaluable—it allows us to optimise our habits not in theory, but in lived reality.

Perhaps the most underrated aspect of consistency is its impact on confidence. When we keep promises to ourselves, even small ones, we build self-trust. That trust becomes the foundation for taking on bigger challenges. A person who proves they can wake up ten minutes earlier each day develops the belief that they can structure their time more intentionally. That belief opens the door to more ambitious goals. The compounding power of consistency is not just behavioural—it is psychological. It strengthens the inner infrastructure required to pursue meaningful change.

Consider, too, the cumulative effect across multiple areas of life. A consistent morning routine might improve sleep patterns, which enhances focus, which leads to better work performance, which reduces stress, which improves relationships. These are not isolated wins—they are cascading benefits. And they all stem from the humble act of doing something small, repeatedly, over time.

This principle was embodied by Kavita, a single mother who wanted to reclaim a sense of agency in her life. She began with a micro habit: tidying one corner of her flat each evening. It was a small act of order in a world that often felt chaotic. Over months, this practice grew. She began waking ten minutes earlier to plan her day. She resumed her creative writing, one paragraph at a time. The flat became more organised. Her mental space cleared. Opportunities that once felt out of reach—applying for a new job, pursuing further study—suddenly felt possible. None of this happened overnight. It happened through small, consistent actions that built momentum, confidence, and clarity.

Consistency, then, is not glamorous. It does not make headlines or garner applause. But it is the quiet architect of meaningful change. It bypasses the volatility of emotion, the fickleness of motivation, and the illusion of shortcuts. It works slowly, steadily, beneath the surface—until the surface itself is transformed.

To embrace consistency is to invest in the future. It is to trust that what feels small today will grow large tomorrow. That what seems insignificant now will shape the contours of our life in the years ahead. And that through the power of repetition, we can build something greater than the sum of its parts—not through force, but through faith in the process. That is the true compounding power of consistency.

The Ripple Effect Across Life Domains

When we adopt a new habit—no matter how small—we rarely do so in a vacuum. Human behaviour is not neatly compartmentalised; our physical, cognitive, emotional, and social selves are intricately interwoven. This is why consistent improvement in one aspect of life often exerts influence far beyond its original intent. A daily walk for physical health, for instance, might also lift mood, improve focus at work, and enhance interpersonal patience. These interconnections are often subtle and cumulative, but over time they form what could be described as the ripple effect: the spreading impact of micro habits across multiple life domains.

Understanding this phenomenon requires a shift in how we view behavioural change. Most people approach habits with a siloed mindset. They aim to get fit, be more productive, or save money—as though these goals occupy isolated islands. But the human system does not operate in such a fragmented manner. Small inputs in one area have knock-on effects, influencing seemingly unrelated outcomes. And the mechanism behind this isn't merely psychological optimism—it is deeply rooted in the way systems behave. Behavioural systems, like biological ecosystems, exhibit emergent properties. A change in one variable can trigger systemic reorganisation.

Take, for instance, the case of Vikram, a thirty-eight-year-old finance professional who took up early-morning stretching to alleviate persistent back pain. His goal was purely physical. But within a month, he noticed he was sleeping better, which made him more alert at work. The increased alertness improved his decision-making, and his calmer mornings made him more patient with his children. Eventually, he reported feeling "less overwhelmed overall," though the only deliberate change he made was a five-minute physical routine. This kind of multi-domain benefit is not unusual—it is typical when consistency is maintained over time.

Physiologically, this interconnectedness is supported by the fact that the body and brain operate through shared systems. Exercise, for example, doesn't just build muscle; it boosts levels of brain-derived neurotrophic factor (BDNF), a protein that supports neuroplasticity and cognitive function. Improved sleep doesn't just combat fatigue—it regulates cortisol and insulin, thereby enhancing emotional regulation and energy availability. Likewise, eating better improves not just physical health but also gut-brain communication, which plays a significant role in mood and focus.

The impact on productivity is particularly striking. When individuals adopt habits that improve sleep, diet, or physical movement, they often report improved mental clarity and efficiency, even though they haven't explicitly changed their working methods. That's because the brain performs better when its baseline needs are consistently met. You don't need to learn new time management hacks when your brain has the bandwidth to think clearly. The micro habit of daily hydration, for example, can lead to sharper attention and fewer headaches—both of which directly affect work performance.

There's also a psychological dimension to the ripple effect, rooted in what behavioural scientists call "self-efficacy"—our belief in our own ability to effect change. When someone successfully maintains a habit in one area, their self-efficacy increases. This enhanced sense of control often carries over into other areas. A person who sticks with a budgeting app for a month may feel more confident tackling meal planning or daily exercise. This is not just a coincidence. Success breeds confidence, and confidence fuels initiative. The micro habit becomes a keystone behaviour—a foundational practice that supports and inspires further change.

Identity reinforcement plays a major role here. As individuals adopt a new habit and maintain it consistently, they begin to internalise a new narrative. They start to see themselves differently—not just as someone who eats well, but as someone who cares about wellbeing. That subtle shift colours decisions across domains. They may be more likely to say no to social engagements that conflict with sleep. They might begin speaking up more at work, now buoyed by a stronger sense of discipline and agency. These are not decisions they planned in advance. They are decisions made by a person with a changed view of self.

Relationships, too, benefit from this inter-domain influence. When people improve their internal conditions—by sleeping better, reducing stress, or developing mindfulness practices—they show up more presently in their interactions. They listen more attentively, respond with greater patience, and are less reactive to conflict. Many therapists note that clients who begin exercise or mindfulness routines, even without addressing their relationship challenges directly, report feeling more satisfied in their partnerships. This is not because the habits fix the relationships, but because they fortify the individuals within them.

Consider Anika, a teacher who adopted a short evening journalling habit to manage stress. She intended to reflect on her classroom experiences, but found herself processing personal frustrations in the same space. Over time, she became less emotionally reactive at home and noticed her relationship with her spouse improving. She communicated more clearly, recognised patterns in her own behaviour, and began expressing appreciation more often. None of this was part of her original goal. The act of journalling for five minutes simply opened a cognitive and emotional valve that flowed into other areas of life.

Social influence can amplify this ripple further. When people witness someone close to them maintaining a healthy habit, they are more likely to try it themselves. This is known as behavioural contagion. Children mimic the habits of their parents. Colleagues adopt each other's productivity cues. Friends often align on health routines or digital boundaries. One person's consistency can catalyse another's transformation—not by instruction, but by example. This communal dimension adds depth to the ripple effect: what starts as a private act may eventually contribute to collective wellbeing.

Even financial habits exhibit cross-domain spillover. A person who begins tracking their spending may find themselves managing time more wisely, establishing boundaries more confidently, or consuming content more selectively. These effects arise because both money and time management rely on similar cognitive skills—delayed gratification, strategic planning, and prioritisation. Strengthening those skills in one context inevitably enhances them elsewhere.

This systems-thinking approach to habit development stands in stark contrast to the reductionist model that dominates self-improvement discourse. It moves beyond the checklist mentality of doing more in isolated silos. Instead, it views behaviour as relational—each habit existing within a broader network of patterns, values, emotions, and environmental cues. From this perspective, a single micro habit has the potential to rewire the network. The effects may not be immediate or obvious, but they are real. And over time, they can shift the entire architecture of a life.

It's worth noting that the ripple effect doesn't always run in a positive direction. Negative habits, when left unchecked, can cascade as well. Poor sleep leads to lower energy, which leads to irritability, which harms relationships, which increases loneliness, which reduces motivation. This downward spiral is the inverse of the upward spiral described above. But the mechanics are the same. Behaviour spreads. Patterns compound. Small inputs lead to big outcomes. The difference lies in intentionality. When we choose our habits deliberately, we regain control of the system.

That's why the focus on micro habits is so powerful. It recognises that you don't need to overhaul your entire life to see meaningful change. You need only commit to one small behaviour that aligns with your values—and let time, consistency, and connection do the rest. The ripple will take care of itself.

In the end, the ripple effect across life domains is not a metaphor. It is a lived phenomenon. It is what happens when we stop seeing change as confined to checklists and start seeing it as systemic. Every micro habit—if rooted in care and repeated with intent—becomes more than itself. It becomes a lever for transformation. Not because it changes everything at once, but because it gently, persistently, changes everything it touches.

Chapter 7
Applying Micro Habits to Key Life Areas

The real strength of micro habits doesn't just lie in their neat packaging or the psychological elegance with which they work—it's in their astonishing versatility. Once grasped, these modest behaviours can be woven into nearly every thread of daily life. They're not confined to narrowly scoped goals like shedding a few kilos or straightening out your inbox. No, they have a way of infiltrating how we move through the world—how we think, how we relate to others, how we feel in our skin, and even how we manage our time and money. This chapter opens the lens a little wider, offering a glimpse of how micro habits play out across five foundational areas: health and fitness, work and productivity, relationships, emotional well-being, and financial life.

We live in a web of overlapping decisions, routines, and reactions. Because of this interconnectivity, a shift in one domain often nudges others along with it. The problem is, most people don't fail for lack of motivation—they're simply overwhelmed. The burden of reinvention is paralysing. Grand declarations and sweeping resolutions tend to collapse under their own weight. Micro habits offer a way out: start small, keep it up, and let the momentum do the rest. It's not glamorous, but it works. Real change, as it turns out, doesn't require drama—just dedication.

Let's begin with the body—because health and fitness is where many turn first when contemplating change. But here too, the popular narrative is rife with intimidation: strict meal plans, gruelling gym regimens, expensive gear. The very thought can be enough to make people retreat. Now imagine something much simpler. A glass of water first thing in the morning. That's it. No kale smoothies, no wearable tech. Just water. Yet this one act rehydrates your system, signals attentiveness to your well-being, and, interestingly, tends to encourage further healthy choices as the day unfolds. Likewise, two minutes of stretching might not turn you into a yogi, but it eases stiffness, resets your posture, and clears your head. A brisk walk after lunch? Good for digestion, better for mood, and often a quiet spur for creative thought. They're small acts, yes—but stack them, and they begin to shift the trajectory of one's health meaningfully.

When it comes to professional life, micro habits offer something many productivity systems lack: humanity. Much of modern work culture is obsessed with optimisation, output, efficiency. But true productivity has less to do with hacking time and more to do with maintaining consistency and clarity of thought. Writing a single sentence each day may look inconsequential on the surface—but it preserves the creative thread. It keeps you in motion. One morning priority—clearly defined—can give the rest of the day a surprising coherence. These aren't overhaul strategies; they're nudges. You don't have to reinvent your workflow. You just have to keep showing up in small, purposeful ways.

It gets even more compelling when you apply this approach to the relational fabric of life. Relationships, after all, aren't built in grand gestures or dramatic reconciliations. They're built in the in-between: the text you didn't have to send but did, the question you remembered to ask, the way you chose to truly listen when someone spoke. A message of appreciation each day may not be remembered in isolation, but its cumulative emotional impact is undeniable. A child told "I'm proud of you" every evening won't remember each utterance—but they'll grow up with that truth embedded in their sense of self. Micro habits are the quiet architects of enduring bonds. They cultivate emotional safety in a world that often pulls us apart.

The same principle applies—perhaps even more poignantly—to mental and emotional health. Here, we often wait until we're on the verge of collapse to intervene. But resilience isn't built in crisis; it's built in maintenance. A few minutes of deep breathing can soothe the nervous system. Jotting down one bright spot from your day trains your brain to scan for the good. These are not heroic acts. But they're effective ones. More importantly, they're sustainable. You don't need a breakthrough or a retreat to tend to your inner life. You need tiny, regular practices that reconnect you to yourself—no fuss, no flourish.

And then there's money—often the quiet source of disproportionate stress. We tend to believe that financial change requires big leaps:

better income, shrewd investments, complex budgets. While those strategies can help, real financial grounding starts with awareness. Track just one expense a day. Save a token amount—fifty rupees, say—each morning. These acts are symbolic, yes, but also behavioural. They shape your self-conception: not just someone who wants to save, but someone who does. Over time, these behaviours expand, taking root and reshaping habits around spending, planning, and ultimately security. And when money feels more manageable, it's astonishing how much calmer everything else begins to feel—sleep, relationships, choices.

Crucially, none of this hinges on perfection. That's not the promise here. Micro habits are forgiving by design. They don't collapse when life does. They're portable, flexible, and quietly tenacious. You don't need ideal conditions. You don't need to feel inspired. You just need to return, again and again, to the small act you've chosen. And if you miss a day, you start again. No drama. No judgment.

In the pages ahead, we'll dive more deeply into each of these five life domains, drawing on research, lived experience, and real-world examples to show how micro habits operate within them. What will become clear is that while the scaffolding remains consistent, the expression of these habits is entirely personal. Your version of a health practice might look nothing like mine—and that's exactly as it should be. There's no prescription here, only a perspective: that change, lasting change, begins with something that fits you. Something that feels doable on your worst day, not just your best.

By the time you finish this chapter, the aim isn't just that you'll understand the mechanics of micro habits. It's that you'll see your own life differently. That you'll feel a sense of possibility—not because the road ahead is short, but because you know where to place your foot next. It's not about turning your world upside down. It's about tipping it, gently, one small act at a time. And from those acts, the shape of a more grounded, intentional life begins to emerge—quietly, steadily, and entirely on your own terms.

Health and Fitness

Among all the domains where micro habits exert their influence, none are more immediately felt—or widely misunderstood—than health and fitness. For many, the notion of getting healthier is associated with sweeping lifestyle overhauls, intensive exercise regimes, or rigid dietary restrictions. These perceptions, while pervasive, often create more psychological resistance than results. In reality, sustainable health transformation is not driven by radical change, but by persistent, manageable action. This is where micro habits offer a refreshing and deeply effective alternative. Their simplicity doesn't diminish their impact; rather, it makes them viable over the long haul.

The human body is an adaptive system. It responds to patterns more than peaks. Just as muscle is built through consistent resistance rather than occasional exertion, health is cultivated through repeated signals of care. Drinking more water, stretching for two minutes, or taking short walks may sound too modest to matter. But these actions, when embedded in daily life, become behavioural triggers for larger shifts—both physical and psychological. They lower the activation energy required to make healthier choices and reduce the reliance on willpower by creating a baseline of physiological self-regulation.

Consider hydration. Most people intellectually understand the importance of drinking water, yet they don't consistently do it. This is rarely due to ignorance and more often a result of neglecting to build it into the fabric of their day. A micro habit such as drinking a glass of water first thing in the morning may seem inconsequential. But this single act sets a physiological tone for the rest of the day. It rehydrates tissues, jump-starts metabolism, and often leads to increased awareness of other health behaviours. Moreover, it provides an early psychological win—proof that one has taken a step towards wellbeing before the day has properly begun.

Likewise, the practice of stretching for two minutes offers an outsized return on investment. Especially for individuals with sedentary jobs, those two minutes can counteract some of the muscular rigidity caused by prolonged sitting. But beyond biomechanics, stretching offers a brief window of mindfulness. It brings attention to the body, grounds the nervous system, and interrupts the often unconscious stress accumulation that characterises many modern workdays. Over time, this micro habit has the potential to evolve into longer mobility routines or spark interest in practices like yoga or pilates. The stretch itself is a beginning, but its value lies in its consistency and capacity to grow.

Short walks represent another deceptively powerful intervention. The modern lifestyle, increasingly defined by digital interfaces and stationary behaviours, has created an epidemic of physical inertia. We move less, and as a result, we feel less energised, less focused, and more prone to chronic health issues. A short walk—five to ten minutes—doesn't just burn calories. It stimulates circulation, enhances mental clarity, and elevates mood through the release of endorphins. Even more importantly, it introduces movement back into daily routines without requiring time-intensive gym sessions or structured workouts. For someone overwhelmed by the idea of getting "back into shape," walking becomes a doorway rather than a demand.

These micro habits also contribute to the development of what might be called embodied awareness. When we repeatedly engage in small physical actions that are good for us, we begin to re-attune to our bodily signals. We become more aware of hunger and satiety, of tension and relaxation, of fatigue and vitality. This awareness is a form of intelligence—one that gets dulled when health is approached only through metrics and external benchmarks. Micro habits reconnect us with the body's internal feedback systems, allowing for more intuitive and effective self-care.

The psychological reinforcement of these habits cannot be overstated. Each time an individual follows through on a micro habit, they reinforce a narrative of agency. They are not passively hoping to become healthier—they are actively proving it to themselves. This matters enormously in an age where health is often framed as either genetic destiny or the result of punishing discipline. Micro habits offer a third path: autonomy through consistency. The cumulative effect is not only physical resilience but psychological empowerment.

Let's take the example of Raj, a mid-level executive in his forties who had become increasingly sedentary and reported feeling chronically fatigued. Raj had neither the time nor the inclination to begin a rigorous fitness programme. Instead, he began incorporating a two-minute stretch every morning, a brisk five-minute walk after lunch, and a rule to drink a full glass of water before every meal. Within two months, he reported increased energy, reduced neck and back pain, and improved concentration at work. None of these outcomes required a single session in a gym. They were the result of sustained, low-friction behaviours that recalibrated his body and mindset.

Micro habits also help to circumvent the common psychological traps associated with health behaviour: perfectionism, guilt, and all-or-nothing thinking. The problem with traditional fitness resolutions is that they are fragile. Missing one workout or indulging in a less-than-ideal meal often triggers a cascade of self-criticism, followed by disengagement. Micro habits, by contrast, are built on the principle of accessibility. Because they demand so little time or energy, it is easier to resume them after disruption. This builds a sense of resilience and lowers the psychological cost of "starting over."

From a broader health perspective, these habits also serve a preventive function. Chronic diseases such as cardiovascular conditions, Type 2 diabetes, and hypertension do not develop overnight. They are the result of prolonged behavioural patterns. Micro habits, when sustained, alter those patterns early. A short walk after meals helps regulate blood sugar. Consistent hydration supports kidney function and cellular efficiency. Gentle stretching improves circulation and reduces inflammation. None of these effects are dramatic in isolation. But when multiplied across days, weeks, and years, they build a different health trajectory altogether.

There's also a social dimension to consider. Health behaviours, especially when visible, influence others. A parent who consistently drinks water, takes walks, or stretches in the morning normalises those behaviours for children. A colleague who steps outside for a short walk during breaks may encourage others to do the same. These behaviours become signals—small, quiet declarations that health can be integrated into ordinary life, without the fanfare of dramatic transformation.

For individuals who struggle with body image or disordered eating, micro habits offer a particularly compassionate approach. Because they are not fixated on weight loss or aesthetic outcomes, they allow for health to be pursued without reinforcing toxic metrics. Stretching because it feels good, walking because it clears the mind, drinking water because it supports energy—all of these are rooted in self-respect rather than self-rejection. This reframing is not only healthier—it is more sustainable.

It's also worth recognising that micro habits often serve as behavioural anchors. That is, they stabilise routines and make it easier to add new practices over time. Drinking water in the morning can become the cue for taking vitamins. A short evening walk might lead to earlier bedtimes. Stretching before sleep may evolve into a full bedtime ritual. These anchor habits don't just improve health—they create a scaffold on which other habits can be built.

Ultimately, the question is not whether small health behaviours matter. The evidence—scientific, anecdotal, and intuitive—is overwhelming. The better question is whether we can give ourselves permission to value them. In a culture that often idolises extremes, the quiet, repetitive act of walking for ten minutes or stretching for two may feel insufficient. But that is a cultural illusion. The body does not respond to intensity—it responds to consistency. And when that consistency is built on habits that are easy to start, pleasant to maintain, and meaningful in effect, transformation is not only possible—it becomes inevitable.

Health and fitness are not destinations to be reached through acts of discipline or denial. They are patterns to be lived, and micro habits offer the most accessible way to establish those patterns. The invitation, then, is simple: begin where you are, do what you can, and do it often. The rest will take care of itself.

Productivity and Career

In today's fast-paced, information-saturated world, productivity is often mistaken for constant motion—being perpetually busy, filling one's calendar with back-to-back tasks, or racing against self-imposed deadlines. Yet meaningful productivity is not about how much we do, but rather how effectively we manage our attention and how deliberately we act. This distinction is crucial in both personal and professional life, particularly in a work culture that rewards output without always evaluating its quality or sustainability. Micro habits provide a way to reclaim agency, focus, and creative energy in a context that is increasingly fragmented by digital noise, competing priorities, and decision fatigue.

Productivity, at its core, is about consistent progress in meaningful work. But the conditions necessary for such progress—mental clarity, task prioritisation, emotional regulation—are not always available in large quantities. This is where micro habits become essential. They don't attempt to overhaul your work ethic or restructure your entire day. Instead, they serve as strategic behavioural levers, subtly nudging your attention towards what matters most, and anchoring your productivity in habits that are realistic and sustainable.

One of the most effective micro habits in this context is the act of writing just one sentence a day. At first glance, this might seem trivial—hardly enough to move a project forward or meet a deadline. But its value lies not in volume, but in maintaining creative continuity. For writers, strategists, researchers, and professionals involved in cognitive work, the hardest part is often not the execution, but the initiation. By lowering the threshold for starting, this tiny commitment bypasses procrastination and maintains a rhythm of thought. Once a sentence is written, a second often follows. But even if it doesn't, the mental connection to the work is preserved, making re-engagement the next day much easier. This approach transforms productivity from a sprint into a cadence.

The same logic applies to the micro habit of daily task prioritisation. Every morning, before diving into emails or meetings, taking two minutes to identify and articulate the most important task of the day can significantly alter the direction and quality of your work. This habit helps mitigate the productivity trap of 'reactive busyness,' where your entire workday is spent responding to others' demands rather than advancing your own priorities. Clarifying what matters—especially in a work environment cluttered with competing stimuli—

restores focus and protects cognitive bandwidth. Over time, this habit cultivates strategic thinking, clearer boundaries, and a more intentional work ethic.

The benefits of micro habits in the context of career growth are also psychological. Consistently following through on small commitments enhances self-efficacy, which is the belief in one's ability to influence outcomes. This belief is foundational to sustained motivation. When people feel capable, they engage more readily, persevere longer, and recover faster from setbacks. A professional who begins the day with five minutes of review or reflection, for example, may start to see patterns in their work, recognise opportunities for improvement, or uncover new directions. These insights don't always emerge from formal planning—they often come from micro practices that promote regular engagement with one's goals and environment.

The compounding power of micro habits is particularly important in a professional landscape shaped by constant change. Career paths are no longer linear. Skills evolve, industries shift, and adaptability is as critical as expertise. Micro habits offer a flexible, modular way to keep learning and developing without requiring large investments of time or energy. Reading one paragraph of a professional book, watching a short educational video, or journalling a reflection at the end of each workday—these small actions maintain a state of professional curiosity and readiness. They prevent stagnation and help build a portfolio of micro-skills that collectively support long-term advancement.

Take the example of Imran, a software developer who wanted to improve his public speaking skills to prepare for a leadership role. Instead of enrolling in an intensive course, which he couldn't accommodate alongside his workload, he started a simple habit: recording a sixty-second summary of his daily progress into his phone. He did this privately, with no audience. At first, his delivery was hesitant and filled with filler words. But within a month, his speech became more fluid. By the third month, he began practising short impromptu talks in team meetings. What started as a private, low-pressure exercise eventually translated into visible professional growth—all without disrupting his existing responsibilities.

Micro habits also support emotional regulation in the workplace, which is an often overlooked component of productivity. The ability to remain calm under pressure, respond constructively to feedback, and recover from disappointment is essential for professional resilience. A brief breathing practice before important calls, a habit of writing a gratitude note to a colleague each week, or simply pausing for thirty seconds before replying to a challenging email—these micro interventions create space between stimulus and response. That space is where reflection happens. And reflection, more than reactivity, is what allows for thoughtful, effective action.

From a managerial perspective, micro habits can be used to model behaviour, reinforce culture, and support team development. Leaders who consistently start meetings with a clear agenda, who regularly check in on their team members' well-being, or who reflect openly on lessons learned after a project, create an environment of intentionality and psychological safety. These are not time-consuming practices, but they have an outsized impact on team morale, trust, and collective focus. The best teams don't operate on urgency—they operate on shared rhythms of communication, review, and renewal.

Technology can both support and undermine productivity, and here too micro habits serve as a form of calibration. Checking email only at designated intervals, silencing notifications during deep work, or taking digital sabbaths for five minutes each hour can help reclaim attention in a world built to steal it. These digital micro habits aren't about rejection of tools, but about mindful use. They introduce behavioural boundaries that protect cognitive resources, making it easier to produce high-quality work in less time.

Importantly, micro habits allow professionals to build a personalised productivity system that reflects their values and constraints. One person may thrive by starting their day with movement and journaling. Another may prefer a late-evening review of progress and lessons learned. The framework is flexible enough to accommodate different rhythms, but the underlying principle is consistent: meaningful work is built on small, sustained acts of clarity, focus, and intention.

The effectiveness of micro habits in enhancing productivity is not speculative. It is supported by decades of research in behavioural science, cognitive psychology, and occupational health. Studies show that habits are more likely to stick when they are specific, easy to implement, and tied to existing routines. Micro habits meet all these criteria. They are frictionless, context-sensitive, and designed to create behavioural inertia—momentum that builds with each repetition, making the habit harder to break than to maintain.

The professional world will always place demands on your time. Deadlines will tighten, expectations will rise, and the tools you use will change. But amidst all this flux, micro habits offer something stable: a structure of small, reliable actions that keep you aligned with your purpose, engaged with your work, and connected to your own potential. They teach you that productivity is not a trait, but a practice—and that mastery is not found in grand efforts, but in the quiet, daily act of showing up with intention.

What emerges from these practices is not just more output, but better output. Not just faster results, but more meaningful ones. And not just professional success, but personal satisfaction—a sense that your work is an authentic expression of your values, your strengths, and your commitment to continual growth. In this way, micro habits don't just enhance your productivity. They transform your relationship with your career itself.

Relationships and Social Life

Of all the domains that shape human flourishing, relationships stand paramount. Our social lives—whether grounded in romantic partnerships, family ties, friendships, or collegial networks—constitute not only a source of emotional richness but also a cornerstone of psychological and physical wellbeing. Yet, in the busyness of modern life, maintaining and deepening these connections can often feel like another item on an ever-growing to-do list. Here, micro habits offer a vital reframing. Rather than waiting for grand gestures, elaborate conversations, or milestone events to express care, micro habits focus on consistent, meaningful behaviours that, over time, reinforce trust, affection, and emotional intimacy.

The strength of any relationship lies in its dailiness—the steady accumulation of small acts of recognition, respect, and reciprocity. Large, infrequent efforts may dazzle, but it is the quiet constancy of showing up, of paying attention, that nourishes the roots of human connection. A short message of appreciation. A moment of undivided listening. A touch on the shoulder while passing. These are not trivial acts; they are foundational. They serve as emotional deposits in the relational account, building a sense of safety, goodwill, and mutual regard that weathers more turbulent moments.

One of the most accessible and impactful micro habits in this space is the daily expression of gratitude. Taking a few seconds each day to thank a friend, partner, sibling, or colleague for something they did—or simply for who they are—can shift relational dynamics in profound ways. Gratitude has been shown to enhance empathy, reduce resentment, and even trigger reciprocal kindness. But beyond the psychological data, its power lies in its emotional clarity. When people feel seen and appreciated, they soften. They open. They lean in. And over time, relationships marked by consistent gratitude develop a deeper emotional tone—one that is harder to erode, even under strain.

Take the example of Kavya, a freelance graphic designer living with her ageing mother. As their roles shifted—Kavya becoming more of a caregiver, her mother less independent—tensions naturally surfaced. Rather than addressing this dynamic with intense conversations, Kavya began a quiet practice: each evening, she left a handwritten note on the kitchen table, expressing appreciation for something specific her mother had done that day. Some notes were heartfelt, others humorous. But every note was sincere. Over weeks, the emotional climate of the house changed. Their conversations became more affectionate, their disagreements less reactive. The practice didn't fix everything, but it recalibrated the emotional tone of their interaction.

Another transformative micro habit is active listening. In theory, everyone understands its value. In practice, few people consistently do it. Most conversations are filled with interruptions, assumptions, and a subtle race to respond. Active listening, as a micro habit, begins with a simple principle: offer undivided attention for a short span—

just one or two minutes of full presence. This means putting the phone down, maintaining eye contact, and withholding judgement. It's not a script. It's a posture. And when done regularly, it creates a psychological space where the other person feels heard and valued.

The effects of this are cumulative. A spouse who feels regularly listened to is more likely to express vulnerability. A colleague who is met with presence, rather than impatience, is more inclined to collaborate. A friend who experiences consistent empathy is more likely to reach out in times of need. Listening is not a passive act—it is an active offering of attention, and its impact on relational depth is difficult to overstate.

Technology, for all its relational advantages, has also introduced new forms of distraction and disconnection. Social media, text messaging, and video calls enable constant contact but often dilute the quality of our interactions. Micro habits can counterbalance this by reintroducing intentionality. Sending one thoughtful message a day—not a meme or a reply, but a genuine expression of interest or affection—can restore the depth that digital communication often lacks. These moments create what psychologist John Gottman has called "bids for connection": small attempts to engage that, when reciprocated, significantly strengthen relational bonds.

For those struggling with social anxiety or introversion, micro habits offer a manageable way to build social resilience. Starting a conversation with a colleague, offering a compliment, or maintaining eye contact for a few extra seconds can serve as daily exercises in interpersonal engagement. These micro interactions, while brief, gradually reshape social confidence. They reinforce a sense of competence and reduce the fear of social rejection. Over time, the person doesn't merely act more confidently—they begin to internalise a more socially capable self-image.

Relationships also benefit from predictability. While spontaneity can bring excitement, trust is built on the assurance that the other person will show up in consistent, caring ways. Micro habits provide that structure. A nightly text to check in. A weekend call. A shared morning coffee, even in silence. These rituals, often unremarkable on the surface, become emotional anchors. They create a rhythm that signals reliability, which in turn fosters emotional security.

Let's consider the case of Arjun and Priya, a married couple navigating demanding careers and raising two children. Their days were full and fragmented, their evenings often spent in parallel exhaustion. Despite being deeply committed, they began to feel emotionally distant. Rather than waiting for the right time to 'have a talk'—a conversation that never seemed to arrive—they began a micro habit: five minutes on the sofa each night with no agenda, no screens, and no interruptions. Some evenings they spoke, others they simply sat. But the consistency of this brief shared pause re-established emotional proximity. It wasn't dramatic, but it was dependable—and that made all the difference.

Micro habits are also effective in mending strained relationships. When trust has been eroded, grand apologies may feel hollow or overwhelming. But a consistent pattern of small, respectful actions—being on time, following through on commitments, making eye contact—can slowly rebuild credibility. These habits demonstrate, rather than declare, change. They offer proof of reliability, not just intention.

In professional settings, micro habits shape culture. Saying thank you, acknowledging someone's contribution in a meeting, or simply greeting colleagues by name fosters a sense of belonging. These are not empty gestures. They affirm presence. They remind people that their work—and their person—matters. Over time, these small acts create a culture of mutual respect and trust that cannot be imposed from the top down but must be lived day by day.

It's also worth noting that micro habits often reveal what we truly value. We may say that relationships are important to us, but our daily behaviour often prioritises productivity, distraction, or withdrawal. When we embed relational micro habits into our routines, we align our actions with our stated values. That alignment generates integrity. And integrity, lived consistently, becomes the soil in which trust and affection grow.

Moreover, these habits are not dependent on others' responses. You don't need someone to reciprocate a thank you to feel good about expressing it. You don't need a deep conversation every evening to feel connected. The power of micro habits is that they are intrinsically rewarding. They reinforce who you want to be, regardless of how others respond. This reduces emotional dependency and fosters a healthier form of interpersonal engagement—one that is generous, not transactional.

Ultimately, the quality of our relationships is not defined by the occasional holiday, the grand gesture, or the rare breakthrough conversation. It is shaped by what we do repeatedly. By the moments we choose to be present, the words we choose to offer, and the time we choose to share. Micro habits are not a lesser version of love or friendship or connection. They are its quiet, enduring architecture. And when thoughtfully chosen and consistently practised, they do more than maintain relationships—they deepen them, ground them, and make them resilient in a world that too often pulls us apart.

Mental Health and Well-Being

Mental health is often discussed in abstract or clinical terms, yet it is lived intimately—in the small rituals that ground us, the thoughts that repeat silently through our minds, and the ways we respond to life's inevitable stressors. It is not a fixed trait or the outcome of one-time interventions, but a dynamic state shaped by daily behaviours. In this sense, emotional resilience, mindfulness, and psychological balance are not reserved for the especially disciplined or spiritually inclined. They are accessible to anyone willing to adopt small, purposeful habits that gradually fortify the mind against turbulence and foster moments of calm within the chaos.

Micro habits offer a particularly effective entry point for improving mental well-being because they bypass the common barriers that hinder long-term emotional growth. Often, people delay attending to their mental health because the solutions they've been offered seem too time-consuming or emotionally demanding. The idea of meditating for thirty minutes a day, journalling for hours, or overhauling one's lifestyle can feel overwhelming to someone already burdened by anxiety or burnout. Micro habits, by contrast, start where people are—not where they think they ought to be. They provide realistic, achievable actions that restore a sense of agency and self-trust.

Mindfulness, often misunderstood as a lofty or esoteric concept, becomes entirely approachable when framed as a micro habit. At its core, mindfulness is the practice of paying attention to the present moment with intention and without judgement. While formal meditation is one way to cultivate this skill, it is not the only way. Pausing for a single conscious breath before opening an email, noticing the taste of the first sip of coffee in the morning, or simply placing a hand on the heart when feeling overwhelmed—all of these can be micro habits of mindfulness. These acts do not demand silence, a cushion, or an app. They require only a willingness to notice and to return—to the body, to the breath, to the now.

The neurological benefits of such moments are well documented. When the mind is drawn back from rumination or projection into the immediacy of the present, the sympathetic nervous system—the branch responsible for the fight-or-flight response—begins to quiet. Heart rate slows. Cortisol levels drop. Cognitive clarity improves. Over time, these physiological shifts become more accessible, as the nervous system learns to regulate more efficiently. But the habit must be repeated. This is where the consistency of micro habits matters more than duration. A one-minute body scan every day can be more effective than a twenty-minute meditation done once a fortnight.

Stress reduction, similarly, is often approached as something to be achieved through escape: holidays, spa days, extended breaks. While such experiences have their place, they are episodic. What is needed is not occasional relief but daily regulation. Micro habits provide this. Taking a slow breath before answering a phone call. Naming an emotion before acting on it. Stepping outside for one minute to feel the air on your skin. These are not dramatic acts, but they interrupt the automaticity of stress responses and reintroduce choice. They create micro-moments of spaciousness in otherwise constricted days.

Consider the case of Naveen, a high-performing consultant whose workdays were marked by constant stimulation and pressure. He frequently felt on edge, snapping at colleagues and struggling to sleep despite feeling exhausted. Traditional stress management advice—exercise more, cut caffeine, get better sleep—felt abstract and unreachable in his packed schedule. Instead, he began with a micro habit: each time he closed his laptop, he would stand, stretch his arms overhead, and take three deep breaths. This practice, which took less than thirty seconds, served as a reset. Over time, it became a cue for psychological decompression. Though subtle, this habit helped Naveen begin regulating his stress before it accumulated. He later added a brief gratitude note to his end-of-day routine, further reinforcing a shift from urgency to reflection.

Emotional resilience—the ability to recover from setbacks, adapt to change, and maintain equilibrium under pressure—is another capacity that benefits immensely from micro habits. Resilience is often mistaken for innate toughness, but in reality, it is a learnable set of skills, many of which can be cultivated through deliberate, repeatable behaviours. One such behaviour is naming one's experience. Simply articulating what one is feeling, even internally, helps to metabolise emotion. "This is anger." "This is sadness." "This is disappointment." Labelling emotions activates the prefrontal cortex, reducing the intensity of limbic activity and restoring cognitive control. Making this a habit—pausing to name emotions during daily transitions or after stressful moments—builds emotional fluency, which is the foundation of resilience.

Another powerful micro habit is reframing. This involves consciously choosing a different perspective on a challenge, not in a way that denies difficulty, but that reinterprets it constructively. For instance, instead of thinking "I failed that meeting," one might say, "I didn't present as clearly as I wanted to, but I know what to improve." The habit of catching and reframing unhelpful thoughts can be as simple as writing down one such shift each evening. Over time, this not only reduces negative self-talk but also builds a mindset oriented towards learning and growth rather than perfection and performance.

Real-world applications of these habits abound. For example, Meera, a secondary school teacher navigating the emotional load of her profession, began a practice of closing each teaching day by writing down one positive interaction she had with a student. Initially, she did this to counteract the heaviness she felt after difficult classroom moments. But within weeks, the habit reshaped her overall narrative of the day. She no longer saw her work through the lens of challenges alone, but also through the lens of connection and impact. This shift fortified her sense of purpose and reduced emotional fatigue—both critical components of resilience.

It is also worth emphasising that micro habits function best when embedded into existing routines. Attaching a two-minute breathing practice to brushing one's teeth, or a moment of gratitude to the act of locking up for the night, turns abstract aspirations into integrated rituals. This is how habits are sustained—not by willpower, but by design. The more seamless a habit is to implement, the more likely it is to endure.

Culturally, there is still a lingering perception that mental health requires major intervention—therapy, medication, or crisis response. And while these forms of support are indispensable for many, they are not the only tools available. Micro habits represent a preventative, self-directed approach. They do not replace clinical care, but they significantly reduce the likelihood of escalation by maintaining baseline emotional and physiological health. They are, in essence, acts of mental hygiene—just as brushing our teeth protects oral health, these small daily acts protect and strengthen the psyche.

The language we use around mental health also begins to change through the adoption of micro habits. Rather than thinking in binaries—well versus unwell, strong versus broken—we begin to view mental health as a continuum, shaped by small, everyday choices. This perspective fosters compassion, both towards oneself and others. It allows for nuance, for fluctuation, for the reality that some days we cope better than others—and that's not a failure, but a reflection of being human.

Ultimately, micro habits for mental health and well-being are not about doing more. They are about doing differently. They invite a relationship with the self that is attentive rather than reactive, grounded rather than hurried. They remind us that stability is not the absence of challenge, but the presence of practices that help us return to centre. And most importantly, they prove—day after day, breath after breath—that mental wellness is not a distant goal, but a living, breathing practice. One that begins not with transformation, but with a moment. Repeated. With care.

Financial Habits

Money is one of the most emotionally charged aspects of adult life, and yet it remains one of the least discussed in everyday terms. Financial health, like mental or physical well-being, is shaped less by dramatic windfalls or grand strategies than by the small, repeatable actions we take on a daily basis. These actions—tracking an expense, saving a small amount, reviewing a bank balance—may not seem revolutionary, but when practised consistently, they rewire both behaviour and belief systems. At the heart of sustainable financial wellness is not complexity, but consistency. And this is precisely where micro habits become indispensable.

The modern individual is inundated with financial advice: invest early, diversify assets, cut discretionary spending, build multiple income streams. While much of this guidance is valid, its breadth and complexity often overwhelm more than it empowers. Financial literacy is not just a knowledge issue; it is a behavioural one. Most people are not undone by a lack of information, but by a lack of habits that allow that information to be used effectively. Micro habits serve as a behavioural infrastructure. They do not replace strategic planning or professional advice, but they provide the behavioural scaffolding upon which more advanced financial decisions can rest.

Tracking one expense per day is a good example of this. On the surface, it appears inconsequential—recording the cost of a coffee or a bus fare. But this act has layered benefits. First, it builds awareness. Much of overspending is not the result of extravagance, but of mindlessness. People simply don't realise where their money is going. By writing down a single transaction, the brain begins to pay attention. This awareness activates the prefrontal cortex, the part of the brain responsible for decision-making and long-term planning. Over time, this habit creates what psychologists call "salience"—the mental prominence of an idea. Money moves from the periphery of consciousness to the foreground, making intentional spending more likely.

There is also a psychological component. When individuals begin tracking spending—even at a micro level—they experience a shift in self-identity. They no longer see themselves as passive spenders, but as active stewards of their resources. This change in self-concept may seem subtle, but it has cascading effects. It makes people more likely to set goals, to resist impulsive purchases, and to delay gratification—all of which are central to financial resilience.

Saving a small amount regularly operates on the same principle. The amount matters far less than the behaviour. Someone who saves fifty rupees a day builds not just a balance, but a habit. They begin to see saving as something they do—not something they intend to do when circumstances improve. This shift is powerful because it breaks through the all-or-nothing thinking that traps so many would-be savers. Waiting until there's "enough to save" often leads to saving nothing at all. But saving a small, manageable amount trains the brain to think in terms of accumulation. It builds financial momentum, which often leads to further positive behaviours such as budgeting, investing, or debt reduction.

The compounding effect of these habits is not only mathematical but behavioural. Someone who saves one per cent of their income every week may increase that amount over time, not through force, but through alignment. Their identity shifts, their confidence grows, and their habits evolve. Eventually, what began as a micro habit becomes a macro result. And this transformation is far more sustainable than sudden, drastic changes, which often falter under emotional or logistical pressure.

Consider the story of Harish, a logistics supervisor in his early thirties who had struggled with money for most of his adult life. He often ran out of funds before payday and had accumulated small debts on multiple credit cards. Traditional budgeting systems never seemed to stick. Then a colleague suggested a simple experiment: write down one thing you spend money on each day, and save twenty rupees in a jar. Harish agreed, mostly out of curiosity. Within a few weeks, he began noticing patterns—daily snacks, impulse buys, rounding up ride fares. The act of writing them down made him more conscious, and the physical act of saving became oddly satisfying. Over three months, he had saved more than a thousand rupees and reduced his unnecessary spending by a third. More importantly, he described feeling "in charge" of his finances for the first time in years. What changed was not his income, but his behaviour—and that started with two micro habits.

Another underappreciated micro habit is the act of reviewing one's bank balance or financial dashboard once a day. Not obsessively, not with anxiety, but with curiosity. This habit builds what behavioural economists call "feedback loops"—real-time insights that allow for course correction. When people avoid looking at their accounts, often out of fear or shame, they also lose the opportunity to make proactive decisions. But when checking in becomes a habit, emotional reactivity decreases. The numbers may not always be pleasant, but they are known—and what is known can be managed. Over time, this practice also desensitises the emotional spikes often associated with money, creating a more stable and empowered relationship with one's finances.

Micro habits also help navigate the emotional layers of money—fear, shame, envy, scarcity. Financial decisions are rarely rational. They are driven by unconscious narratives about what money means: success, security, freedom, self-worth. When people begin small financial practices—tracking, saving, reviewing—they begin to unearth these narratives. A person might notice that they spend impulsively after a stressful meeting. Or that they avoid saving because it feels futile compared to larger debts. These insights do not emerge from reading personal finance books alone. They emerge from behavioural engagement. Micro habits act as mirrors, reflecting not only what we do with money, but why we do it.

Importantly, financial micro habits are not only for those in crisis. They are equally valuable for those seeking to optimise, grow, or plan. A high-income professional might use micro habits to automate incremental increases in investment contributions. A young student might use them to track textbook spending and build awareness of cost-benefit choices. A retiree might adopt a habit of reviewing expenses weekly to maintain clarity and confidence. The beauty of micro habits lies in their scalability. They can be adapted to any financial context because their power lies in repetition, not magnitude.

Technology can be both an ally and an obstacle here. Budgeting apps, digital savings tools, and automatic alerts can facilitate micro habits by reducing friction. A daily push notification reminding you to log one expense or save a small amount can anchor behaviour in the rhythm of daily life. However, the habit must remain conscious. Automating savings is beneficial, but if it becomes invisible, it may lose its psychological reinforcement. The goal is not just financial growth, but financial literacy and agency—and that requires awareness.

Social context also matters. Financial behaviour is shaped not only by personal choices, but by cultural norms, family dynamics, and peer influences. Micro habits offer a subtle way to challenge unhelpful narratives or inherited patterns. If one grew up in a household where money was a source of conflict or secrecy, small habits of transparency—such as talking openly about a spending choice or sharing a saving goal—can begin to rewrite that script. These changes may feel small, but over time they reshape the emotional landscape of money.

At its most fundamental level, money is a tool. It is not moral, it is not fixed, and it is not beyond influence. The way we relate to it is entirely trainable. And that training does not require a financial degree, a windfall, or a breakthrough. It requires a habit—a small act, done often, with intention. Whether it's tracking one purchase, saving one note, or reviewing one statement, these actions compound not only in wealth, but in wisdom. They build a sense of order, clarity, and calm in an area of life that too often feels chaotic or shame-laden.

Financial well-being, like physical or mental health, is not the result of occasional intensity. It is the reward of sustained attention. And in a world where so much about money feels urgent or overwhelming, micro habits offer a rare gift: they make the complex feel manageable, the abstract feel concrete, and the overwhelming feel possible. They remind us that financial strength is not a destination, but a practice—and that every choice, no matter how small, is a step towards stability, sovereignty, and peace of mind.

Chapter 8
The Identity Shift – Becoming the Person You Want to Be

Real change—change that lasts, that sinks into the bones—is never just about doing things differently. It's about becoming someone new. Beneath the daily actions we repeat lies something deeper: the gradual, often quiet, remaking of identity. We're not just cultivating habits when we strive to improve ourselves; we're shaping how we see ourselves and how we move through the world. And this is where the idea of identity-based change enters with force: it urges us to think beyond outcome-driven goals and focus instead on the kind of person we're becoming through what we repeatedly do.

Too often, we're told to fix our lives by chasing visible results—slimmer bodies, fuller wallets, neater calendars. These are fine aims, to be sure. But they're flimsy scaffolding if not anchored to a deeper sense of self. Goals divorced from identity tend to wobble. They lean on fleeting willpower or the high of progress. And when the dopamine wanes—or worse, when the goal is reached and nothing inside has changed—so do the habits. But if a behaviour stems from the belief that this is simply who I am, it's no longer a tactic. It becomes a truth in motion. Subtle difference in language, dramatic shift in effect.

Every repeated act, no matter how trivial it may appear, casts a vote for the identity we are building. A single run isn't about fitness; it's a quiet reaffirmation: I'm someone who moves, who values strength. One written paragraph, even a clumsy one, signals: I'm a writer. Not because I publish, but because I persist. In those early, fragile days of habit-building, what matters most is not volume or intensity—it's consistency. The real magic lies not in what you do, but in what it starts to mean about who you are.

This isn't just poetic musing—it's backed by psychology. Self-perception theory, to name it properly, suggests that we learn who we are by observing what we do, especially when our identity in a particular area is still forming. Start tracking your spending each evening—even if finances have always felt alien to you—and, over time, you may begin to believe you're someone who's financially responsible. In this way, micro habits—those tiny, nearly forgettable actions—quietly lay the groundwork for the kind of person you're becoming. They're not just self-help strategies; they're instruments of self-definition.

This chapter aims to explore how micro habits, applied through the lens of identity, become more than routine—they become declarations. And central to this is the idea that progress outweighs perfection. Perfectionism is a saboteur disguised as high standards. It whispers that if something can't be done flawlessly, it isn't worth doing at all. The micro habit mindset refuses this binary. It insists that excellence is born of rhythm, not of spotless execution. To keep going, even messily, is to affirm a deeper commitment. And this isn't just feel-good reasoning—it's effective. The more frequently we act in alignment with who we hope to become, the sturdier that identity becomes.

Consider Ravi, a young entrepreneur at the threshold of launching his consultancy. He was paralysed—by self-doubt, by the weight of what he imagined a "real" leader ought to be. He didn't try to overhaul his schedule or mimic someone else's formula. Instead, he began each morning by writing a single sentence about the kind of leader he wanted to grow into. Two minutes, perhaps less. But those sentences became a mirror, a guide, a daily reorientation. They helped him sift through priorities, delegate with intention, and navigate the bumps and bruises of a fledgling business—not because he became perfect, but because he slowly began to believe he was the sort of person who could lead.

That, in essence, is what gives habits staying power: alignment with personal values. If a habit isn't rooted in something you genuinely care about, it won't survive friction. Performative habits—those done to impress, to fit in, to tick a box—can run for a while, propelled by external praise or novelty. But they usually peter out when life gets demanding. Habits born of value, on the other hand, don't just endure—they deepen. If you cherish creativity, then a daily sketch—however rough—feels less like a duty and more like a reclaiming of self. If you hold integrity close, then a brief moment of evening reflection becomes not a task, but a return to centre.

To bring this value-habit connection into sharper focus, many behavioural coaches suggest crafting what's called an identity statement. The structure is simple: "I'm the kind of person who..." The completion is yours. Perhaps: "...keeps promises, even small ones." Or "...moves my body every day, even when it's just a walk." These aren't grand declarations. They're gentle commitments—grounded, believable, repeatable. Spoken aloud or held quietly, they gain force when paired with action. And over time, they begin to feel less like aspirations and more like truths.

Still, it must be said: identity-based habits are not immune to resistance. They require scaffolding—practical, emotional, environmental. One frequently overlooked barrier is what psychologists call emotional friction. We don't always drop habits because we forget; we drop them because they begin to feel heavy, unrewarding, or tainted by past failures. This is where micro habits shine. Because they're intentionally small, the cost of resuming them is low. Miss a day? No crisis. It's only two minutes. That lack of drama provides a cushion—a kind of psychological grace—that makes returning to the habit far more likely.

Ultimately, what sustains change isn't grit—it's design. Systems that reduce friction and encourage follow-through make all the difference. Leave your journal on your pillow. Switch off notifications before your creative work. Surround yourself with people who live the way you want to live. The idea is to remove as many internal negotiations as possible. When the path is clear, walking it becomes not only easier, but almost inevitable.

"You are what you repeatedly do"—the phrase is often quoted, but perhaps still underappreciated. It's not just philosophy; it's neurology. The brain, through repetition, rewires. Neural pathways strengthen with use. Habits, repeated often enough, move from effortful to automatic. In essence, they become us. And this is the quiet genius of identity-based micro habits: they automate the becoming.

But let's not pretend this process is tidy. Identity is not a fixed point. It evolves. And the beauty of micro habits is precisely that they leave space for this evolution. They don't demand reinvention overnight. They offer a method of editing the story, paragraph by paragraph. You're not trapped by your past patterns. You are, at every moment, one small act away from shifting the narrative.

By the end of this chapter, one truth should land with clarity: every micro habit is a tiny stake in the ground—a vote for the version of you that you are actively choosing. With time and repetition, these votes accumulate—not just into better routines, but into a more coherent, more intentional self. You'll notice the shift not in some grand epiphany, but in the way you show up to your day—with more direction, more conviction, and perhaps most of all, more congruence between who you are and who you wish to be.

Habits Shape Identity

The human sense of self is not static, but a living narrative shaped over time through reflection, experience, and behaviour. While identity is often perceived as something innate or discovered, it is in fact continually constructed—layer by layer, decision by decision. Nowhere is this more evident than in the influence of habits. These small, repetitive actions, often performed without much conscious thought, play an outsized role in forming our self-perception. Over time, what we do becomes who we believe we are. Our habits, in essence, cast votes for the type of person we think we are becoming. And once that identity begins to solidify, it becomes a powerful driver of future behaviour.

Psychologists have long studied the relationship between action and self-concept. One of the most compelling insights comes from self-perception theory, which suggests that individuals come to understand themselves by observing their own actions, particularly in ambiguous or uncertain contexts. Rather than forming beliefs first and acting second, the process is often reversed. A person who donates to charity repeatedly may come to see themselves as generous, even if generosity wasn't part of their self-definition beforehand. Likewise, someone who consistently rises early to read or write may eventually adopt the identity of a disciplined or studious individual. It is the recurrence of these actions—not their scale or external recognition—that forges the internal belief.

This process is subtle but incredibly consequential. Each time you engage in a specific habit, you are reinforcing a particular narrative about yourself. The person who walks daily for ten minutes may start to believe they are someone who cares about their health. The individual who ends every day by writing a single line in a gratitude journal gradually begins to see themselves as more appreciative. Identity is not declared in moments of inspiration—it is constructed through repeated demonstration.

Real-world examples bring this concept vividly to life. Consider the case of Anika, a mid-level executive who, after years of self-doubt and perceived underperformance, began the micro habit of preparing for each meeting the evening before. Initially, the habit was purely pragmatic—born out of frustration with feeling disorganised. But as it became consistent, her internal narrative began to shift. She started seeing herself as someone who is competent, prepared, and professional. This new self-concept began influencing other behaviours: she became more confident in speaking up, more proactive in offering ideas, and more resilient under pressure. The habit was small, but the identity shift was significant. Through action, she rewrote the story she had been telling herself.

The same principle applies to habits with negative valence. A person who repeatedly breaks promises to themselves—skipping workouts, ignoring budgets, avoiding difficult conversations—begins to erode their own self-trust. Even if these actions are rationalised or justified externally, they accumulate internally as a quiet undermining of one's perceived integrity or reliability. Over time, the identity that takes hold might be one of someone who is undisciplined or inconsistent, regardless of intent. The behaviour doesn't just reflect the identity; it informs and reshapes it.

This is why efforts at self-improvement so often falter when they are goal-based rather than identity-driven. Goals are useful for direction, but they are fleeting by nature. Once a goal is achieved—or worse, abandoned—the motivation behind it often dissipates. A person might aim to run a marathon, and indeed complete it, but without a deeper identity shift, they may never run again. Contrast this with someone who builds the identity of being a runner—someone who laces up their shoes daily, regardless of distance or pace. The former achieves a task; the latter sustains a transformation.

Understanding the identity-forming power of habits invites a different approach to change. Rather than asking, "What result do I want?" a more powerful question becomes, "Who do I want to become?" This reframing shifts the focus from distant outcomes to present-tense behaviours that are accessible and affirming. It also provides a more stable foundation for perseverance. When actions are anchored in identity rather than outcomes, they are less likely to be derailed by temporary setbacks or lack of external validation.

Adopting this mindset also mitigates the perfectionism trap. When people set goals based on performance rather than identity, they tend to view any slip-up as failure. But when the goal is to reinforce a particular self-concept, consistency matters more than flawlessness. Missing a day at the gym doesn't mean you're not an athlete; it's a temporary break, not a broken identity. This distinction allows for a more compassionate and sustainable approach to habit maintenance. It normalises variability while preserving the underlying narrative of who one is becoming.

There is also a neurological dimension to consider. Neuroscience has shown that habits create neural pathways that strengthen over time with repetition. This is often referred to as Hebb's law: neurons that fire together, wire together. The more often a habit is performed, the more automatic and engrained it becomes—not only in behaviour but in brain structure. This biological embedding reinforces identity at the cellular level. You are not just thinking differently—you are literally becoming different.

One must also acknowledge the social reinforcement of identity-based habits. When others begin to recognise and reflect your habits back to you—calling you organised, creative, thoughtful—it further cements the identity you are building. Social validation can be a double-edged sword, but in the context of positive identity reinforcement, it acts as a mirror that strengthens internal belief.

However, the most enduring identities are not those formed for others' approval, but those aligned with personal values and aspirations.

Of course, identity is multi-dimensional. We are not just one thing—we are a collection of roles, desires, fears, and values. But habits offer a way to shape each dimension intentionally. A parent might adopt habits that reinforce their identity as a nurturing presence. A manager might build routines that affirm their commitment to ethical leadership. A student might create micro habits that reinforce their curiosity and intellectual resilience. These identities are not imposed from outside—they are cultivated through choice, repeated consistently.

This perspective also invites a more forgiving view of past behaviour. Many people carry the weight of identities formed in reaction to earlier failures or disappointments. They might believe they are "not good with money," "lazy," or "disorganised"—not because these traits are fixed, but because previous patterns have reinforced them. The good news is that just as old habits shaped these identities, new habits can reshape them. Change is not about becoming someone entirely different; it's about remembering and reinforcing the best parts of who you already are—and choosing behaviours that make that version of yourself more visible.

Habits, then, are not just practical tools for efficiency or discipline. They are instruments of self-creation. Every repetition is a brushstroke in the portrait of who you are becoming. And while that picture is never fully finished, each deliberate act adds clarity, depth, and intention.

Ultimately, the question is not whether your habits are shaping your identity—they are. The only question is whether you are doing so consciously or by default. The invitation is to reclaim that process. To move beyond passive repetition and into purposeful practice. To choose, again and again, the kind of person you wish to be—and to let your habits tell that story, one small act at a time.

The Micro Habit Mindset

At the heart of lasting behavioural change lies not only a set of practices but an entirely different orientation to progress. The micro habit mindset is not a collection of techniques; it is a psychological framework that redefines how we approach growth, discipline, and self-improvement. It asks us to trade perfectionism for consistency, grand ambition for small action, and all-or-nothing thinking for something more humane and sustainable. By doing so, it helps dissolve the paralysis that often accompanies the desire to improve. It allows us to move, even if only slightly, in the direction we want to grow—and to feel that movement as real, worthwhile, and empowering.

Perfectionism is among the most persistent enemies of behavioural change. It disguises itself as a high standard or noble intention, but its true nature is far more insidious. It promotes a binary view of success: you either execute flawlessly, or you have failed. This thinking not only discourages experimentation but also makes relapse or inconsistency feel catastrophic. As a result, many people abandon habits not because they lack ability or desire, but because they lack tolerance for imperfection. The micro habit mindset dismantles this barrier. It teaches us to embrace incrementalism—not as a compromise, but as a strategy grounded in behavioural science and real-world applicability.

The psychology of habit formation reveals why this approach is so effective. When we engage in small, repeatable actions, we begin to experience a sense of momentum. That momentum reinforces belief and builds self-efficacy—the conviction that we are capable of making choices that align with our goals. Each act, however modest, becomes a vote for the type of person we are becoming. Over time, this consistency trumps intensity. A two-minute practice done daily often yields more sustainable transformation than a 30-minute effort done sporadically.

Consider the example of Lata, a medical student who wanted to incorporate mindfulness into her daily routine to manage stress. Initially, she envisioned a 30-minute seated meditation every morning. But between early classes, long shifts, and fatigue, she quickly fell off track. Frustrated, she began to feel that she simply wasn't the "meditating type." A mentor then suggested a micro habit: close your eyes and take three slow breaths before opening your laptop each day. This took less than 30 seconds, but it was something she could maintain. More importantly, it kept her anchored to her original intention. As the habit took root, she began to expand it naturally—first to a few minutes, then to a consistent five-minute evening routine. But the critical shift wasn't in the duration; it was in the mindset. She stopped measuring her worth by how perfectly she followed a prescribed routine and began valuing the simple act of showing up.

This mindset also has profound implications for how we interpret setbacks. When we value progress over perfection, failure ceases to be an identity and becomes part of the process. Missing a day does not erase the previous six. Struggling one week doesn't negate the progress of the month before. The micro habit mindset replaces guilt with curiosity: What made it difficult to act today? What would make it easier tomorrow? This orientation keeps us emotionally engaged with the process of habit building, rather than emotionally depleted by it.

Another feature of this mindset is its emphasis on identity rather than outcome. When people chase goals from a place of deficiency—wanting to be "better," "more disciplined," or "successful"—they often reinforce a sense of inadequacy. But when habits are approached as expressions of an evolving identity, they become acts of affirmation. A person who writes one sentence a day is not failing to be an author—they are *being* one. A person who saves fifty rupees each morning is not failing at wealth-building—they are embodying financial attentiveness. This shift reframes the purpose of habit not as achievement, but as alignment.

Moreover, the micro habit mindset champions flexibility. Life is inherently unpredictable—schedules change, energy fluctuates, crises arise. The rigidity demanded by perfectionism is incompatible with this reality. Micro habits, by contrast, are designed to bend rather than break. Their small scale makes them adaptable, and their simplicity allows them to persist even in chaotic conditions. If a person's usual routine is disrupted by travel, illness, or unforeseen obligations, a micro habit can often be modified or relocated without collapsing entirely. This resilience makes habit continuation not only possible but likely.

The mindset also fosters a more compassionate internal dialogue. Often, the voice that sabotages change is not laziness, but shame. People tell themselves stories: "I never stick to anything," "I always lose momentum," "I'm not cut out for this." These narratives are rarely true, but they are reinforced each time a lofty intention falls apart under the weight of its own ambition. Micro habits interrupt this cycle. They create daily evidence that a different story is possible—that you are someone who can commit, follow through, and make gradual improvement. Over time, the internal critic becomes quieter, replaced by an inner coach who recognises and celebrates progress.

We must also consider the cultural significance of adopting such a mindset. We live in a society that glorifies extremes—overnight success, dramatic transformations, peak performance. The micro habit mindset resists this narrative. It insists that ordinary acts, repeated with care, can produce extraordinary outcomes. It recognises that the most meaningful changes are often invisible at first: the emotional strength built through tiny acts of discipline, the self-trust rebuilt through a streak of small wins, the quiet pride of staying consistent when no one is watching. These are not trivial achievements—they are the bedrock of long-term growth.

Importantly, this mindset allows room for joy. When the pressure to be perfect is lifted, habit formation becomes more playful, more creative. People feel freer to experiment, adjust, and personalise their routines. A micro habit can evolve as you do—shaped by your energy, your context, your preferences. This autonomy enhances intrinsic motivation. Rather than feeling controlled by a rigid system, you feel supported by a flexible structure that works with you, not against you.

One particularly insightful aspect of the micro habit mindset is how it rewires our relationship with time. Often, people overestimate what they can do in a day and underestimate what they can do in a year. Micro habits reverse this miscalculation. They leverage the compounding power of time—tiny acts multiplied over days, weeks, and months to produce changes that seem invisible until, suddenly, they are undeniable. Just as a single drop of water seems insignificant until it becomes a steady stream, so too does a micro habit seem minor—until it rewrites a self-concept, transforms a pattern, or alters a trajectory.

Take the story of Jay, a 58-year-old accountant who had struggled for decades to write creatively. After years of abandoned drafts and crushed confidence, he began a new practice: writing one sentence per day. That was it. Just one. Some days, the sentence was clumsy or dull. Other days, it opened the floodgates to more. But he never skipped it. Within a year, he had completed a collection of short stories. More importantly, he now introduced himself as a writer—not because of external validation, but because of daily proof. He had become what he had only dreamed of being. Not through radical overhaul, but through patient, persistent commitment.

The micro habit mindset, then, is not merely about doing less. It is about doing with more intention, more compassion, and more consistency. It is about releasing the myth that we must change everything to change anything. And it is about trusting that the person we hope to become is already within us—waiting not for a grand transformation, but for a daily invitation to emerge.

By embracing this mindset, we free ourselves from the tyranny of all-or-nothing thinking. We begin to see every small act as a meaningful step. We realise that progress, no matter how modest, is always worth celebrating. And we learn that becoming who we want to be is not an event—it is a practice. One habit. One moment. One decision at a time.

Aligning Habits with Core Values

True behavioural change does not begin with the mechanics of action, but with meaning. When habits are disconnected from personal values, they become performative—mechanical tasks pursued more out of obligation than conviction. But when they are rooted in what matters most to us, they become expressions of identity, integrity, and purpose. Designing habits that reflect one's values is not just an exercise in productivity—it is a deliberate act of alignment, an ongoing process of ensuring that how we live mirrors what we believe. In this way, the act of habit formation becomes not merely a strategy for self-improvement, but a pathway to greater authenticity.

Many people find themselves caught in a cycle of starting and abandoning habits, not because the habits are inherently unsound, but because they are misaligned with their values. Take the example of someone who resolves to wake at 5 a.m. to go for a run, not out of a love for movement or a desire to be healthy, but because they admire people who do it. Their commitment is aspirational, but extrinsic—it is grounded in the idea of who they *should* be, rather than who they truly are. When the initial motivation fades, the habit collapses, because it was never deeply tethered to something meaningful. This is the critical distinction between discipline and alignment. The former can be enforced for a time. The latter is sustained through resonance.

The process of aligning habits with values begins with self-inquiry. Before we decide what to *do*, we must clarify what we *stand for*. This means asking questions that cut beneath the surface of goal-setting: What do I care about? What kind of life am I trying to create? What principles do I want to embody, even when no one is watching? These are not easy questions, nor do they yield immediate answers. But the clarity they produce is indispensable. When our habits reflect our values, even the most modest actions feel significant. They carry emotional weight. They reaffirm a narrative we believe about ourselves—and aspire to make true.

Consider the case of Elena, a corporate strategist who struggled for years to build a regular writing practice. She admired thought leaders and aspired to contribute to her field, but each attempt to develop a content routine faltered. It wasn't until a coach asked her what she *most valued* about her work that something shifted. She realised that what energised her wasn't visibility or influence—it was insight. She valued depth, not attention. With this in mind, she restructured her habit. Rather than committing to publish weekly blog posts, she adopted a micro habit of writing one thoughtful paragraph each morning on a topic that intrigued her. She shared none of it publicly, at least initially. But she began to feel creatively fulfilled and intellectually engaged. Over time, her insights evolved into articles and talks—but the habit endured because it was grounded in her value of intellectual curiosity, not external affirmation.

The alignment of values and habits also acts as a filter. It helps us say no with confidence, because it clarifies what we are saying yes to. A person who values connection may choose to limit evening screen time in favour of a brief, daily call with a family member. Someone who prizes creativity may carve out five quiet minutes each day to sketch or free-write, even amid a demanding schedule. These actions, small though they may be, carry disproportionate meaning. They reinforce an internal coherence—a sense that one's time and energy are being invested in a life that feels honest and worthwhile.

Of course, values are often abstract, while habits are concrete. The bridge between the two is *translation.* Values such as compassion, resilience, integrity, or growth need to be articulated in behavioural terms. What does compassion look like in action? Perhaps it is the habit of asking one thoughtful question each day to someone in your care. What does growth look like? It might be reading one paragraph of a challenging book each night. The habit does not need to be dramatic to be effective. It needs only to be specific, repeatable, and emotionally resonant. Over time, these acts become symbols—rituals that reinforce what we care about.

The benefits of this approach extend beyond motivation. When we engage in habits that are aligned with our values, we experience a psychological state known as *integrity congruence.* This refers to the alignment between our internal beliefs and our external behaviours. Studies in psychological well-being show that people who experience high congruence report greater satisfaction, lower stress, and stronger resilience. They are also more likely to persist in their habits over time, not because they feel obligated, but because they feel internally rewarded.

Take the story of Arvind, a software developer who struggled with time management. Every attempt to implement productivity hacks left him feeling pressured and robotic. Then he reframed the issue:

his core value was *presence*—being mentally and emotionally available in each context, whether at work or at home. With this lens, time management was no longer about efficiency for its own sake, but about creating the mental clarity needed to be present. He developed a habit of ending each workday with a two-minute reflection on what felt most meaningful. This simple act improved not only his planning, but his sense of satisfaction. It became a way to reaffirm his value, not just complete a task.

One might object that this process seems slow, especially when compared to more aggressive self-optimisation models. But slowness is not a weakness—it is a kind of depth. When habits are built too quickly, without reference to values, they may appear productive but remain hollow. When they are built with care, they become durable—not because they are perfectly executed, but because they are meaningfully chosen.

Another virtue of value-aligned habits is that they are more resilient in the face of adversity. Motivation will inevitably waver. Circumstances will change. What remains constant is the value. If your habit is merely to go to the gym, you may stop when it becomes inconvenient. But if your habit is grounded in the value of vitality—of showing up for your body so you can show up for others—you will be more likely to adapt the form while maintaining the function. You might go for a walk instead. Or stretch for five minutes in your living room. The shape shifts, but the soul of the habit remains intact.

It's also important to understand that this alignment is a living process. Our values evolve as we grow. What mattered deeply a decade ago may no longer hold the same weight. Life transitions—parenthood, loss, career shifts—can dramatically reshape our priorities. Habits must evolve alongside them. Periodic reflection ensures that we are not blindly repeating behaviours that no longer serve us. A monthly review, even just a quiet evening of honest self-questioning, can reattune our habits to our values. This is not indulgent introspection—it is maintenance for the self.

One of the most overlooked aspects of this approach is its impact on relationships. When people live in alignment with their values, they become more trustworthy—not because they are flawless, but because they are coherent. Their actions reflect their beliefs. Their commitments feel sincere. In a world where dissonance is often normalised, coherence stands out. It becomes a form of leadership—not hierarchical, but moral. People feel safer around those whose habits reflect their principles, because it signals integrity.

Ultimately, the process of designing value-aligned habits invites us into a deeper engagement with our own lives. It asks us not only what we want to *do*, but who we want to *be*. It bridges the gap between the ideal and the actual. It transforms everyday routines into acts of meaning. And in doing so, it allows us to walk through the world with a greater sense of clarity, dignity, and peace.

The habits we choose matter. But *why* we choose them matters even more. When habits reflect our core values, they cease to be tasks. They become a way of living—a quiet, daily affirmation of what we hold sacred, and a blueprint for the person we are becoming. Not through sweeping change, but through steady alignment. Not through grand declarations, but through humble, repeated acts that say, "This is who I am. This is what I care about. And this is how I choose to live."

Creating an "I'm the Type of Person Who..." Statement

Much of personal transformation rests not on what we do, but on how we *see* ourselves. Identity, more than motivation or external reward, drives sustained behaviour. When our habits reinforce a desired self-concept, they become easier to adopt and harder to break. One of the most effective yet overlooked strategies in cultivating lasting change is the use of identity statements—simple, powerful affirmations that begin with the phrase *"I'm the type of person who..."* These statements allow individuals to articulate a vision of who they are becoming through the consistent expression of values, not perfection, and to anchor their actions in a coherent and motivating sense of self.

At its core, the "I'm the type of person who…" statement is a form of identity shaping through habit. Rather than merely focusing on results—such as losing weight, earning more, or being productive—this approach invites individuals to examine the kind of person they believe they are. The framing is subtle but significant. It shifts the conversation from doing to *being*, from outcome to embodiment. When repeated behaviour becomes a form of self-expression, it ceases to feel imposed. It starts to feel like integrity.

Consider the difference between the two internal dialogues: "I need to go for a run" versus "I'm the type of person who doesn't skip movement, even if it's just a short walk." The first is task-oriented and easily derailed by inconvenience or mood. The second is identity-oriented. It is a reaffirmation of a self-image that guides decisions even when enthusiasm wanes. This is not about self-delusion or bravado. It's about reinforcing the behaviour you want to see by embodying the identity that supports it.

Psychologically, this technique draws from the theory of cognitive dissonance—the tension that arises when behaviour and belief are misaligned. When someone identifies as a reader, they are more likely to pick up a book than scroll their phone, not because the action is easier, but because not reading feels inconsistent with their self-image. Over time, the behaviour and belief reinforce one another. Each action strengthens the narrative: *This is who I am.*

Real-world examples of this identity reinforcement abound. Rajeev, an accountant who once struggled with punctuality, decided to shift his approach. Rather than berating himself for being late, he began adopting the statement, *"I'm the type of person who respects others' time."* This simple reframe influenced not only his arrival times, but how he approached meetings, emails, and even family commitments. The identity became a reference point for behavioural decisions. When faced with a choice—leaving on time or lingering—he didn't just consider logistics; he considered whether the decision aligned with who he believed he was.

The power of this identity shift lies in its simplicity. The statements are not grand or rigid; they are flexible frameworks that individuals can adapt across contexts. Someone seeking to improve their focus might say, *"I'm the type of person who protects my attention."* A new parent struggling with exhaustion might tell themselves, *"I'm the type of person who asks for help when needed."* A student battling self-doubt might affirm, *"I'm the type of person who shows up, even when I feel uncertain."* These are not magical incantations—they are behavioural cues embedded in self-talk. They remind us that we are not passive recipients of identity, but active participants in its construction.

This process is particularly effective when combined with micro habits. The strength of the habit lies not just in its ease or frequency, but in what it says about the person enacting it. Brushing your teeth for two minutes doesn't just promote hygiene—it reaffirms, *"I'm the type of person who takes care of their body."* Writing a single sentence each day is not just an exercise in discipline—it supports the narrative, *"I'm the type of person who values my voice."* By deliberately connecting action to identity, we deepen the significance of each habit and increase the likelihood of its continuation.

One of the more poignant examples comes from Amrita, a teacher recovering from burnout. Struggling with self-worth and depleted energy, she began a tiny habit: each morning, before speaking to anyone, she would place a hand over her heart and say, *"I'm the type of person who treats herself with kindness."* The habit itself took seconds, but its emotional weight accumulated. It began to influence her tone of voice, the breaks she allowed herself, and how she responded to mistakes. The statement created an internal reference that anchored her in self-compassion—a value she had long taught to others but rarely extended to herself.

Designing your own "I'm the type of person who…" statement requires honest reflection. The most effective statements are those that resonate with deeply held values and reflect a behaviour you are genuinely willing to practise, however minimally. They are not declarations of who you *wish* you were in an idealised sense, but commitments to a way of being that feels meaningful now. Importantly, these statements do not require perfection. You can miss a habit and still return to it because it is tied not to a streak, but to a sense of self. If you identify as a writer, not writing for a day doesn't invalidate your identity—it simply becomes a pause in a longer rhythm.

This resilience is critical. Many people abandon habits because they tie their success to external outcomes or perfect execution. But when identity is the anchor, temporary setbacks don't unravel the entire structure. Instead, they become opportunities for reaffirmation. Missing a day becomes a chance to say, *"This isn't like me, and I'm ready to return to what matters."* The statement serves not as a standard to be punished by, but as a guide to return to.

There is also a broader cultural relevance to this concept. In a world dominated by performance metrics and social comparison, reclaiming identity as a personal, internal construct is a radical act. It allows individuals to define success on their own terms. You might not write a bestseller, but if you write each day, you are a writer. You might not lead a global initiative, but if you practise kindness in your daily life, you are a leader of compassion. The "I'm the type of person who..." statement returns agency to the individual. It reminds us that identity is not a title granted by others, but a role we step into through daily action.

Critically, these statements can also evolve. Identity is not static; it is developmental. As your circumstances change, so too can your statements. A new parent might begin with, *"I'm the type of person who creates calm in chaos."* Later, they may shift to, *"I'm the type of person who makes time for my own growth."* The flexibility of this tool allows it to accompany us through different seasons of life, providing continuity even as we adapt.

It is also worth noting the relational impact of identity-based habits. When we act consistently with our values, others begin to experience us as more trustworthy and grounded. Our behaviours become predictable in the best sense—not rigid, but reliable. This consistency builds relational capital, deepens trust, and reinforces the feedback loop between action and self-concept. A person who consistently treats others with respect reinforces not only their own identity, but their place in a wider social fabric. The "I'm the type of person who..." statement, when lived out, becomes not just an internal affirmation but a relational signature.

Ultimately, this approach is not about branding yourself with lofty labels. It is about quietly and consistently articulating who you are choosing to be—today, and again tomorrow. It is about replacing vague resolutions with lived values. And it is about trusting that even the smallest act, when tied to a meaningful identity, can catalyse profound change.

Through this lens, every habit becomes a declaration. Every action becomes a brushstroke in the portrait of who you are. And every "I'm the type of person who…" statement becomes both a promise and a practice—an invitation to step not only into a new routine, but into a truer version of yourself.

Sustaining Long-Term Change

The initial thrill of starting something new is often misleading. In the early days of adopting a new habit, motivation is high, the novelty is energising, and the vision of the end result feels tangible. But time is a great leveller. As enthusiasm ebbs and external distractions intensify, the difficulty of sustaining change becomes apparent. The real test of any habit is not whether it can be started, but whether it can be maintained when the emotional tailwinds fade. Sustainable change requires more than discipline or willpower—it demands design, reflection, and a mindset built for the long haul.

Motivation is a famously unreliable resource. It is cyclical, transient, and influenced by countless factors beyond our control: sleep, stress, weather, environment, and mood, to name a few. Relying on motivation to fuel consistent behaviour is like depending on good weather to run a marathon—you might get lucky some days, but the conditions are unlikely to hold. Instead of centring motivation, sustainable habits are built on structure. This structure consists of three foundational elements: environment, identity, and emotional regulation.

One of the most effective ways to reduce dependence on motivation is to build habits that require as little cognitive effort as possible. When habits are simple, clearly defined, and embedded in existing routines, they are less vulnerable to fluctuations in mood or energy. This is why micro habits—tiny, repeatable actions—are so powerful. Their minimal size reduces the barrier to action, making them easier to complete even when we feel unmotivated. A person might lack the energy to write a full journal entry but can usually manage one sentence. That sentence, in turn, maintains the behavioural streak, protecting the habit from collapsing entirely.

Automation is another key strategy. The more decisions we remove from the habit process, the more sustainable it becomes. Decision fatigue—the mental drain that results from making numerous choices throughout the day—can derail even the most well-intentioned routines. Automating a habit might involve setting a fixed time, preparing materials in advance, or linking it to another action. These cues create consistency, helping the behaviour to run in the background of our day without requiring conscious effort or emotional negotiation.

Consider the case of Shalini, a busy mother of two who wanted to incorporate daily exercise into her schedule. Her previous attempts relied heavily on morning motivation, which was invariably undercut by sleep disruption and caregiving duties. She then restructured her approach. Instead of aiming for a full workout, she committed to five minutes of stretching each evening, immediately after her children were in bed. She laid out her mat in advance and kept her phone in another room. The habit was small, automatic, and linked to a pre-existing routine. Over time, the five minutes often became ten or fifteen, but the real triumph was that she no longer depended on mood. She relied on method.

Another underappreciated factor in long-term habit maintenance is the role of identity. When a behaviour is integrated into one's self-concept, it becomes easier to sustain. A person who sees themselves as a runner is more likely to go for a jog on a cold morning than someone who simply has "run more" on their to-do list. This identity reinforcement doesn't require grand gestures. Small, consistent actions—performed regularly—gradually shape how we see ourselves. Each repetition is a reminder: *this is what I do, this is who I am.*

This identity-centric approach also offers psychological insulation against setbacks. When motivation fades or circumstances disrupt a routine, the identity remains. A temporary lapse does not dismantle the self-image. Instead of spiralling into guilt or self-recrimination, a person anchored in identity is more likely to reflect and resume. They say to themselves, *I'm someone who values growth*, or *I'm someone who gets back on track quickly*. This mindset fosters resilience—a quality more crucial than perfection in sustaining change.

Emotional regulation is equally vital. Many habits collapse not because they are too difficult, but because the emotional discomfort they evoke—boredom, frustration, self-doubt—goes unmanaged. Effective habit maintenance requires strategies for handling these internal states. One such strategy is reframing. Rather than viewing a lapse as failure, it can be framed as feedback. What made today harder? Was it poor sleep, an overwhelming schedule, or unclear triggers? This curiosity replaces judgment, allowing for adaptive adjustment rather than abandonment.

Another powerful technique is visual feedback. Tracking habits—even with something as simple as a calendar tick or a digital streak—creates a visual representation of consistency. This representation is motivating, not because it reflects perfection, but because it reflects effort. It provides a record of engagement that can counteract the distorted narratives we often hold about ourselves: *I never stick to anything*, or *I always quit*. When the evidence contradicts these beliefs, they begin to weaken.

The social environment also plays a significant role in sustaining habits. When others are aware of our commitments—or even better, engaged in them with us—accountability increases. This doesn't mean broadcasting every action on social media. It means cultivating a small circle of mutual support, where habits are normalised and encouraged. A study partner, walking companion, or simply someone who checks in weekly can dramatically increase the likelihood of habit persistence. Social reinforcement taps into our innate need for affiliation and approval, making the habit feel shared rather than solitary.

Of course, even the most well-designed habits must evolve. Life circumstances change, priorities shift, and what worked well last month may feel misaligned today. Sustainability, therefore, requires periodic reflection. Are my habits still serving my goals? Do they still align with my values? Have they become stale or burdensome? Reflection does not signal failure—it signals maturity. It allows for recalibration, ensuring that habits remain not only intact, but alive.

Arun, a university lecturer, offers a compelling example. For two years, he maintained a habit of reading ten pages of academic literature every morning. It had become part of his identity as a scholar and a grounding ritual in his day. But when he transitioned into a new role with earlier meetings and heavier administrative responsibilities, the habit became a source of stress. Rather than abandoning it altogether, he revised it: five pages, over lunch, four times a week. This adjustment preserved the essence of the habit—continued learning—while adapting to his new context. The sustainability of the behaviour lay not in rigidity, but in responsiveness.

Lastly, it's important to acknowledge the emotional dimension of long-term change. Sustained habits are not just about doing—they're about caring. When a habit is connected to something meaningful, it is far more likely to endure. This meaning might be deeply personal—a connection to family, health, or spiritual purpose. Or it might be professional—a sense of mastery, contribution, or alignment with one's values. The key is to keep that meaning visible. Write it down. Reflect on it often. Remind yourself *why* the habit matters. When motivation fades, meaning remains.

Sustaining long-term change, then, is less about relentless effort and more about thoughtful design. It is about making the habit so easy that you can do it on your worst day, so aligned with your identity that it feels natural, and so meaningful that it still matters when the initial spark has gone. It is about building a system that supports the person you are becoming, not just the task you are completing. And it is about recognising that consistency is not the enemy of freedom, but the foundation of it.

In the end, the question is not whether you will lose motivation—you will. The real question is whether your habits are designed to carry you through that inevitable dip. If they are, then change is not only possible—it is sustainable. Not through heroics, but through design. Not through perfection, but through presence. One small, deliberate action at a time.

Chapter 9
Real-Life Stories of Transformation

While theories and scientific models offer a sturdy framework for understanding behavioural change, it's the personal stories—the quiet, often unnoticed shifts in daily life—that truly stir belief. It's proximity, not just potential, that moves us. When we encounter people like ourselves—busy, distracted, flawed, human—managing to build and maintain small habits amid the chaos, it lights a small fire within. If they can do it, perhaps so can I. This chapter leans into that sense of recognition. It doesn't peddle tales of overnight turnarounds or cinematic reinventions. These are subtler, sturdier stories—ones shaped by modest, repeated choices that, over time, changed not just behaviour but identity, health, and a sense of possibility.

What makes micro habits compelling is not just their accessibility, but their near-universal malleability. They don't demand ideal conditions. They aren't tethered to a specific profession or temperament. Their quiet strength lies in their ability to meet people as they are. Take, for instance, James—a retired railway engineer navigating the ache of loss in his late sixties. When his wife passed, so did much of his energy. He retreated into solitude, hollowed out by grief. On his daughter's gentle prompting, he began greeting the postman each morning. Just a nod at first. A mumbled "hello." Yet even that small gesture opened a crack in the silence. Over time, it widened: a walk down the road, a shared cup of tea with a neighbour, and eventually, regular afternoons spent at the local men's shed. There was no epiphany, no dramatic plot twist. Just the simple act of stepping outside—repeated, respected, and, ultimately, transformative.

Ananya's world could not have been more different, yet the theme resonates. A gifted architect in a relentless corporate setting, she was running on fumes—chasing deadlines, haunted by inboxes, and slowly eroding inside. She'd attempted the usual fixes: early yoga, unplugged weekends, grand digital sabbaths. None held. Eventually, nudged by a coach, she tried something almost absurdly simple: a two-minute breathing ritual before opening her laptop. Just two minutes. Eyes closed. Inhale, exhale. That pause, slight as it seemed, became sacred. It marked the line between presence and performance. In time, it recalibrated her relationship to work—not by changing the job, but by reorienting her within it.

What binds these otherwise unrelated tales is not circumstance, but structure: micro habits succeed because they favour consistency over drama, simplicity over ambition, and embodiment over abstract aspiration. Their power lies in their doability. When someone succeeds in simply *doing*, belief sneaks in. And belief, more than any clever strategy, is what keeps us going.

Flexibility is another through-line in these stories. Life, as we know, rarely holds still. Babies are born. Jobs shift. Bodies tire. Habits that last are those that flex. Vikram, a secondary school teacher in Pune, found solace in journaling each evening—ten minutes of reflection to digest the emotional clutter of the classroom. Then came fatherhood, and with it, fractured nights and shifting priorities. The journaling could've disappeared. Instead, it morphed. One sentence typed out on his phone, often while pacing the hallway with a drowsy infant. The content remained; the format bent. The result? A habit preserved, and with it, a sense of stability.

These anecdotes reveal a deeper truth: small habits are seldom about the act itself. They are entry points—tiny portals to something far larger. Trisha, a university student shadowed by depression, made a quiet promise to brush her teeth each night. Not for her dentist's approval, but for herself. It was, in her words, a stand-in for hope. That one act, done even on the worst evenings, led—eventually—to bigger changes: eating regularly, short walks, therapy. But it all hinged on that first tiny victory. That symbolic refusal to give up.

And patterns begin to appear. Meaning, for one, is non-negotiable. The most resilient micro habits are never random. They're anchored in something deeper: a yearning, a value, a glimpse of who we wish to be. Second, they are unthreatening by design. A habit that takes thirty seconds doesn't trigger resistance. There's no internal debate, no grand justification needed. And third, once they've taken root, these habits stick—because they start to feel good. Not in a superficial, dopamine-hit way, but in a subtle, emotional sense. Pride.

Calm. A private kind of triumph. This emotional charge deepens the habit's imprint and boosts its staying power.

Some of the most remarkable transformations surface in the most unlikely places. In a women's prison in Kerala, a pilot programme invited inmates to start each morning by writing down one thing they were grateful for. It was voluntary. At first, uptake was minimal. But slowly, participation grew. The gratitude was rarely about grand blessings—often it was the feel of sunlight through a window, or a warm word from a fellow inmate. This tiny ritual, two minutes at most, began to thaw something. Guards noted fewer flare-ups. The women reported a greater sense of calm. It didn't rewrite the injustices of the system, but it returned a measure of agency—of self-regard. A glimmer of freedom inside locked doors.

Across all these accounts, a shared thread emerges: agency. Not control over life in its entirety—that's a myth—but over one corner of it. Micro habits return that sense of authorship, however small. They suggest that transformation isn't reserved for the privileged or the hyper-disciplined. It belongs to anyone willing to begin.

That's what this chapter really extends: an invitation. Not to mimic someone else's journey, but to let these stories inform your own. To see them not as blueprints, but as inspiration. Your life is different. Your pressures are real. But the principles apply: start modestly, show up regularly, adapt with grace. Root your actions in meaning. Define success not by scope, but by presence.

You may not yet think of yourself as a person with a story worth telling. But all stories begin in the murky middle—before we know what they're becoming. The most enduring changes don't look impressive at first glance. They're quiet. They live in the mundane: shutting a laptop with intention, drinking water with awareness, leaving the phone face-down for a moment longer. These acts are unremarkable in isolation. But together, they form a structure. A framework for care. A rehearsal for the person you're choosing to become.

So, as you take in these lived experiences, pay attention not just to what people did, but to how they thought about what they were doing. How they found meaning. How they navigated failure. Let their humanity remind you that change is a process—not a burst, but a layering. And that those who persist, gently and imperfectly, are the ones who build something lasting.

Perhaps today is the start of your own quiet shift. Nothing grand. Nothing worth tweeting about. Just one act, well-chosen and protected. Give it time. Let it breathe. Let it repeat. And you may just discover that from that modest beginning grows an entirely new story—your story—of resilience, clarity, and transformation in the truest sense.

Case Studies of Micro Habit Success

Transformation is often imagined as the result of sweeping action, a grand decision, or a sudden awakening. Yet, beneath most enduring changes lie modest beginnings—small, repeated behaviours that evolve, compound, and eventually redefine the course of a life. While habit theory provides the framework, it is real people and their lived experiences that bring the concept to life. Case studies of individuals across backgrounds, professions, and life stages show that micro habits—far from being simplistic—are both potent and versatile in practice. Their success stories carry important lessons not only about behaviour change but also about resilience, identity, and the human capacity for growth.

Take the story of Meera, a 42-year-old single mother and school administrator based in Chennai. For years, Meera struggled with exhaustion and self-neglect. Her mornings were frenetic, her health declining, and her sense of identity worn thin by responsibilities. Previous attempts to overhaul her routine had failed—gym memberships, elaborate diet plans, even meditation retreats. What finally created change was a micro habit so small it almost seemed trivial: drinking a full glass of water first thing in the morning. That was it. No app, no accountability partner, no motivational poster. Just water.

This single act—simple, immediate, and achievable—became a signal. It reminded Meera each morning that she was worth care.

Over time, she added a two-minute stretch while her kettle boiled. Then, she began journalling a single sentence about her intention for the day. Each of these habits took less than five minutes, but together, they reframed her mornings from chaos to calm. Within a year, Meera reported feeling more centred, more energised, and more capable of supporting not only her family but herself. She had not changed her circumstances—her responsibilities remained the same—but she had changed the rhythm through which she met them.

A very different, yet equally powerful story comes from Tomás, a 26-year-old software developer in Dublin. Tomás battled crippling social anxiety. Though successful in his work, he avoided meetings, rarely contributed in group settings, and struggled with feelings of inadequacy. Encouraged by a mentor, he began a micro habit of saying one sentence aloud during team calls, even if it was just a greeting or an affirmation. The discomfort was real, but the bar was low enough that he could cross it even on bad days. This practice became his ritual of courage.

After three months, Tomás had progressed from monosyllables to short reports. More importantly, his internal dialogue shifted. He no longer saw himself as someone who "couldn't speak up." The habit did not erase his anxiety, but it undermined its power. He went on to volunteer as a mentor himself, helping new hires navigate the very terrain he once found treacherous. His story underscores a key insight: transformation is less about elimination of fear and more about the repeated refusal to be ruled by it.

Then there is Leena, a retired textile designer in Ahmedabad who wanted to return to creative expression after a decade of caring for her ailing parents. At 67, Leena felt unsure about re-entering a world that seemed to have moved on. She no longer had professional ambitions, but a part of her yearned to reconnect with her creative spirit. She started with a micro habit: five minutes of sketching each evening before bed. No pressure to share or complete anything—just lines on paper.

What started as a gentle evening activity gradually awakened her creative intuition. Within a year, she began digitising her sketches.

By the next year, she had built an online portfolio. Her work was featured in a local gallery's senior artist showcase. But perhaps more significantly, Leena reclaimed a sense of joy and agency that had long been buried beneath duty. Her habit was not just a creative revival—it was an act of re-becoming.

What connects these cases is not the magnitude of change, but the design of the habit. Each one was small, strategically placed in the rhythm of the day, and reinforced not by external outcomes, but by internal rewards. These individuals did not wait for perfect conditions. They started with what was available. And they did not demand immediate results—they allowed their habits to take root slowly, trusting that consistency would deliver what intensity never had.

Among the most compelling stories is that of Kareem, a former athlete in his early forties who experienced a career-ending injury. Struggling with depression and weight gain, Kareem felt estranged from the identity he had spent decades building. Physical activity, once the core of his life, now felt like a painful reminder of what he had lost. His turning point came not from a new workout regimen, but from a friend's suggestion that he start with something simpler: putting on his workout clothes each morning—even if he didn't exercise.

At first, the habit felt performative. But soon, it became symbolic. Wearing his gear reminded him of who he once was—and who he might still become in a different form. Within a few weeks, Kareem began walking short distances. Then light bodyweight exercises. Over the course of a year, he built a new routine grounded in movement that honoured his changed body rather than trying to replicate his former one. His micro habit didn't restore his old life—it helped him build a new one.

These case studies also reveal that the context of success is not always linear or obvious. Many of the most effective micro habits emerged in the midst of adversity—bereavement, burnout, self-doubt. They were not polished routines adopted during peaceful times, but survival strategies reimagined as acts of hope. Each person began not with certainty, but with experimentation. Not with transformation in mind, but with the intention to try something that might help.

One of the more unusual stories comes from Gauri, a municipal officer in Bengaluru who applied micro habits to environmental advocacy. Frustrated by the inefficiency of office recycling efforts, she implemented a two-minute habit among her colleagues: everyone would sort one item properly each morning as they settled in at their desks. It wasn't enforced, but it was encouraged. Over a few weeks, participation grew. A small competition emerged. Within six months, the office diverted over 60% of its waste from landfills—up from 10%. What started as a micro habit became a culture shift, demonstrating that even institutional change can begin with individual acts.

Each of these stories illustrates the ripple effect of consistent, meaningful behaviour. The person who takes one deep breath before reacting is less likely to escalate conflict. The person who writes one line of code daily stays connected to their craft. The person who expresses one word of gratitude each night builds an inner climate of appreciation. These habits may not be headline-worthy, but they are profoundly human. They remind us that change is not only accessible—it is already within reach.

What we learn from these case studies is not that certain habits are universally superior, but that successful ones are personally resonant. They align with a person's values, identity, or goals. They are shaped by the realities of the individual's life—not imposed from above, but integrated from within. And above all, they are kept deliberately small—not because people lack ambition, but because they understand the power of momentum.

Micro habit success is not about dramatic before-and-after stories. It is about *during*—the quiet continuity, the gradual reorientation of daily life, the moments where a person chooses, again and again, to show up. These stories honour that process. They are not myths. They are blueprints—proof that transformation does not require a revolution. It requires intention, design, and above all, repetition.

As you reflect on these examples, consider what they awaken in you. Which story feels familiar? Which behaviour feels possible? The habits that change lives are rarely borrowed wholesale—they are adapted, personalised, and embodied. Your micro habit doesn't need to be perfect. It needs to be yours. And as these stories show, that is more than enough.

Lessons Learned from Everyday People

It is often the quiet acts of ordinary individuals that offer the most profound insights into what it means to change—and to do so sustainably. While research and theory provide the necessary scaffolding for understanding habit formation, the lived experiences of real people ground these ideas in authenticity. Their stories reveal more than just outcomes; they illustrate the emotional contours of habit-building, the nuance of setbacks, and the ingenuity required to adapt when life doesn't go according to plan. When examined closely, these narratives highlight a series of powerful lessons—practical, deeply human, and immensely motivating.

One of the most consistent lessons across the stories of micro habit success is that *permission to start small* is transformative. This might sound deceptively simple, but the cultural backdrop against which most people operate is obsessed with dramatic reinvention. Grand goals dominate social discourse, and anything less than perfection is often dismissed as mediocrity. Yet, time and again, individuals who embraced modest beginnings have reported deeper satisfaction and greater longevity in their behavioural change.

Consider the case of Aaron, a civil servant who had long struggled with maintaining an exercise routine. His previous attempts were defined by intensity: committing to long runs, expensive equipment, and strict regimes—all of which collapsed within weeks. His turning point came when he reframed his expectations. Instead of focusing on outcomes, he committed to putting on his running shoes and walking for five minutes outside his door. This act—unimpressive by conventional standards—laid the groundwork for a consistent routine that slowly evolved into meaningful fitness progress. Aaron's story is a reminder that change begins not with monumental effort, but with manageable action. It is not laziness to start small—it is strategic humility.

Another key takeaway is that *emotional context matters as much as the behaviour itself.* Many people assume that success with habits comes down to grit or time management. Yet what we see in the lives of everyday individuals is that emotional alignment plays a central role. When a habit reflects a person's deeper values or self-concept, it becomes inherently more sustainable.

This was evident in the story of Farah, a university lecturer navigating burnout. She wanted to reclaim a sense of calm and presence in her life but found conventional mindfulness practices overwhelming. Through coaching, she began with a micro habit of pausing for a single breath at her desk before opening her email each morning. While almost invisible, this practice reconnected her with her value of intentionality. Over time, it became a cue not only for calm but for self-respect. Farah didn't just learn a breathing technique—she re-established a relationship with her own priorities. Habits grounded in emotional meaning have a gravitational pull; they draw us back even when life gets chaotic.

The third lesson is that *consistency, not perfection, is the engine of transformation.* In many stories, individuals encountered disruptions—travel, illness, family emergencies, or simply a loss of motivation. What separated those who continued from those who quit wasn't willpower or superior strategy. It was mindset. They did not catastrophise setbacks. They returned to the habit not because they were flawless, but because they had made the habit part of their identity.

Take the example of Anita, a young mother who had developed a habit of writing one line in her journal each night. When her newborn arrived, her evenings became unpredictable and exhausting. Rather than abandon the habit entirely, she shifted it—sometimes she wrote a word, sometimes she wrote the next morning, sometimes she simply held the pen. The core principle was not the exact output, but the continuity of engagement. Anita's experience underscores a crucial point: sustaining a habit does not mean adhering to it rigidly, but adapting it intelligently without breaking the thread.

Another powerful insight is that *environment subtly shapes success far more than motivation does.* While motivation is often viewed as the holy grail of behavioural change, those who succeed with micro habits consistently describe how changes in their physical or social surroundings made the behaviour easier to maintain. This was clear in the story of Priya, a graphic designer who wanted to read more. She didn't start by carving out an hour a day or setting reading targets. Instead, she placed a book on her pillow each morning as she made her bed. This simple cue ensured that she read even if only for a few minutes each night. What might appear as discipline was, in fact, design. Her habit thrived because the environment invited it.

The stories also point to an often-overlooked lesson: *shame is a terrible motivator, while self-compassion is a reliable ally.* When people fail to maintain habits, they often fall into a cycle of guilt and negative self-talk. This only deepens avoidance and saps energy for change. In contrast, individuals who viewed their setbacks with curiosity rather than judgment were far more likely to re-engage.

This theme was central in the experience of Malik, a software engineer who had struggled for years with time-blocking his calendar. Every time he missed a slot or overran a task, he would abandon the practice entirely, seeing it as proof of failure. With therapeutic guidance, he began responding differently. When a task took longer than expected, he asked why. Was it poor estimation? Distraction? Emotional avoidance? Rather than condemning himself, he sought insight. This shift—from shame to curiosity—helped him maintain the practice and improve his planning over time. Habits do not survive in climates of self-punishment. They thrive in environments of learning and care.

The stories shared throughout this chapter also remind us that *progress is often imperceptible until it becomes undeniable.* Because micro habits are small by design, their impact may not be immediately visible. This can lead to doubt or abandonment. But individuals who succeeded learned to trust the compounding nature of consistent effort. They celebrated not outcomes, but inputs—the act of showing up.

Ritika, a data analyst, offers an illustrative case. She began a habit of studying one new concept in her field each day—sometimes reading a paragraph, other times watching a five-minute tutorial. Six months in, she didn't feel much different. But when a colleague fell ill and she was asked to lead a project, Ritika realised she was fully prepared. The transformation had occurred silently, almost invisibly, through daily deposits of knowledge. This delayed visibility is both a challenge and a truth: the most significant changes often happen while we're too busy working to notice.

Perhaps the most unifying lesson from everyday people is that *we are all capable of change, but we often need to lower the barrier to entry.* Ambition, while admirable, can be paralysing when it demands too much too soon. Micro habits offer a compassionate alternative: begin where you are, with what you have, and let consistency do the heavy lifting.

What we learn from these stories is not that change is easy, but that it is accessible. People across professions, ages, and circumstances have reshaped their lives not by doing more, but by doing less—consistently, mindfully, and meaningfully. The sophistication of their success lies not in complex systems but in the willingness to begin with small acts and allow those acts to become pathways to larger outcomes.

These lessons are not reserved for a special subset of individuals. They are not contingent on talent, income, or lifestyle. They are principles that anyone can adopt: start small, anchor your habits in values, design for ease, be kind to yourself when you stumble, and remember that repetition—not intensity—is the master key. The stories of everyday people are not anecdotal outliers. They are proof of what is universally possible when intention meets action, and when patience is paired with design.

As we consider these insights, we are reminded that real transformation is not about becoming someone else—it is about returning to the best of who we are, one small act at a time.

The Common Threads

When one studies the lives of individuals who have successfully integrated micro habits into their daily routines, a set of recurring themes begins to emerge—principles that cut across age, profession, temperament, and circumstance. These commonalities are not mere coincidences; they are structural patterns underpinning sustainable behavioural change. While the specific habits may differ wildly—from daily stretching to a single sentence of journalling—the architecture of success is surprisingly uniform. This chapter brings into focus the core elements that consistently appear in the narratives of transformation: consistency, simplicity, and adaptability. Together, they form the backbone of effective habit formation, offering both conceptual clarity and practical guidance for those wishing to build lives of deliberate design rather than reactive motion.

The first and perhaps most fundamental pattern is consistency. Not explosive effort, not heroic gestures, but regular repetition—quiet, rhythmic, often unremarkable. In a culture that romanticises breakthrough moments, the sustained value of showing up day after day is frequently overlooked. Yet, consistency is what transforms an action from an isolated event into a reflexive behaviour. It shifts effort from the conscious to the automatic, embedding the habit into the architecture of daily life.

Consider the experience of Arjun, a logistics coordinator who struggled with chronic stress and scattered attention. After years of cycling through various productivity systems, he committed to one micro habit: closing all browser tabs except the one he was actively using. It was not a radical change, but he did it without fail every day. That single act of digital decluttering significantly improved his focus. Over time, this simple behaviour created a halo effect: his meetings became more effective, his emails more intentional, his afternoons less chaotic. The habit's power lay not in its size, but in its repetition. Consistency allowed it to anchor itself into his working rhythm, transforming how he interacted with his environment.

The second thread—simplicity—is intimately tied to sustainability. Habits that succeed are often defined not by their impact, but by their approachability. The most effective micro habits are those that require minimal cognitive load, physical effort, or preparation. They are frictionless. They do not demand an overhaul of one's day, but instead fit seamlessly into it. Simplicity ensures that even when energy or motivation is low, the habit remains achievable.

Take for instance the story of Ishita, a schoolteacher who wanted to improve her posture. Rather than committing to extended yoga sessions or posture correction programmes, she placed a sticky note on her desk that read "Lengthen spine." Every time she saw it, she took three seconds to adjust. The action was effortless, but its effect was cumulative. Within weeks, the habit had become instinctual. Her awareness of body alignment increased, she reported less back pain, and even her classroom presence subtly improved. Ishita's habit did not require equipment, time blocks, or reminders—just a visual cue and a small correction. Simplicity made it scalable and sustainable.

Adaptability, the third thread, is what allows habits to survive the inevitable fluctuations of real life. No matter how carefully designed, every habit will encounter resistance: travel, illness, shifting priorities, emotional upheaval. Habits that are rigid in design tend to collapse under the pressure of such disruptions. Those that are flexible, however, evolve in response. They bend without breaking.

Ramesh, a mechanical engineer who adopted a reading habit during his lunch breaks, exemplifies this flexibility. Initially, he read for ten minutes each day in the staff cafeteria. When a departmental reshuffle altered his schedule, his lunch window was shortened. Rather than drop the habit, Ramesh adapted. He switched to an audiobook played during his commute. The context changed, but the core behaviour—engaging with new ideas—remained intact. This adaptability preserved the momentum of the habit and prevented the cognitive and emotional disengagement that often follows disruption.

Interestingly, adaptability is not only external but also internal. It involves a shift in mindset—a willingness to see lapses not as failures, but as opportunities for recalibration. This psychological flexibility protects individuals from the perfectionist thinking that derails so many well-intentioned efforts. It reframes a missed day not as a broken streak, but as a temporary pause. From this perspective, the goal is not flawlessness, but return.

These three threads—consistency, simplicity, adaptability—are not just strategic tools; they represent a deeper philosophy of behavioural change. They suggest that transformation is less about forcing oneself into a new mould and more about working *with* the rhythms, limitations, and realities of one's life. They emphasise sustainability over spectacle, endurance over intensity.

Moreover, these patterns speak to the importance of design. Effective habits do not happen by accident. They are the result of thoughtful integration—placing a new behaviour within a familiar context, keeping it small enough to avoid resistance, and allowing for contingency plans when life gets in the way. In this sense, habit design becomes an act of personal engineering—one that respects both the psychology of change and the variability of human experience.

There is also a relational dimension to these threads. When habits are consistent, simple, and adaptive, they tend to radiate outward. They affect not only the individual but their relationships, environments, and communities. Meena, who began with a two-minute habit of greeting her team each morning with presence and positivity, noticed that over time, her office culture shifted. Meetings became more collaborative, morale improved, and turnover declined. What began as a micro habit became a cultural contagion—proof that behavioural change is both personal and systemic.

These threads also reassert the idea that transformation need not feel transformative in the moment. Most of the individuals whose stories are referenced here did not feel particularly different after a week, or even a month. But they kept going. And it is that act—continuing despite the absence of fireworks—that ultimately created change. This long-view perspective is critical. It reminds us that the habits that change our lives most profoundly are often the ones that, at first, feel too small to matter.

What makes these patterns particularly empowering is their accessibility. You don't need to be a productivity expert or possess elite discipline. You need only be willing to start small, repeat with regularity, and allow for imperfection. These are not traits reserved for the few—they are capabilities within reach for anyone willing to engage with themselves with patience and intention.

In sum, the common threads identified here do more than explain why certain habits succeed. They offer a roadmap—a clear, grounded framework for building practices that endure. They challenge the myth that change must be dramatic and offer instead a more compassionate, effective, and realistic alternative. And they affirm something deeply hopeful: that the life we aspire to live is not the product of massive upheaval, but of small, deliberate actions repeated with care.

By understanding and applying these principles, readers are equipped not just with techniques, but with a mindset. One that values effort over performance, process over perfection, and evolution over radical overhaul. These are the true levers of change—subtle, silent, and astonishingly powerful when allowed to work their way over time.

Micro Habits in Unexpected Places

We tend to associate habits with personal improvement—exercise, productivity, self-care, or diet. The conventional image of habit-building is an individual, often in isolation, striving towards betterment. Yet the influence of micro habits extends far beyond personal routines. When thoughtfully implemented, even the smallest actions can have ripple effects in contexts we least expect—workplaces, classrooms, healthcare settings, public institutions, and even digital spaces. These quiet interventions, often overlooked due to their modest scale, can create shifts that are social, structural, and sometimes systemic.

One compelling example comes from a regional hospital in Gujarat, where a senior nurse named Priyanka began a practice that, at first, seemed purely procedural. Every morning before her shift began, she took two minutes to check the stock of essential emergency supplies in the crash cart. It wasn't part of her official role; it was a simple, voluntary habit that stemmed from an incident months earlier when a critical item had been missing during an emergency. Her action—uncompelled, unrewarded—was consistent. Soon, other nurses followed suit, and within a year, the hospital documented a marked improvement in response times during acute crises. The practice became a standard protocol. What began as a solitary micro habit evolved into a cultural norm, reinforcing the idea that patient safety could be upheld through deliberate, low-effort consistency.

The key insight here is that habits, while rooted in individual action, can create structural change when repeated within a social environment. Behaviour spreads. A small act performed in a shared space becomes visible. It creates expectations, inspires imitation, and builds norms. This phenomenon—sometimes called behavioural contagion—helps explain how micro habits can thrive in unexpected places and produce disproportionately large outcomes.

Consider also the story of Dev, a junior graphic designer at a creative agency in Bengaluru. New to the company and eager to make an impression, he felt overwhelmed by the pace and competitiveness of the team. During one particularly stressful week, he began closing each day by writing down the one task he had completed that he felt proud of—just a single sentence. He didn't share it, nor did he think much of it beyond its ability to bring him a sense of closure. But in a meeting weeks later, when asked how he managed stress, he mentioned his practice. Intrigued, his manager encouraged others to try it. Gradually, it spread across departments. A small, private reflection exercise became a shared ritual of acknowledgement. Staff reported feeling more valued and less burnt out. The organisation eventually formalised the practice into a five-minute "daily wins" wrap-up at the end of each week. A micro habit, born from one person's need to self-soothe, reshaped the emotional texture of a workplace.

In education, micro habits can yield similarly surprising impacts. A school principal in rural Maharashtra introduced a practice during morning assembly in which one student, selected at random, would share a two-minute personal story or thought of gratitude. Initially met with awkwardness and hesitation, the habit took hold within weeks. Students began preparing their reflections in advance. Shy students volunteered. The quality of attention among peers improved. Over time, teachers noticed a shift in classroom dynamics—more openness, greater empathy, and fewer behavioural issues. This was not the result of a sweeping curriculum overhaul or an external intervention. It was a micro habit embedded into a ritual that already existed. Its success stemmed not from its novelty, but from its emotional accessibility and social visibility.

What makes these examples noteworthy is not merely the outcome, but the way in which the change occurred. Micro habits thrive in unexpected places because they avoid the cognitive and logistical resistance associated with larger initiatives. A two-minute act is easy to trial, rarely demands institutional approval, and does not provoke defensive responses. Its very smallness is its strength. It flies under the radar until its benefits become too visible to ignore.

Even in digital environments—arguably the least intuitive space for habit-building—micro habits can exert surprising influence. Take the case of a remote software development team spread across three time zones. Communication had become erratic and terse. A team member named Jelani, based in Nairobi, began a practice of starting every group message with a personal greeting and ending it with an encouraging remark. Simple, almost trivial. But after two weeks, others followed. A Slack channel transformed from being purely transactional to something human. Team cohesion improved, misunderstandings decreased, and project delays lessened. It wasn't the tool that changed, but the behaviour within it. A micro habit, implemented with intention and consistency, humanised a medium often seen as impersonal.

Public spaces too can benefit from these habits. At a metro station in Delhi, a group of volunteers initiated a micro habit campaign: they stood near escalators and gently reminded commuters to stand on one side and leave the other free for walking. The interaction lasted no more than five seconds. Initially, the reminder was met with confusion, even indifference. But after weeks of repetition, patterns shifted. Regular commuters began reminding others. The habit transferred from advocacy to self-regulation. Eventually, station signage was updated to support the practice. Flow improved.

Frustration declined. What began as a tiny behavioural nudge became an accepted part of crowd movement. The habit outlived the volunteers.

Such examples call us to rethink the spaces where habit change is possible. We often assume that transformation must be personal and private. But the success of micro habits in communal or institutional settings proves otherwise. These are environments where habits do not only serve the individual—they contribute to a collective rhythm. When that rhythm is influenced by small, positive inputs, the culture itself shifts.

This is especially relevant in contexts where resources are limited, and large-scale interventions are impractical. In healthcare, education, and public infrastructure, small habitual changes can offer outsized returns. A micro habit of greeting patients by name in a crowded clinic. A librarian's practice of placing one engaging book at the front of every shelf. A janitor who ensures the noticeboard in a building is tidy and current. These actions may not seem transformative in isolation. But across time, they shape experiences, improve morale, and build environments that function more fluidly.

Crucially, these examples illustrate a broader truth: micro habits are not just tools for self-improvement—they are acts of quiet leadership. When implemented consistently and thoughtfully, they model a different way of engaging with the world. They invite others to reconsider what is possible. They offer a form of influence that is subtle yet persuasive—not by instruction, but by example.

This understanding has important implications for anyone seeking to lead, manage, or inspire change. Rather than beginning with sweeping reforms or complex systems, what if we started with a small act performed reliably? What if we placed our focus not on transformation at scale, but on action at human scale? These questions are not rhetorical—they are strategic. They offer a lens through which complex environments can be made more humane, more effective, and more resilient.

Micro habits in unexpected places challenge our assumptions about how change happens. They show us that significance is not a function of size. That progress is not always visible at first. And that the most meaningful shifts often arise not from what we implement broadly, but from what we repeat quietly.

By embracing the potential of these small acts, we unlock a form of agency that is both accessible and enduring. Whether in a hospital corridor, a classroom, a digital chat, or a public square, the right habit—done consistently—can tip a system. The lesson is simple: never underestimate the power of a few good seconds, repeated with care. The impact may be far greater than expected.

Your Story Begins Now

Every story in this book has served a purpose—not merely to inform or entertain, but to illustrate that profound change is not reserved for the extraordinary. It is accessible to anyone willing to begin, however modestly. The final story, and arguably the most important one, is yours. This chapter is not an end. It is an invitation—an open page awaiting your pen, your intention, and your willingness to take the smallest step forward. It is about becoming your own case study, not through dramatic overhaul, but by applying what you now know about micro habits: that they are achievable, sustainable, and surprisingly transformative when practiced with consistency and care.

It's tempting to think that the people who succeed at change are different in some fundamental way—more disciplined, more organised, more motivated. But this book has made it clear that such assumptions are not only misleading, they're counterproductive. The individuals whose stories you've encountered faced the same limitations, doubts, and setbacks that most of us contend with. What distinguished their outcomes was not talent or intensity, but intention expressed repeatedly through small, consistent actions.

Take Shreya, for example, a 38-year-old HR manager who spent over a decade battling cycles of burnout. After reading about the two-minute rule, she decided to begin a micro habit of breathing deeply for sixty seconds before each meeting. Initially, the effect seemed negligible. But over time, this brief ritual grounded her. She became less reactive, more attentive, and more present. Colleagues noticed. She felt it too—not as a lightning bolt of insight, but as a gradual unburdening. That one practice, easy to execute and impossible to excuse, eventually became the cornerstone of a broader shift in how she managed her energy and her expectations. Shreya didn't become a different person. She became more aligned with the person she already wanted to be.

Now it's your turn to discover what that alignment looks like in your context. No one can prescribe the exact habit you should start with. That's the beauty and the responsibility of this process. You are the architect. The question is not, "What's the best habit to begin with?" but rather, "What's one small action that reflects who I want to become?" The answer to that question doesn't need to be clever or impressive. It only needs to be repeatable.

Perhaps you've always wanted to be someone who reads regularly, but never found the time. Could you start with reading one paragraph a day? Or maybe you want to prioritise your relationships. Would you be willing to send a short message of appreciation to one person each evening? These are not trivial gestures. They are expressions of value, embedded into time. They are statements of identity made tangible through behaviour. Over time, they become patterns. And patterns become stories.

The shift from reader to participant is subtle but significant. It requires no fanfare, no formal announcement. What it asks for is commitment—not to a result, but to a practice. That is where the real power lies. Once you adopt this mindset, you begin to see the world differently. You stop waiting for the right moment or the perfect conditions. You realise that the only thing required to begin is the willingness to do something so small it's almost impossible to fail.

Consider Amit, a university student juggling academic pressure and part-time work. For years, he aspired to write creatively, but felt overwhelmed by the blank page. After encountering the idea of identity-based micro habits, he began writing one sentence each night before bed. Some nights it was all he could manage. Other nights it led to paragraphs. What mattered wasn't the output, but the act of showing up. Within six months, he had a folder filled with story fragments. By the end of the year, he had completed three short stories. He hadn't set out to become prolific. He had simply decided to become someone who writes daily—and the rest followed.

You too have the capacity to shape your narrative, not by declaring it, but by living it one small act at a time. That means embracing a long-view mindset. Results may be delayed, and motivation will inevitably waver. But that's precisely what micro habits are designed to withstand. Their simplicity makes them durable. Their size makes them manageable. And their repetition makes them meaningful.

This is not to say that every habit will succeed immediately. Some may need to be adjusted. Others may reveal that your real priority lies elsewhere. That's part of the process. The goal is not perfection, but engagement. Pay attention to how each habit feels. Observe what energises you, what creates resistance, what fades, and what sticks. In doing so, you become both the practitioner and the researcher of your own behavioural experiments.

One of the most powerful outcomes of becoming your own case study is the way it shifts your relationship to effort. Rather than seeing hard work as a grind, you begin to appreciate effort as a form of alignment—your daily actions matching your deeper values. This sense of congruence is not only satisfying; it's psychologically sustaining. It builds self-trust. You start to believe, not because of some abstract affirmation, but because you have evidence—habitual, behavioural evidence—that you are capable of change.

And that belief spreads. It spills into other areas of life. When you consistently do something small in one domain, you become more likely to try something new in another. A person who builds a habit of drinking water first thing each morning may find it easier to add a stretch. A person who begins with two minutes of meditation may gradually develop more emotional awareness throughout their day. These spillover effects are not engineered; they're emergent. They arise from the sense of coherence that comes from acting in accordance with your intentions.

As you begin crafting your own micro habits, remember that visibility matters. Track your habit. Create a visual cue. Share it with a friend if you feel comfortable. These small reinforcements amplify the behaviour and signal its importance to your subconscious mind. Over time, these cues create momentum, which leads to identity reinforcement, which in turn sustains the behaviour. It's a virtuous cycle, quietly set in motion by the act of beginning.

This process also brings into focus the importance of self-compassion. You will miss days. You will forget, falter, and occasionally feel frustrated. That's part of the story. What matters is not that you avoid setbacks, but that you return after them. Resilience is not the absence of error—it is the willingness to begin again without judgement. And every time you do, you reinforce your belief that you are someone who shows up. That is the true gift of micro habits: they provide endless opportunities for renewal.

The choice to begin your story is not about ambition—it is about authorship. Are you willing to write the next chapter of your life with clarity, intention, and care? Are you ready to see your life not as something that happens to you, but as something you co-create through small, repeated actions?

You have the knowledge. You have the tools. You've read the stories. Now is the moment to take that first step—not tomorrow, not next week, but now. Not because you have to, but because you can. Because every great transformation, without exception, begins with a single act. Yours might be as small as tying your shoes and stepping outside. Or switching off your phone for two minutes. Or writing one word.

Whatever it is, do it with awareness. Let it be your declaration. Let it be your beginning. Your story is not behind you—it is unfolding beneath your feet. And from this moment onward, you are not merely a reader of other people's change. You are the protagonist of your own.

Conclusion
Your 2-Minute Transformation Starts Today

The words you're reading were never intended to sit still on these pages. They are designed to move—into your thoughts, your decisions, and the rhythm of your everyday life. At the heart of this book lies a deceptively simple idea: small actions, performed consistently, can lead to remarkable change. And now, as we near the end of this exploration, the real work begins—not in theory, but in practice. Your two-minute transformation doesn't hinge on how much discipline, energy, or motivation you have at this moment. It begins with one small, intentional act that you can do right now, regardless of where you are or what you've done before.

Throughout this book, we've peeled back the layers of habit formation—the processes by which behaviours take root, grow, and become ingrained. We started by rethinking what change really means. Instead of relying on sheer willpower, we looked at how micro habits work by reducing friction, bypassing resistance, and making behaviour feel natural rather than forced. With the cue-routine-reward loop as our guide—a framework grounded in psychology and neuroscience—we discovered that every habit follows a predictable pattern, one that we have the power to consciously reshape.

We've also discussed why motivation is often an unreliable force, particularly in those moments when we need it most. Instead, we've presented more reliable alternatives: designing your environment, aligning with your identity, and simplifying your actions. Through the Two-Minute Rule—choosing habits that take two minutes or less to perform—we've explored how even the smallest rituals, whether it's writing a sentence, stretching briefly, or drinking a glass of water, can serve as gateways to lasting change. These actions, seemingly insignificant, have the power to build momentum. And momentum, as you'll see, has a compound effect.

In our exploration of the science behind change, we've encountered key ideas from behavioural economics—concepts like loss aversion and default bias that shape the way we make decisions. We've examined how the brain's reward system responds to small wins, particularly the role dopamine plays in reinforcing our actions. But perhaps most crucially, we've uncovered the identity loop: every small action you take is, in a sense, a vote for the kind of person you believe yourself to be. Your habits don't just reflect who you are—they help shape who you are becoming.

The stories woven throughout these chapters have been both evidence and inspiration. They've shown how people from all walks of life have used micro habits not just to change their routines, but to transform their mindset, their confidence, and their sense of agency. Take, for instance, the weary teacher who found joy again through a daily gratitude practice. The overwhelmed professional who regained her focus by starting each day with a moment of intention. The isolated retiree who reconnected with his community by simply greeting his neighbour. None of these transformations required a radical upheaval—just a commitment to something small, done regularly, over time.

Now, as we transition from learning to action, the question becomes pointed: What will your two-minute habit be? What's one simple action you can begin today—yes, today—that will serve as the starting point for broader change? This isn't a rhetorical question; it's a genuine prompt. The answer might seem obvious, or it might require some reflection. Either way, the habit should be so easy, so frictionless, that there's no excuse for not doing it.

Maybe it's a morning ritual—placing your phone face down while you make a cup of tea. Perhaps it's a quick posture adjustment—sitting up straight every hour and taking a single deep breath. It could be something social, like sending a brief message to someone you appreciate, or something more reflective, like jotting down one thing you've learned each day. The exact habit isn't what matters most. What matters is the consistency with which it is practised. The real transformation lies not in the habit itself, but in the identity it begins to reinforce: I am someone who shows up for themselves.

What you'll discover, often within just a few days, is that completing this tiny habit starts to shift how you see yourself. You begin to trust yourself more. You no longer wait for some monumental change or surge of motivation. Instead, you become the kind of person who creates progress intentionally, not through wishful thinking. This internal shift, though subtle, is incredibly powerful. It influences how you tackle challenges, how you bounce back from setbacks, and how you approach long-term goals.

Let's take a moment to clarify what this approach isn't. Micro habits aren't a magical solution. They won't eliminate all difficulties, nor will they guarantee smooth, linear progress. But what they do offer is something far more dependable than fleeting inspiration: reliability. When everything around you feels uncertain, when your energy is running low, and the world feels heavy, micro habits remain. They are a lifeline, a steady path to follow, a gentle reminder that you are not powerless. You always have the ability to take one small action.

And that one small action is more significant than you might realise. The compound effect of these tiny, positive actions is profound. You won't always see the results immediately, and in fact, many people give up on their habits because the change doesn't feel instant. But micro habits follow a delayed curve. Their impact builds quietly, beneath the surface, until one day you realise that you've become someone who reads every day, who moves regularly, or who takes a deep breath before reacting. And that realisation—that you've already changed—is what makes you believe in what's possible next.

This, in essence, is the larger arc of this book. It's not about reinventing yourself or becoming someone radically different; it's about uncovering the potential that has always been there, waiting for the right conditions to emerge. Micro habits are simply the tools that dismantle resistance, smooth the path to action, and reinforce the values you already hold dear. They show us that change isn't about striving for the extraordinary—it's about staying consistent in small, meaningful ways.

So, as we wrap up this chapter, let this be your beginning. Choose something, no matter how small, and start today. Not tomorrow, not when life calms down, not when your calendar has room. Today. Two minutes is all it takes to signal to yourself that you're ready—that you're engaged, that you're not waiting for change, but actively participating in it.

Your story is not fixed. It's unfolding. Each small action you take is a line of dialogue, a paragraph, a phrase. Over time, these moments accumulate. They become habits, and those habits weave together to shape your life. And that life, shaped by deliberate, conscious action, becomes your transformation—not because it arrived suddenly, but because it was built steadily over time.

Let that be your takeaway. You don't need to overhaul your life to change it. You simply need to begin with what you can do, where you are, with what you have. Because the real difference between intention and transformation is action. And action begins with something you can do in two minutes or less.

Start now. Because, really, now is always the right time.

Recap of Core Concepts

As we draw the book towards its final reflections, it's important to revisit the central ideas that have shaped the narrative throughout. While each chapter has offered unique insights and practical strategies, they all revolve around one unifying premise: transformation does not demand dramatic overhauls, but rather emerges from small, intentional actions sustained over time. The concept of micro habits—simple behaviours that take two minutes or less—serves as the foundational mechanism through which this transformation becomes accessible, repeatable, and enduring.

The book opened by dismantling the conventional model of behaviour change, which too often hinges on grand intentions, high motivation, and inflexible goals. These traditional approaches, though aspirational, tend to collapse under the weight of their own expectations. Life, with all its fluctuations and unpredictability, rarely accommodates rigid blueprints. Micro habits, in contrast, are malleable. Their beauty lies in their simplicity and their genius in their subtlety. They reduce resistance, sidestep perfectionism, and plant the seeds of identity-based transformation—quietly, but powerfully.

We explored the mechanics of habit formation, beginning with a clear definition of what a habit is: a behaviour repeated consistently enough to become automatic. Habits are not simply tasks we perform; they are the architecture of daily life. Much of what we do, think, and feel is driven by them, often below the level of conscious awareness. Understanding this, we unpacked the habit loop—cue, routine, and reward—a model that clarifies how behaviours are initiated, sustained, and reinforced. By learning to manipulate the elements of this loop, readers discovered how to replace unhelpful patterns with ones that better align with their values and aspirations.

Delving into the psychological underpinnings, the book highlighted the role of the brain's reward circuitry—especially the function of dopamine—in reinforcing behaviours. We discussed how even the smallest wins can stimulate a sense of accomplishment and prompt the brain to repeat the action. This neurological feedback loop is one of the reasons micro habits work so well. A two-minute behaviour that generates a tiny success sets off a reward response, which then encourages repetition. Over time, this pattern strengthens neural pathways and paves the way for more substantial habits to grow organically.

We also touched on the concept of neuroplasticity—the brain's capacity to change through experience. Every time we repeat a micro habit, we are physically rewiring our neural networks. This knowledge alone is profoundly empowering. It shifts change from something abstract to something tangible. The brain is not fixed. Behaviour is not destiny. Through micro habits, we can reprogramme ourselves, one decision at a time.

A central idea repeated throughout the book is that motivation, while useful in spurts, is inherently unreliable. Too often, people wait for the perfect mood or the right level of inspiration to act. But behaviour research consistently shows that action precedes motivation more often than it follows it. This book encouraged readers to discard motivation as the primary driver and instead rely on structure, design, and environmental support. When the context is primed for success—when cues are visible and habits are simple—behaviour change becomes less dependent on internal states and more dependent on external systems.

To support this, we introduced the Two-Minute Rule—a principle stating that any habit should be executable in two minutes or less. This constraint, rather than limiting, liberates. It eliminates excuses, overcomes inertia, and creates a psychological foothold. Readers learned that folding one shirt is enough to build a habit of tidiness, that writing one sentence can lead to completing a novel, and that standing still for a single breath can evolve into a meditation practice. The power lies not in the action's magnitude, but in its consistency and identity alignment.

Identity itself became a recurring theme. We examined how habits do more than produce results—they shape self-concept. Every action we take is a vote for the type of person we believe we are becoming. By focusing not on outcomes, but on identity—on being the kind of person who exercises, who plans, who listens—we anchor change in a deeper motivation. Goals may come and go, but identity, once internalised, continues to influence behaviour long after the original objective has faded. This concept of "I'm the type of person who…" has been shown to produce a more robust commitment to habits, as it bypasses superficial compliance and speaks directly to values.

Another core pillar was environment design. Rather than depending on discipline, readers were encouraged to manipulate their surroundings in ways that make desirable behaviours easier and undesirable behaviours harder. A kitchen counter cleared of clutter invites healthier food preparation. A book placed on the pillow invites night-time reading. These small shifts reduce friction and enable automaticity. The environment becomes a silent partner in your behavioural contract—supportive, responsive, and persistent.

We also discussed the role of social context. Habits don't exist in a vacuum; they are influenced, shaped, and sometimes sabotaged by the people around us. Social reinforcement, accountability, and cultural norms all affect how easily a habit takes root. Whether it's adopting a positive habit through peer modelling or anchoring behaviour in communal practice, micro habits that are socially embedded tend to flourish more easily than those pursued in isolation.

The book dedicated space to understanding the common barriers to habit formation: procrastination, perfectionism, and fear of failure. Rather than simply diagnosing these issues, it offered counter-strategies—like commitment devices, habit stacking, and visual tracking—to neutralise their power. Readers learned that perfection is not only unnecessary but often an obstacle to progress. Instead, it is through repeated imperfection—small attempts, course corrections, and persistent engagement—that mastery is developed.

Throughout the chapters, stories were used not as embellishments, but as evidence. Real people, in varied contexts, demonstrated how micro habits can lead to significant changes—not overnight, but over time. Their experiences underscored a key truth: the principles in this book are not hypothetical. They are proven, lived, and replicable.

One of the most encouraging takeaways is that habits scale. What begins as a micro habit has the potential to expand naturally. A reader who starts with one push-up may find themselves completing a full workout six months later. Someone who commits to saving ten rupees a day may end the year with a renewed sense of financial agency. These are not fairy-tale stories. They are common outcomes for those who start small and persist.

We also explored how different domains of life—health, relationships, productivity, mental well-being, and finances—can be shaped through micro habits. Practical examples were offered not to prescribe behaviour, but to inspire creativity. The goal was not to create carbon copies of routines but to help readers discover the habits that resonate most personally and meaningfully with them.

In the final chapters, we considered the broader implications. Micro habits not only change behaviour—they change narratives. When a person commits to a small action, they are doing more than performing a task. They are rewriting a story that may have been stuck in patterns of frustration, stagnation, or shame. They are building self-trust. And as they succeed—even incrementally—they begin to believe in the possibility of change.

That belief is perhaps the most powerful habit of all.

What this book has aimed to offer is not just a system, but a philosophy. One that respects the constraints of modern life, honours the individuality of each reader, and values progress over perfection. A philosophy that asserts, confidently, that anyone can change—without waiting for motivation, without chasing extremes, and without needing to be extraordinary.

If there is a single message to take forward, it is this: small is not trivial. Small is strategic. And when practiced with consistency, small becomes unstoppable. Your two-minute action, repeated over weeks and months, becomes not just a habit, but a life structure. It becomes evidence of your values, a reflection of your priorities, and a cornerstone of your future.

As you step into that future, do so with intention. Let the insights you've gained move from the page into your behaviour. Let them become embedded in your mornings, your work, your conversations, and your rest. Every two-minute habit is a choice to act with purpose. And every choice, no matter how small, is a thread in the fabric of the life you are now designing—thoughtfully, skillfully, and entirely on your terms.

A Call to Action

There comes a moment in every act of learning when contemplation must give way to action. The insights, frameworks, and stories presented throughout this book have been carefully constructed not merely to inform, but to initiate a shift—a practical, grounded, deeply personal movement from awareness to application. That moment, if it hasn't arrived already, arrives now. This is not a rhetorical gesture or a literary device. This is a real and pressing call to act, to commit to one micro habit that signals the beginning of something intentional, sustainable, and profoundly transformative.

Change, as we've established, does not erupt from sudden epiphanies or dramatic declarations. It grows incrementally, through deliberate, manageable behaviours repeated consistently. This may be one of the most liberating ideas in the modern landscape of self-improvement—that you do not need to overhaul your life to change it. You do not need to be energised, inspired, or flawless. You need only begin.

That beginning does not have to be bold. In fact, it should not be. The genius of micro habits lies in their unassuming scale. A single push-up. One mindful breath. The act of filling a glass with water. The discipline of writing one sentence. These are not finish lines. They are behavioural entry points. They ask almost nothing of you, which is why they are so powerful. They bypass internal resistance and external excuses, offering a path forward that is immediate and doable.

So, what will your two-minute habit be?

It is a question only you can answer. Yet it is not a question to be postponed. Too often we delay change because the path appears complicated. We fear commitment. We search for the perfect strategy. But perfection is the enemy of progress, and micro habits expose that illusion. You don't need the perfect habit—you need a starting one. A habit so small it feels almost ridiculous to say no to it. And from that first act, momentum builds.

Consider Ravi, a junior lawyer overwhelmed by the pressures of long hours and constant deadlines. His health had taken a back seat. Motivated by the idea that even the busiest people can build micro habits, he decided to do one wall sit every morning before leaving for work. It took less than thirty seconds. Within weeks, he added a stretch. Eventually, he was completing short mobility routines that helped reduce his chronic back pain. The first habit didn't require gym clothes, extra time, or any major lifestyle shift. It required presence. A choice. Repeated.

Or look at Alina, a graphic designer whose creative spark had dulled under the weight of monotonous client work. Rather than wait for inspiration to return, she created a rule: she would doodle one object every evening. Just one. Some nights, it was a coffee mug or a tree. Others, a simple abstract shape. This practice reawakened her curiosity. It had no commercial goal, no artistic benchmark. Yet it led her to rediscover her joy in creating—and eventually sparked a personal illustration project that evolved into a freelance offering.

These are not dramatic tales. That is precisely what makes them compelling. They reflect the ordinary, the real, the human. They demonstrate that the architecture of a transformed life often begins with behaviours so small they seem trivial. Yet they are anything but. They are the proof that change is accessible, not aspirational.

If you are still unsure where to start, reflect not on what you want to achieve, but on who you wish to become. Identity precedes outcome. Do you want to be someone who is present, healthy, focused, kind, or creative? Choose one aspect. Identify one behaviour that reinforces that identity. Then scale it down until it fits into two minutes or less. It might not feel meaningful at first. But meaning emerges through repetition. The act becomes symbolic. It becomes a declaration: *I am choosing to show up for myself.*

It's worth noting that the world will rarely make space for these quiet commitments. There will always be something more urgent, louder, or seemingly more important. That's why the act of establishing a micro habit is so significant. It's not about time—it's about priority. You are telling yourself that even in a chaotic, demanding world, you are not lost in it. You are creating a point of stability—a ritual of self-alignment.

There is also a hidden benefit. The act of doing a small thing regularly recalibrates your trust in yourself. Many people carry around the quiet shame of broken promises—to exercise, to write, to meditate, to save. These accumulated lapses erode self-belief. But micro habits offer a chance to rebuild that trust. Each time you complete a small action, you reinforce the narrative that you are capable, that your word holds weight. And when that trust returns, so does your confidence in what else is possible.

None of this requires external validation. You don't need to post about it, announce it, or wait for recognition. The true reward is internal. It's the satisfaction of being in motion, of acting in a way that aligns with your values. Over time, others may notice. Your energy may change. Your focus may sharpen. But that is a by-product, not the purpose. The purpose is to become the kind of person who takes action—even tiny action—without waiting for the perfect conditions.

That is the invitation of this moment. To stop reading, reflecting, or planning—and to act. Choose one habit. Decide when and where it will happen. Anchor it to something you already do—waking up, brushing your teeth, brewing your coffee. Then begin. Not with force, not with urgency, but with clarity. Make it so easy that success feels inevitable. And when you complete that first action, notice what happens. Not outside you, but within. The subtle but powerful recognition that you are in motion. That your story is not abstract. It's unfolding.

And if you miss a day? Begin again. That is the beauty of micro habits—they forgive lapses. They do not demand perfection. They are resilient by design. What matters is not whether you never falter, but whether you return. Every act of return strengthens the identity you are building. You are not just someone who acts—you are someone who returns. That is a deeply powerful narrative to carry.

This call to action is not about speed. It is about direction. You may move slowly, but you are moving deliberately. You may not feel different immediately, but change is already underway. You have taken the hardest step: deciding that a better life is not out of reach, not locked behind motivation, but built through moments of intention.

So take that moment now. Not later. Now. Decide what your two-minute act will be. Do it today. Then do it again tomorrow. Let it become your anchor. Let it reshape how you see yourself. Let it spark other shifts, quietly and naturally.

Because this is how transformation begins—not with a grand gesture, but with one small action, repeated with care. This is your call to act—not because everything is ready, but because *you* are ready to begin.

The Journey of a Thousand Miles

Every long-term transformation, no matter how extraordinary its eventual shape, begins with a modest origin. This truth is so universal that it has been immortalised in the ancient proverb often attributed to Lao Tzu: "A journey of a thousand miles begins with a single step." And yet, despite its familiarity, this insight is frequently misunderstood or overlooked in our haste for results. We are conditioned to celebrate milestones, breakthroughs, and grand achievements—while giving far less attention to the small, often invisible, decisions that made those outcomes possible.

This chapter serves as a reminder that the single step is not merely the starting point—it is the essence of sustained change. It is the most repeatable, the most reliable, and the most empowering component of growth. One micro habit, performed consistently, has the power to outpace intermittent ambition. And in a culture saturated with the spectacle of overnight success, reclaiming the dignity of the small step may be the most radical act of all.

The entire premise of micro habits rests on this foundational principle: you do not need to see the whole staircase to take the first step. More importantly, the effectiveness of the first step does not depend on its magnitude but on its repeatability. An act that requires little effort but signals a shift in mindset is far more potent than a monumental effort performed once in a burst of enthusiasm.

Consider the experience of Hari, a logistics manager from Pune, who had struggled for years with poor sleep habits. Having read extensively on sleep hygiene, he had compiled a long list of changes he intended to make—cutting screen time, changing his diet, purchasing blackout curtains. Yet these plans always remained theoretical. Overwhelmed by the prospect of doing everything at once, he did nothing. That changed when he decided to commit to one action: dimming the lights at 9:30 p.m. every evening. It was small. Almost comically simple. But it was enough to mark a turning point. The early cue created a domino effect. Over time, he adjusted his wind-down routine, began sleeping earlier, and woke with more energy. The large-scale change came not from tackling everything, but from doing one thing—repeatedly.

What makes this approach so powerful is that it respects the realities of human psychology. When we perceive a task as too large, too complex, or too uncertain, we hesitate. We procrastinate not because we are lazy, but because our brains interpret ambiguity as a threat. A large change effort, even when rooted in good intentions, can trigger a fear response. The beauty of micro habits is that they fly under the radar of our resistance. A two-minute action feels safe. It feels manageable. And once we are in motion, our perception shifts. Behaviour shapes emotion. Action generates clarity.

This concept of beginning small extends beyond the personal. It has been adopted in various professional and institutional contexts. In the early 2000s, the British Cycling team, once considered a perennial underperformer, began applying the principle of marginal gains—a concept closely aligned with micro habits. Under the leadership of Dave Brailsford, the team introduced dozens of 1% improvements, from adjusting bike seats to hand-washing techniques to reduce illness. Each change was minor. None made headlines. But collectively, they produced historic success, including multiple Tour de France victories and Olympic medals. The transformation was not triggered by any single revolution but by the aggregation of many small, deliberate steps.

There is something fundamentally human about beginning small. Children do not learn language by memorising grammar rules—they begin with sounds. Writers do not complete books by staring at a blank screen—they begin with a sentence. Musicians do not perform symphonies on their first attempt—they begin with a single note. Yet as adults, we often lose patience with incrementalism. We want to leap, not step. We want the destination without the discomfort of the path. But in doing so, we bypass the psychological scaffolding required to sustain meaningful change.

The process of taking a small step does more than move us forward—it builds self-trust. It allows us to observe our own behaviour and say, "I did what I said I would do." That experience, repeated, is the foundation of confidence. Not bravado. Not ego. But genuine belief in one's ability to act with consistency. This is what gives micro habits their extraordinary leverage. They don't just produce outcomes; they rewire our sense of identity. We begin to see ourselves differently—not as someone who struggles to change, but as someone who follows through.

This perspective becomes especially vital when we face setbacks. Because we inevitably will. Life will interrupt our best intentions. Sickness, stress, or circumstance may derail progress. The traditional model of goal-setting often collapses under such disruption. But micro habits are inherently resilient. They do not demand intensity. They require presence. Even on a difficult day, performing a two-minute action can keep the habit alive. This continuity sustains the pattern until motivation returns. It transforms lapse into pause rather than failure.

Another powerful aspect of starting small is that it allows us to calibrate. Often, our assumptions about what we need are inaccurate. We might think we need to exercise for an hour a day, when in fact a 10-minute walk significantly improves our focus. We might assume we need to overhaul our finances, when tracking one expense daily is enough to shift awareness. By starting small, we create feedback loops. We learn, we adapt, and we grow with precision rather than force.

The metaphor of a "journey" is not inappropriate, but it needs refining. Change is less like a straight road and more like a series of loops—acts repeated, refined, and reconnected. The first step does not lead forward so much as inward. It is a declaration of willingness. It invites you into a conversation with your future self, not as a critic or taskmaster, but as an architect of daily behaviour. And it does so without demanding perfection, only participation.

For those who have read this book and are wondering where to go from here, the answer is deceptively simple. Do one thing. Do it today. Make it small, make it meaningful, and make it yours. Whether it is placing a book beside your bed, preparing your clothes for a walk, or closing your eyes for a moment of stillness, let the action be real. The point is not the act itself, but the identity it represents. You are becoming someone who acts, someone who honours intention with behaviour.

The accumulated wisdom of behaviour science, personal narratives, and cognitive psychology all point toward the same truth: real change is not reserved for the rare, the gifted, or the unusually disciplined. It is available to anyone willing to begin. And that beginning is often humble. But what matters is not its scale. What matters is that it happens.

So, wherever you are, start there. Not because it is easy, but because it is possible. Let your transformation begin not with a roar, but with a whisper of action. The kind that slips past resistance and builds a foundation so quietly, you hardly notice it—until one day, you do. Until one day, you look back and realise that what seemed like a small step was, in fact, the most significant one of all.

Final Words of Encouragement

There is something profoundly empowering about knowing that real, lasting change does not demand heroics. It does not require radical upheaval, sheer force of will, or waiting for some elusive ideal moment. Rather, it begins with the smallest of actions—an intention translated into behaviour, a quiet decision honoured in the midst of a noisy world. That is the legacy of the micro habit. And that is what this book has set out to affirm: that within the ordinary lies the extraordinary, waiting patiently for your participation.

As you arrive at this final reflection, pause for a moment—not to look forward with anxiety, nor backward with self-judgement, but to recognise that you now carry something that many people spend years searching for. You have a framework, not only for understanding behaviour, but for shaping it. You have a method that is grounded in evidence, supported by real-world application, and—most critically—customisable to your unique life. This is not an abstract theory. It is a practice. One that meets you where you are, and grows with you over time.

If there is one message to take from these pages, let it be this: small is not insignificant. Small is powerful. Small is sustainable. And small, when sustained, becomes unstoppable. The most transformative shifts rarely begin with a dramatic pivot. They begin with a quiet, almost imperceptible choice to show up. To take one breath. To write one line. To move for two minutes. These acts may seem trivial in isolation, but stacked over time, they become proof of character, resilience, and personal authorship.

Consider the story of Priya, a new mother navigating the chaos of early parenthood. Overwhelmed and sleep-deprived, she struggled with the dissonance between who she had been—a meticulous, high-achieving academic—and who she now felt she was becoming. Amidst the haze, she chose one habit: each night, before collapsing into bed, she would jot down one thing she had done well that day. Sometimes it was as simple as "kept the baby alive." Other times, it was "replied to an email." What mattered was not the magnitude, but the recognition. This two-minute act reconnected her with her competence and eventually served as a bridge back to her confidence. The habit did not change her circumstances, but it changed her narrative. And that made all the difference.

These kinds of transformations—quiet, steady, deeply human—are within reach for anyone. Including you. Perhaps especially you. Because if you have read this far, you are not merely curious. You are committed. You are willing to act not out of urgency, but out of intention. That is the beginning of all meaningful change.

There will still be challenges. There will be days when you forget, days when you doubt, and days when it feels easier to slip back into old patterns. But your strength is not in never wavering. It is in returning. That return—again and again—is what builds discipline, not punishment. It is what builds identity, not idealism. A micro habit offers you a place to return to. It is not fragile. It is forgiving. And that is why it works.

Some people will underestimate the value of small actions. Let them. You will know better. You will know that success is not determined by how much you do in one day, but by what you consistently repeat. That real confidence is not built through performance, but through practice. That you can change your life not by doing everything, but by doing one thing well—and then doing it again.

Take Raj, a middle-aged finance officer whose sedentary routine had begun to erode his vitality. Intimidated by gyms and uninspired by diets, he chose a single habit: standing up for two minutes every hour to stretch. It felt almost absurd at first. Yet over months, the habit evolved into short walks. Then longer ones. Eventually, it became a non-negotiable daily routine. He didn't begin with a wellness plan. He began with a stretch. The stretch became a habit. The habit became a rhythm. And the rhythm reshaped how he moved through his days.

The beauty of this approach is that it scales without force. When you act consistently, your brain adapts. Your identity shifts. And from that new identity comes a new level of engagement. Habits that once felt foreign begin to feel familiar. Then they feel essential. This process is not linear. It is iterative. And it is deeply personal. There is no template, only tools. No rules, only principles. You shape them to your context. And you do so with trust—in yourself, in the process, in the power of repetition.

Let this chapter serve not as a conclusion, but as a continuation. A reaffirmation that you are capable of extraordinary things—not because you have to force them, but because you are willing to begin with what is possible. The two-minute habit is not a gimmick. It is a gateway. A way of anchoring your highest values in your smallest actions. A way of aligning your aspirations with your behaviour in a manner that is honest, achievable, and lasting.

So choose something. Not everything. Just something. Let that act be your first move, your quiet rebellion against overwhelm, against doubt, against the inertia that so often paralyses ambition. Let it be your reminder that change is not something that happens to you—it is something you participate in.

As you move forward, you may wish for results. That's understandable. But let your real satisfaction come not from the outcome, but from the act of showing up. From the knowledge that you are doing something today that your future self will thank you for. That is a kind of success far more profound than metrics. It is integrity in motion.

This is your moment. Not to do more. But to begin. To begin again, if you must. To choose presence over perfection. To choose direction over speed. To choose one small act and invest in it, not because it will change everything overnight, but because it represents everything you are willing to stand for—quietly, consistently, and fully.

There are no fireworks here. No final flourish. Just a human being, capable of change, invited to act. Let that be enough. Because it is. Because you are.

And because everything that matters—every story of strength, of clarity, of transformation—starts small.

So go ahead. Take the smallest step. And keep taking it.

You already know what to do. Now do it.

About the Author

Lina Vermeer is a behavioural change specialist and life strategy mentor with a passion for making transformation simple and attainable. Drawing from neuroscience, habit psychology, and decades of coaching experience across Europe and Asia, Lina champions the philosophy that big change starts small. Her work bridges science with daily life, helping readers develop powerful routines through the art of consistency and micro actions. Through her writing, Lina empowers everyday individuals to reclaim control, build momentum, and shape a life of clarity and purpose—two minutes at a time.

www.ingramcontent.com/pod-product-compliance
Lightning Source LLC
Chambersburg PA
CBHW031342230926
51848CB00002B/342
* 9 7 8 9 3 6 2 9 2 1 7 2 7 *